# Chicanas in Charge

# Chicanas in Charge

*Texas Women in the Public Arena*

José Angel Gutiérrez,
Michelle Meléndez,
and Sonia Adriana Noyola

ALTAMIRA
PRESS

A DIVISION OF
ROWMAN & LITTLEFIELD PUBLISHERS, INC.
Lanham • New York • Toronto • Plymouth, UK

AltaMira Press

A division of Rowman & Littlefield Publishers, Inc.
A wholly owned subsidary of The Rowman & Littlefield Publishing Group, Inc.
4501 Forbes Boulevard, Suite 200, Lanham, MD 20706
www.altamirapress.com

Estover Road, Plymouth PL6 7PY, United Kingdom

British Library Cataloguing in Publication Information Available

**Library of Congress Cataloging-in-Publication Data**
Gutiérrez, José Angel.
  Chicanas in charge : Texas women in the public arena / José Angel Gutiérrez,
Michelle Meléndez, and Sonia Adriana Noyola.
      p. cm.
  Includes bibliographical references and index.
  ISBN-13: 978-0-7591-0560-7 (cloth : alk. paper)
  ISBN-10: 0-7591-0560-X (cloth : alk. paper)
  ISBN-13: 978-0-7591-0561-4 (pbk. : alk. paper)
  ISBN-10: 0-7591-0561-8 (pbk. : alk. paper)
  1. Women in politics—Texas—Biography. 2. Mexican American women—Political
activity—Texas—Case studies. 3. Mexican American women politicians—Texas—
Biography. 4. Women civic leaders—Texas—Biography. 5. Women in public life—
Texas—Biography. 6. Leadership in women—Texas—Case studies. I. Meléndez,
Michelle. II. Noyola, Sonia Adriana. III. Title.

  HQ1236.5.U6G88 2007
  976.4'004687200922—dc22
  [B]
                                                                    2006028131

Printed in the United States of America

♾™ The paper used in this publication meets the minimum requirements of
American National Standard for Information Sciences—Permanence of Paper
for Printed Library Materials, ANSI/NISO Z39.48-1992.

Gracias to Tonantzin, who forever has watched over me, and Maria and Pedro Hernandez, a precursor shared-leadership, husband-and-wife team from Lytle, Texas, who defended children's rights and our Mexicaness to their dying breaths from the early 1900s to the 1970s; plus all the Chicanas in this volume whose narrative of their personal life stories made it possible.

José Angel Gutiérrez

To all the Chicana/*Mexicana* warriors in my life; to the men who are being led by them; to my daughters for being the natural born leaders that they are; to my mother; my grandmothers, and great grandmother. And to my father, for taking me to MALSA meetings and marches on the steps of the capitol.

Michelle Meléndez

*Para mi amá y apá, Daniel y Alma Noyola, gracias por todo el amor y el apoyo que me han dado en mi vida . . . les amo.*

Sonia Adriana Noyola

*Maria Hernandez*

# Contents

# PREFACE

~

# Political Ethnography and Oral History

The 1960s was an era of activism, particularly marked by the outpouring of sociopolitical protest by the nation's ethnic and racial groups, namely Chicanos, Native Americans, African Americans, and Puerto Ricans. White youth actively supported these groups and initiated their own counterculture social movement of protest as hippies and peaceniks. Civil rights and self-determination in the public arena were the primordial concerns of these groups, as was the increasingly costly war in Southeast Asia. Women were deeply involved in the respective struggles of their communities. Yet the role of Chicanas, women of Mexican ancestry born in the United States, in the civil rights movements of the era, lay subsumed and invisible to most Americans, as did the cause of Chicanos generally. Their contributions, their stories, their narratives were made invisible by nonreporting and by the lack of academic study of their contributions.[1] This book is about Chicanas who became leaders in their communities, and thereby in the Texas political arena. The mini-ethnographies presented here are our summaries of the narrative of each woman, certainly not the full story, much less biography. We gleaned this material from the complete political ethnography and oral history video interview for each public figure. The entire collection of interviews is on deposit with the Special Collections Department of the General Libraries of the University of Texas at Arlington.

We have attempted to bring to print, in some cases decades later, the struggles, contributions, narratives, and stories of twenty-five Chicanas in Texas active from 1964 to the present. Some are deceased, others have retired from public service, and many remain active. "Central to the reclaiming of the Mexican past was the narrative habit of remembering oneself within a community of the past," wrote an autobiography scholar.[2] He was describing the task of the narrator in reconstructing oneself in the present about the past despite the efforts of others to distort, erase, discredit, and discontinue histories of persons not credited with roles in the making of history or social life. In the view of some, ethnic group members do not have a history worth repeating, much less remembering. "It is though individual Mexican Americans had never set their lives to paper, had lived and then disappeared from history without a trace."[3]

## Methodology

Our attempt is interdisciplinary, employing two main approaches: ethnography and oral history.[4] During videotaped interviews, usually an hour or longer, the women in this study were asked to self-identify themselves. The overwhelming number chose Chicana over Hispanic or Latina. The words *Chicana* and *Chicano* come from the root word *mexika*, (meh she kah) which is the Náhuatl name for the original inhabitants of the Valley of Mexico. This reclaiming of the past by use of this self-descriptor was instrumental in tying the Mexican American population to their historical roots on this continent, and in establishing relationships with other Native American activists. They were asked to tell about their family biography and early childhood. They were asked to describe their political work. The ethnographic narratives about their major life components formed the basis of our data. The interviews are oral history data, and they are the expressions of a woman's perspective in a male-dominated world. As Emma Pérez puts it, "For the most part, male immigrant experiences have been written in such a way that they seem to be the normative experience, thus denying and negating women's experiences and their differences."[5] In these interviews, Chicanas give meaning and emphasis to their stories. History is nothing more than stories. By synthesizing their interviews, we added our emphasis and meaning to what we thought was important to relate to the reader. That is our bias. The manuscript is divided into four parts. Each part contains the summary of select Chicanas, representative in our view of the active women of that era. Many Texas women were not included in this selection because of space and time limitations. In the larger study of 175 persons, about 68 are Chicanas. Women appointed to public office and influential in the business world, for example, are not profiled in these pages. We wanted to write about the social activists and political doers among Chicanas in Texas from the mid-twentieth century to the present. In 1950 there were few women of Mexican ancestry holding public office in the state. By 1972 there were only 28 Chicanas among the 736 Spanish-surnamed elected officials in Texas. A mere two decades ago there were only 591 Chicanas and Latinas holding public office in the United States. By 2005 in Texas alone there were 592 Chicanas and Latinas holding public office. The women of La Raza now constitute 30 percent of all Latino/a elected officials in the country.[6] The Chicanas presented here live in all geographic regions of the state. They span the range of ages, educational attainment, marital status, and category of public office held or sought. In order to view the image of those interviewed, both men and women, hear them tell their story, and read the transcript for 77 of the interviews that are digitized and on the Internet go to http://www.libraries.uta .edu/tejanovoices/.

Alessandro Portelli, the leading scholar utilizing oral history, describes the intersection of history and biography this way: "How historical is private life? How personal is history? The oral history genre flows between biography and autobiography, personal and social, narrator and interpreter. Oral history stays in between *life and times* of the subject. The key word in *life and times* is the one in the middle."[7] Portelli has developed some theoretical underpinnings for oral history in the course of his work among Italians in World War II. He believes that there is a time for telling and a time for history, the key difference between narrating and narrated, the dialectics of story and history. The narrative of the interviewee prompts the memory of the interviewer and both become involved in the developing of the narrative and later the text, as we have. Our short political ethnographies of these Chicanas are expressions of meaning, theirs and ours, and practice. Meaning and practice are inseparable, even for the most objective of scholars. Interpretation begins at the moment the interview begins, and all representations made by questions, answers, stories, anecdotes, interruptions, and silence or pauses are all interpretations. The interviews are a process where one has a story to tell and the other with a history to reconstruct. And we had a broad choice from which to pick material for inclusion here: "Either the story was well told or the life is meaningful."[8]

## Context

This book spans the political arena in Texas during the 1960s to the present time. Early feminist writings, mostly by white women, in the twentieth century delineated three currents of thought prevalent among women in the public arena: suffrage, reform, and partisan political activity; the latter were known as party women. By the twenty-first century, feminists were no longer suffragettes or reformers; mostly they were party women and gender-based ideologues.[9] Chicanas, by and large, did not identify with the white feminists of the twentieth-century.[10] Suffrage movement in the United States did not seek to include Chicanas. Mexican women migrating to the United States, particularly after the Mexican Revolution of 1910, did not expect to vote and did not make suffrage a central issue of concern. Moreover, there was no tradition of female suffrage in Mexico. Mexican women did not get the right to vote until 1953 in that country. In the late 1970s, during the national conference held in Houston, Texas, in conjunction with the International Year of the Woman, Chicanas were not included in the U.S. delegation nor selected as U.S. delegates to the world gathering held in Mexico City. It was the Mexican government that saw to it that Chicanas were included in the Mexican delegation to that important summit. During the 1970s, the Raza Unida Party was born out of the Chicano Movement, a liberating experience for most Chicanas, participants and observers alike, in that they were able to establish a caucus within the political party and assume leadership roles in party positions and as candidates. Within the nascent but growing academic discipline of Chicano Studies in the 1980s, Chicanas fought not only for equal footing among male peers within the professional organization but also for intellectual respect and autonomy from peers, male and female, for Chicana feminist thought.[11] Chicanas have stepped front and center into the public arena since that era.

The most recent demographic projections developed by Jeffrey S. Passel of the Urban Institute, in collaboration with Roberto Suro of the Pew Hispanic Center, posit that Latinos[12] in the United States population are growing at unprecedented rates.[13] This growth will continue well into 2020. The striking difference between Hispanic population growth of the 1990s and that in the 2000s is the role of the second-generation Mexicans, that is to say, those born in the United States with at least one foreign-born parent. Putting it another way, the Pew Hispanic Center's researchers found that between 1970 and 2000 the Hispanic population grew by 25.7 million, and immigrants, mostly from Mexico, accounted for 45 percent of that increase, while the second generation accounted for 28 percent. In the 1980s the second generation's growth began to outdistance that of immigrants, 52 percent. By 1990 the population increase attributed to second-generation Latinos reached 63 percent. Passel estimates that the number of second-generation Latinos in U.S. schools will double and the number in the U.S. labor force will triple between 2000 and 2020. These U.S. born Hispanics, mostly Mexicans, are citizens and will be eligible to vote and hold public office. Also, these second-generation Mexicans are mostly female. During the 1960s, 1970s, and into the 1980s before the identity labels of Hispanic and Latina came into vogue, these females of Mexican ancestry called themselves Chicanas. At the same time that the greater

Raza community reaches population numbers in the 60 and 70 million range and percentages of the U.S. population of 25 to 30 percent, Hispanic women will be our leaders, not men. This gender shift in leadership will be transcendental and transformational at the same time. Between now and then, Latinos will have to learn how to follow women. Latinas will have to learn how to lead as women, not simply imitating male-centered leadership roles of the past. Research by the National Center for Education Statistics[14] reveals a widening gap in educational attainment and achievement between genders. Girls are doing better academically and graduating at greater rates than boys. The findings of this gender gap hold true not only for white and black girls but also Hispanics. Black girls have achieved academically over black males for a long time. But white girls had not and neither had Hispanic girls until the late 1980s. In 1977, boys (white, Hispanic, Asian, and Native American) out-performed academically and graduated in higher numbers than girls. In the late 1980s, according to *Business Week's* article on the gender gap, the girls leaped ahead and the gap continues to widen. The educational attainment gap will continue to grow in this decade and the foreseeable future. For example, in 1999–2000 for every 100 men that obtained bachelor's degrees in the United States, 133 women did so. In obtaining master's degrees, the women beat out the men 138 to 100. It is estimated that for every 100 men obtaining bachelor's degrees in 2009–2010, 142 women will do the same, and for every 100 men obtaining master's degrees, 151 women will do so. Half of the law students in 2004 were women. In the male-dominated fields of medicine, engineering, and science women are closing the gap rapidly. College diplomas for women in the United States went from 39 percent in 1960 to 57 percent in 2000, PhDs went from 11 percent in 1960 to 49 percent in 2000. The reading scores for girls surpassed those for boys in tests administered to fifteen-year-old students abroad, 517 to 485, and in the United States 518 to 490.[15] In the Hispanic community, the same trend is evident. Moreover, Latinas vote more often than Latinos, and in greater numbers. Latinas outnumber Latinos in the population. Hispanic women live longer than Hispanic men. Chicanas are entering the labor force in greater and greater numbers. The Bureau of Labor Statistics projects that the female Hispanic labor force will grow "to about 8.5 million in 2008—an increase of 48 percent. That represents the greatest growth among all female ethnic groups."[16]

And Chicanas are increasingly taking leadership roles at younger ages. Chicanas and other Latinas will be the dominant force in the public arena in the years to come. This study is but an introduction to those first Texas women that entered the public arena during 1964 to the present time. Michelle Meléndez wrote the section on Women Warriors—discussing the duality of the Meso-American world view and the first female Mexican leaders recorded in history. Sonia Adriana Noyola wrote the section that poses the question: Where are the Chicanas? She also wrote the mini-biographies of Rose Herrera, a school board member in Fort Worth; Diana Flores, a community college trustee in Dallas County; and Lena Levario, a former district court judge in Dallas County. Michelle Meléndez wrote the biographical vignettes for Alicia Chacón, the first Chicana ever to be elected as a county judge in Texas; Trini Gámez, farmworker activist and organizer in the Pan Handle; Norma Chávez, state representative from El Paso; Norma Villarreal, former county judge in Zapata County; Alma Canales, first woman and Chicana candidate for lieutenant governor in Texas; Severita Lara, 1969 school walkout leader and former mayor of Crystal City; Socorro Medina, the first *Mexicana* county commissioner in Potter County, which comprises the city of Amarillo; Elfida Márquez Gutiérrez, an educator and trustee on the El Paso Community College Board; and María Jiménez, director of the American Friends Service Committee. José Angel Gutiérrez wrote the preface and the selections for Virginia Muzquiz, first Chicana to run for state representative in Texas; Irma Mireles, former member of the San Antonio River Authority; María Escobar and Rosa Tijerina, mother and daughter, involved with the Land Grant Recovery Movement in the United States; Elvira Reyna, first Republican Hispanic state representative in the state; Leticia Van de Putte, state senator from San Antonio; Hilda Tagle, first Chicana federal judge in the state; Linda Reyna Yáñez, appellate court justice in the Rio Grande Valley; María Antonietta Berriozabal, a San Antonio city councilor for ten years and one-time mayoral candidate; Rosie Castro, a Mexican American Youth Organization organizer whose two sons followed her example and became elected representatives; Gloria De León, cofounder of the National Hispanic Institute, which has trained thousands of young Chicanos in leadership; Anita Martínez, the first Mexican American elected to the Dallas City Council; and Olga Peña, who organized Chicanas into the Bexar County Democratic Women's Club and built the local network to elect and reelect her ex-husband, Albert Peña Jr.

## Notes

1. Suzanne Oboler, *Ethnic Labels, Latino Lives: Identity and the Politics of (Re)Presentation in the United States* (Minneapolis: University of Minnesota Press, 1995), p. 44–45.

2. Genaro M. Padilla, *My History, Not Yours: The Formation of Mexican American Autobiography* (Madison: University of Wisconsin Press, 1993), p. 29.

3. Padilla, *My History*, p. 3.

4. Oral history as a research method and a strategy for both teaching and learning has not been as examined or utilized by political scientists as it has by historians, sociologists, and anthropologists. See Alma M. Garcia, *Narratives of Mexican American Women: Emergent Identities of the Second Generation* (Walnut Creek, CA: AltaMira Press, 2004) for the use and application of oral history to explore the ethnic construction of a social identity among second-generation female children of Mexican immigrants in the United States. She conducted twenty-five interviews for her study.

5. *The Decolonial Imaginary: Writing Chicanas into History* (Bloomington: Indiana University Press, 1999), p. 79. Pérez posits a typology of how we study history in the United States, usually linearly and from a "great man" perspective, ignoring women. That is to say, historians trained in Western institutions go from this happened, then this happened, and that happened, all along an obsession with chronology on a horizontal plane. In opposite fashion, Michel Foucault introduced a vertical approach, from digging into the past to projecting into the future, but in stages and eras or epochs. Pérez prefers the cyclical approach of pre-Columbian civilizations, where events seem to repeat themselves and return again and again with no beginning, middle, or end. See her introduction for this commentary, pp. xiii–xix.

6. National Association of Latino Elected and Appointed Officials (NALEO), 1997, 2005. *National Directory of Latino Elected Officials*, Washington, D.C.

7. Alessandro Portelli, *The Battle of Valle Giulia: Oral History and the Art of Dialogue* (Madison: University of Wisconsin Press, 1997), p. 6.

8. Alessandro Portelli, *The Battle of Valle Giulia: Oral History and the Art of Dialogue* (Madison: University of Wisconsin Press, 1997), p. 19 but his entire Introduction in this book and Chapter 1. Oral History as Genre must be read to fully conceptualize his ideas about the method.

9. As the twentieth century began, there were three major types of female political activists: feminists, reformers, and party women. Feminists, aka suffragists and reformers, emerged in the nineteenth century; party women came out in the late nineteenth century and by the twentieth were out in full force. Party women hold partisan loyalty to political parties and their philosophies. Reformers worked for the issue of suffrage. Feminists promoted the interests of women. With passage of the Nineteenth Amendment, realignment took place. The reformers sought new issues framed within a woman's agenda. Party women sought positions of power with the political parties, and feminists pushed for solidarity within the gender. See Jo Freeman, *A Room at a Time: How Women Entered Party Politics* (Lanham, MD: Rowman and Littlefield, 2000). This book ignores Latinas altogether. In order to find Latinas in the global literature, see Jennifer Abbassi and Sheryl L. Lutjens, eds., *Rereading Women in Latin American and the Caribbean: The Political Economy of Gender* (Lanham, MD: Rowman and Littlefield, 2002) particularly the annotated index on women and gender, pp. 361–74 that covers the period 1974 to 2001.

Theoretical movements surrounding the study of women are several. See Joan Scott, *Gender and the Politics of History*, rev. ed. (New York: Columbia University

Press, 1988), p. 2, for an analysis of gender versus woman, as concepts. Gender is the "social organization of sexual difference" whereas woman is a biological-based category. Gender is a social construction that precedes and proscribes behaviors and places, and their power is masculine and feminine.

10. The feminist movements that began in the United States and Europe in the 1960s and 1970s were labeled "Second Wave Feminism." These proponents introduced the "personal is political" sphere, critiquing the personal sexism of the New Left activists and identifying patriarchy as a universal system of power and domination. See Mary Daly, *Gyn/Ecology: The Metaethics of Radical Feminism* (Boston: Beacon Press, 1978), p. 5. Chicanas and other feminists of color responded with criticism of their own against these white radical feminists. See Chela Sandoval, "Feminist Forms of Agency and Oppositional Consciousness: U.S. Third World Feminist Criticism," in *Provoking Agents: Gender and Agency in Theory and Practice*, ed. Judith Kegan Gardiner, pp. 208–26 (Urbana: University of Illinois Press, 1995). Sandoval charged Second Wave U.S. feminists with middle-class, white prejudices that damaged their feminist theory and its practices. Sandoval proposed an emergent Third World Feminism to force attention to the intersection of gender, race, class, and sexuality, and the subsequent transformation of political strategies.

11. *Mujeres Activas en Letras y Cambio Social* (MALCS) was established in 1983 and dedicated "to the documentation, analysis, and interpretation of the Chicana/Latina experience in the United States." See Adela de la Torre and Bearriz Pesquera, eds., introduction to *Building with our Hands: New Directions in Chicana Studies* (Berkeley: University of California Press, 1993), p. 5.

12. The persons profiled in this text use the terms *Latino, Hispanic, Mexican American, Mexican, Mexicano, Chicano*, and *Chicana*. We will used them interchangeably, but more often than not we will use either *Chicana*, referring to women, or *Chicano* when referring to males or the greater community. We will also use the term *Raza* or *Mexican* to refer to the greater community.

13. See www.pewhispanic.org and see Roberto Suro and Jeffrey S. Passel, "The Rise of the Second Generation: Changing Patterns in Hispanic Population Growth," October 2003. See also www.tsdc@tamu.edu for access to the Texas State Data Center and population projections for Texas.

14. See www.nces.org and see also Michelle Conlin, "The New Gender Gap," *Business Week*, May 26, 2003, 75–80, 84.

15. The phenomenal advances in female attainment and achievements are not only found in the United States but also in forty-two of the industrialized nations of the world. The Organization for Economic Cooperation and Development (OECD), a think tank on global social issues, reported these statistics in "Education at a Glance 2003." See www.oecdwash.org for the study. See also Alaina Sue Potrikus, "Girls Pulling Ahead of Boys in Academics, Study Finds," *Fort Worth Star Telegram*, September 20, 2003, p. 1, 17A. Andrew Hatcher has forthcoming *Mismatch: The Growing Gulf Between Women and Men*.

16. *Hispanic Business*, April 2003, p. 31.

~

# Acknowledgments

This manuscript would not have been possible without the collaboration of those interviewed, *Gracias*. The three of us acknowledge each other for the assistance in writing and division of labor that made this book possible. The Special Collections Department staff at the University of Texas at Arlington library made possible the digitization of the some interviewees and their digital photo images. Thank you Gerald Saxon, Ann Hodges, Carolyn Kadri, Julie Williams, Scott Holmes, Jonathan Scott, Kristen Swenson, Joshua Dugdale, Sarah Jones, and Marie Irwin. The Visual Arts Department of the University of Texas at Arlington copied from video to digital image the other photos, except Rosa Tijerina. Her photograph was made possible by Jack Newsome of Albuquerque, New Mexico. Students in Dr. Gutiérrez's political science classes at the University of Texas at Arlington during the Fall 2003 semester helped update information on some of the interviewees. Some students wrote papers on some of these Chicanas: David J. Jusiewicz, Nicolas Pyeatt, and Gerald L. McAllister in Public Policy and the Mexican American Community, a graduate course, and many undergraduates in the class Texas Politics and Government. Thank you students for turning in your work on time and readable, particularly Waqar Ghani, Antonio López, Tutrinh Thi Vo, Wesley Nesbitt, Christine Tsuchiya, and Chasity Turner. And thank you prior students who also had to read, write, and analyze some of these persons.

As the first deadline neared, Dr. Gutiérrez's wife, Gloria, and daughters Andrea, Clavel, and even "adopted" daughter Jasmín Mendoza, read some of the work. Thank you for your editorial comments and suggestions for improvement. As the final deadline neared, Michelle Meléndez took responsibility for rewriting some chapters, editing all the chapters but her own, and for pulling the final manuscript together in the publisher's format. Thank you. At the last minute, Michelle's coworker, Francisco J. Ronquillo Domínguez, made Spanish grammatical corrections, while preserving the words and sentiment of the women as they spoke them. *Gracias.*

We thank Rosalie Robertson, senior editor at AltaMira Press, for her faith in our project, patience with us as the deadline for submission neared, and her careful review of our manuscript. Her guidance, keen observations, and gentle editorial persuasion made this a better product than we expected. Toward the end of the process, the invaluable assistance from Bess Vanrenen and Alden Perkins, editors at Rowman & Littlefield, helped birth this book. Thank you both.

# INTRODUCTION

~

# Women Warriors

Mexican civilization has a long history of female leadership and female equality.[1] Meso-American (Toltec and forward) teachings about the creation of the world and about the origin of people are preserved in codices, both pre-Columbian and post-Columbian. Spanish friars who assisted the Spanish invaders of the sixteenth century further recorded the stories. More important, the teachings have been collected in oral histories by eminent *Mexica* scholar Arturo Meza Gutiérrez.[2] According to the Codex Borbonicus, before the world was created, there were primordial female and male creative forces, *ome tecuhtli* (dual male) and *ome cihuatl* (dual female). The energetic manifestations of all natural elements in Anahuac (Náhuatl word for the North and Central American continents) cosmology (often misinterpreted as Rain God, Sun God, Earth Goddess, etc.) contain complementary male and female forces.[3] The earth is affectionately called *tonantzin coatlicue* (Our Mother, she who wears the skirt of serpents) as a metaphorical representation of the earth, which is teaming with life-giving waves of energy resembling the slither of snakes.[4] But *coatlicue* also represents the transformation of life, which to some is death, in that our mother earth entombs our bodies when we die. Perhaps the most eloquent teaching about the duality of the universe is related in Arturo Meza Gutiérrez's work, *Mosaico de Turquesas*. When asked how the people in an indigenous village in the state of Mexico say *Dios*, or God, in Náhuatl, an elder responded, "*No tenemos el nombre en nuestra lengua. No tenemos por qué ponerle nombre . . . todo lo que ven sus ojos, las piedras, la hierba, las nubes, los animales, la gente, las montañas, el cielo, los ríos, los árboles, todo, todo lo que nos rodea, es, y está formado de partes hombre y partes mujer.*"[5]

This cosmology contrasts that of ancient Mesopotamia, which stresses the opposing nature of the masculine and feminine forces struggling for each other's destruction.[6] This difference in worldview may help explain why the female disappeared from the historical record after the Spanish invasion, because the Spanish drew their worldview from the Catholic Church, which regards the supremacy of the Holy Father and Son and reduces the role and status of women. Before the Spanish invasion, Aztec women had their own governance structures called *cihuatlahtocan* (council of women), who along with a council of men, advised the *tlahtoani* (speaker or leader).[7] The *cihuatlahtocan* was made up of fourteen women chosen through popular election. It held court, carried out laws, and passed judgment independently from the men. The council also governed over female warrior societies and guilds such as weavers, artists, jewelers, and other merchants who conducted business. Women had their own schools called *Ichpochkalli* (house of young women) that, like the *Telpochkalli* for boys, were dedicated to the philosophy of *tezcatlipoca*, or the smoking mirror, which is a metaphor for self-awareness, inner consciousness, and self-reflection. Young women also attended schools of higher education, called *Calmecac*, where they alongside young men learned to read, write, and interpret the calendar systems and history books (codices), sacred songs, and poetry. The foundation of *Mexica* communities was the family. The women acted as administrators of the family. The same worldview and organizational structure is found throughout Meso-American civilizations. *Mixteca* and *Zapoteca* governance structures also were dual. The famous female leaders of the *Mixteca* are well known.

One of the earliest recorded histories of a female Aztec leader was of Malinalxochitl, the sister of Huizilopochtli.[8] Sister and brother led the eight *Náhuatlaca* (Náhuatl-speaking) tribes out of Aztlán in the year AD 1064 and migrated, separately, to the Valley of Mexico. This journey was recorded in the Codex Boturini. Malinalxochitl is said to have broken off from her brother's group, and to have led her group of migrants to found the city of Malinalco, southwest of Tenochtitlan, where Huizilopochtli's *Mexicas* eventually settled in 1325. Some interpretations of the codex imply that Malinalxochitl did something to upset the balance in Huizilopochtli's group, and was banished. But it is unclear where that interpretation came from and whether the interpretation was post- or preinvasion.

Some two hundred years later, in 1521, another Aztec leader is noted in historical records. Cuayaotitalli was the mother of Cuauhtemoc, the last *tlah-*

*toani* (leader) of the Mexika people.[9] She took up arms against the Spanish when her son was captured. The brief history recorded about her says women and children fought alongside men against the Spanish, using the weapons of the men who had fallen in battle. Even though it wasn't customary in *Mexica* warfare, the women shot Spanish invaders in the back in a last ditch effort to save their people. The women and children had fought similarly, once before, in revenge for the well-documented slaughter of Toxcatl, in which hundreds of *Mexica* were ambushed during a feast ceremony marking the beginning of summer. The Spanish named the event "La Noche Triste" because so many Spanish died. To the *Mexica*, it is known as the night of victory.

A contemporary of Cuayaotitalli was Malintzin, perhaps the most infamous Mexican woman in history. She went down in history as "La Malinche,"[10] a term that came to mean traitor. Malintzin was captured by or sent to live with Hernán Cortés shortly after he landed in the Yucatan.[11] She became his translator, since she spoke Náhuatl, the language of Central Mexico, and Chontal Maya, which was also spoken by Jerónimo de Aguilar, one of Cortés's men. Much of what is known about her comes from the writings of Bernal Díaz del Castillo, a Spanish conquistador who chronicled his participation in the Spanish conquest in the book, *The Discovery and Conquest of New Spain*. In Díaz's account, Doña Marina, as Malintzin was called in Spanish, was of royal lineage, but because of her father's death and her mother's remarriage (a union that produced a son), Malintzin never assumed her rightful place as ruler of the tribe she was born into. Instead she was sold into slavery to a Mayan tribe, given to a Tabascan tribe, and finally offered at the age of fourteen to Hernán Cortés along with twenty other young women. Malintzin is said to have given birth to a son, Don Martín, who has been called the first *Mestizo*, or mixed-blood person in Mexico. Today, the term "malinchista" refers to a person who has betrayed or "sold out" their people or country. A feminist interpretation of "La Malinche" emphasizes her leadership qualities, courage, resilience, intelligence, and compassion. After Malinche, there is a long gap in the recorded history of Mexican women. During this gap, mothers, sisters, and grandmothers kept Mexican families together as best they could as Mexicans were sold into slavery, forced to adopt Christianity, and stripped of their indigenous roots and language. The women are largely responsible for keeping Mexican traditions and culture alive, sometimes hidden, and sometimes cloaked in Spanish/Catholic custom. These traditions include the *quinceañera*, the piñata, music, dance, and of course, the food. The fighting spirit of Mexican women endured and emerged, here and there. But one had to look.

## Where are the Chicanas?

It was not until I went to college that a new world began to open, the world of Mexicans and their progeny in the United States: Chicanos. Research libraries, advanced courses, and technology provided me with essential information on my special topic of interest: my people. At universities across the country, beginning in the late 1960s and early 1970s, students like me could enroll in Mexican American Studies and Chicano Studies classes to learn about their history and current situation. The opportunity to learn about Chicanas began to be a reality. Growing up in South Texas, I recall hearing *cuentos* (stories) recounted to me by my parents, grandparents, and *tías y tíos* (aunts and uncles) about great Chicanos. This was history that was not taught in any of our social studies classes. I remember detailed stories of the vigor and tenacity with which these Chicano leaders fought for justice: César Chávez and the United Farm Workers movement, Dr. Hector P. Garcia's[12] founding of the American GI Forum, and José Angel Gutiérrez's[13] founding of La Raza Unida Party just to name a few. When I asked my teachers for more information about those heroes, they would only give me a sentence or two, if they knew anything at all about the people I was interested in learning about. Back home I would hear *esos cuentos de mi raza* (those stories of my people) that I couldn't get in school. The caress of those words on my soul and the vision of those brown faces in my mind were enough to keep me from climbing the walls. But only for a short while. Soon I began to ask, "*¿Dónde están las mujeres; las mujeres cafecitas, hermosas y fuertes?*" (Where are the women, the strong beautiful brown women?) My family was at a loss to tell me. They knew a few stories of great women from Mexico—Sor Juana Inez de la Cruz,[14] who challenged the Church's hierarchical structure by writing and publishing her works on topics ranging from science to poetry; and *Las Adelitas*,[15] the soldier women who came to symbolize the women of the Mexican Revolution and who fought valiantly alongside the men. Not wanting to leave me disappointed with such a few stories, my family turned to a logical solution—"*La biblioteca! Debemos de encontrar algo en la biblioteca.*" (The library! We should be able to find something in the library.)

So we got *en la troca* (in the truck) and drove to the downtown library. After an initial card catalog search, we took down the call numbers of a dozen or so books and began to search the shelves. I found a few books about Chicanos. Each repeated the stories of the same great men that my family had told me. Generally, work on *las mujeres* (women) was sparse and anecdotal. It was as if Chicanas were a side note to history. How could my beautiful brown Chicana sisters be a side note to history? Sadly, my parents knew that

the answer was right in the front of each book we read. They were all written by men. My parents told me, "*Así es a veces, pero si quieres cambiarlo, lo
tienes que hacer tú misma.*" (That's the way it is sometimes, but if you want to
change it, you are going to have to write them yourself.) These words stung
me at the time, but later served as inspiration.

The goals my parents set for me were to do well in school so that I would
never have to depend on a man for my livelihood and to change those things
about society that I did not like. So I concentrated on my studies during junior high and high school and learned what I could about Chicana leaders in
my community. One of those women was Doctor Cleo Garcia, the sister of
Hector Garcia of the American GI Forum. Dr. Cleotilde P. Garcia was an incredible role model and cornerstone of strength for many Chicana/os in the
Corpus Christi area. She came from a family of civil rights leaders and stood
out in her own right. Dr. Cleo, as she was fondly referred to, was born in Ciu-
dad Victoria, Tamaulipas, Mexico, on January 9, 1917. She earned a bachelor of arts degree in 1938 and her master's in education in 1950, both from
the University of Texas in Austin. In 1954 she graduated from the University of Texas Medical Branch in Galveston and began practicing medicine in
Corpus Christi. Dr. Garcia later became involved with higher education. She
was elected to public office as a trustee of the Del Mar College (community
college). She won reelection for over twenty years. She received numerous
awards for her service to the community, including induction into the Texas
Women's Hall of Fame. Her gift to us was through her role as an educator
(historian, author, teacher, principal) and medical professional who cared for
thousands of patients (and delivered over 10,000 babies). She also was the
founder of the Carmelite Day Nursery Parents and Friends Club and the
Spanish American Genealogical Association. While we have a record of her
accomplishments, her story must be told in print and video format so that future generations understand the struggle and fortitude of Chicanas who came
before. She was a woman in charge of her destiny. She utilized her influence,
personal wealth, and knowledge to assist others. Dr. Cleotilde Garcia served
not only as an example of a strong female role model, but also of the reality
that women, even strong ones, are often overlooked. Her story is often a side
note to the accomplishments of her brother, Dr. Héctor Pérez García.

## Leadership Studies

Women have often been overlooked in leadership studies due to male bias in
definitional and theoretical constraints, as leadership studies have focused on
what are considered masculine traits of white males.[16] Very little research exists

on Chicana leadership models because of the bias of researchers and omission by feminists. Women leadership studies often focus on gender differences without regard to ethnicity and class. Chicanas have long opposed such a narrow view and included in their analysis the intersection of race/ethnicity and class. As Eden E. Torres writes about her experimental course at the University of Minnesota called "Chicana/Latina Quarter," offered by the women's studies department, "Jane can never become part of the culture that tantalizes her. She is locked in a worldview that does not question the construction of whiteness as dominant and brownness as subordinate. . . . Even as we confront the mixture that exists in our very bodies, we Chicanas can never forget that *mestizaje*, border crossing, and hybrid identities are also the history of the rape of brown women."[17]

Opportunities for women to participate in the public arena have opened greatly over the past few decades. Over half of the women in the world who have served as top public officials (presidents, prime ministers) came into office in the 1990s.[18] However, it is important to note that the study of Chicana leadership will be determined primarily by new scholars who are interested in pursuing such knowledge and/or experienced researchers' making adjustments in their research to include and examine these often overlooked areas.

## Chicanas and the Struggle to Lead

Marta Cotera, a prominent Chicana scholar, was a pioneer in documenting and providing a profile of Mexican American women so that curricula could be developed for and about Chicanas.[19] Her book *Diosa y Hembra* took a stand against the "myths and stereotypes [that] abound because very few resources have been allocated to objective research and to documenting historical fact."[20] Not only did this book provide the illumination of Chicana history from the colonial period in Mexico to the 1960s in the United States, but it also discussed the socioeconomic circumstances of Chicanas in the United States. Cotera discussed Chicana historical accomplishments, family, stereotypes, and the future of Chicanas. Cotera predicted that Chicanas would have to acquire positions of leadership in order to more effectively push their agenda. Cotera also opined that in order to change the dominant culture's image of Chicanas as slovenly, brazen, and undesirable, they had to become activists.

Cotera's work *The Chicana Feminist* asserts that Anglo feminist pioneers at the turn of the twentieth century assisted in the creation of Chicana stereotypes by not documenting Chicana feminist activities.[21] Cotera in this book also explored the racist and sexist forms of Anglo oppression and the added burden of classism on Chicanas. Chicanas have a feminist heritage and legacy in their own history, but the world would not know it from reading white women's versions of struggle for equality. Cotera cites Beverly Hawkins and Charlotte Bunch as proof of this "guilt by omission and commission." Beverly Hawkins describes how societal improvements made in the name of "Woman" were not shared or distributed equally among all women, certainly not brown or black women. Bunch's discussion of "privileged passivity" details how Anglo women in positions of power take for granted their position and therefore fail to take risks or tough stands on issues regarding all women. This bestowed upon white women the privilege of their color. While white women were not given the same privileges as white males, they still were endowed with "white privilege." In a nutshell, white privilege can be summarized as a set of freedoms and advantages bestowed upon people whose skin is white that is not afforded to people of color, such as (but not limited to): the ability to avoid people who you have been trained to mistrust, being able to shop without having to worry about being harassed by security guards or police, being able to possess ill manners (talking with your mouth full, not saying please or thank you, etc.) without having it attributed to your race, and the ability to worry or not worry about such topics as racism.[22] In *White Women's Rights*, author Louise Newman discards the idea that feminism was a movement centered on egalitarian principles. Instead white women viewed themselves as the appointed "civilizers" of the inferior beings such as immigrants, enslaved blacks, and Native Americans. When we discuss Chicana leadership, we cannot take for granted the experiences of both racism and sexism that she has had to overcome in order to pursue her leadership goals.

During the Civil Rights era of the 1950s and 1960s, Chicanas, Native American, and black women were not only engaging in tremendous battles for their basic civil rights but were also struggling to serve in prominent roles within those movements. Many Chicanas were involved in the fight for both racial and gender equality. In the Chicano Movement, Chicanas fought for an end to various forms of racial discrimination in the fabric of everyday life (segregation, substandard housing, low wages, English-only public schools, and police brutality, for example.) In the (white) Women's Movement, Chicanas fought to end pervasive sexual discrimination; for equal pay, against the glass ceiling; for expanded child care; and for control over their bodies. Chicanas were involved and torn between both struggles. Chicanas suffered from "Triple Oppression,"[23] which entailed the burden of being discriminated against based on class (socioeconomic status), race/ethnicity, and gender. In addition to this triple oppression, there exists for Chicanas another form of oppression. The oppression comes from other women and from within their own cultural sphere. Women who were taking leadership roles in the fight against injustice on multiple fronts were criticized for drawing attention away from or not being completely loyal to the Women's Movement or to the Chicano or Black Power Movement. However, each movement neglected one or more essential pieces of Chicana liberation.[24] Middle-class white feminists lacked insight into the issues of racial discrimination, which Chicanas shared with their male counterparts, and Chicano men could not fully grasp the plight of women within a male-dominated society.[25]

Chicanas are at a disadvantage in their access to economic resources; they still suffer from being limited to gender-specific jobs and lower wages relative to men.[26] They also have a long and vibrant history with leadership roles from organizing strikes and assisting with issues in their communities to running for elected office. Recent insightful works that document the activism of Chicanas within their places of employment and communities have arisen, but more are still needed.[27] Chicanas enter the political arena to assist their community as well as for the conventional motivations that drive women to serve in political office.[28] Chicanas focus on interdependence and collectivism in their leadership style, and they do not place as much emphasis on hierarchy as would their male counterparts but instead utilize a less rigid, less formal style of leadership.[29] One such woman is the remarkable Representative Irma Rangel, who passed away in March of 2003. This amazing Chicana was described as a "Texas Trailblazer" in MALDEF's (Mexican American Legal and Educational Fund) Winter 2003 newsletter for her incredible role as an advocate for higher education and her twenty-five years of public service. It was Representative Rangel who was crucial in acquiring almost half a billion dollars for South Texas universities. Here is the perfect example of a Chicana who contributed to future generations, and we should ask ourselves: What will be our contribution to the next generation?

## The Next Step

*"Cuando reclamamos nuestra historia, afirmamos nuestro futuro.*[30] (When we reclaim our history, we affirm our future.) Long before my birth, the battle for the opportunities I have received was waged. The mere fact that there are words on this page, written by a Chicana, speaks to the lasting power of those fierce and courageous women who broke down barriers, created inroads, and paved the way unselfishly for the generations to come. Within the brief history of the United States, there have been numerous Mexican American

women activists who have served as role models for modern-day Chicanas. They include labor leaders Lucia Gonzalez Parsons, Maria Hernandez, Emma Tenayuca, and Virginia Musquiz, to name a few.

Sadly, for every success story that is told there remain countless others that have gone untold. Activism on multiple levels: social, political, and economic, is occurring daily, but its documentation has yet to be made. How can we begin to study women who have contributed so much of their lives and sacrificed for the good of the community? Documentation and analysis is the answer. We cannot rely on others to document our stories. In 1969, the National Women's Hall of Fame (NWHF) was created to honor the achievements of women in various fields from the humanities to science, from education to politics. The NWHF has honored Chicana activists such as Dolores Huerta and Linda Alvarado but still has not made room for others mentioned in this essay. The need to preserve the history of a greater number of Chicanas is essential if we wish to provide future generations the inspirational stories of their predecessors.

It is with this in mind that *Chicanas in Charge: Texas Women in the Public Arena* celebrates the accomplishments of modern Chicanas in their various leadership roles and assists in the documenting of those achievements for future generations. *Chicanas in Charge* seeks to retrieve and preserve vivid accounts of Chicana leaders who have and continue to lower barriers for the rest of us. In reading the accounts of their past and the success of unrelenting courage, we must never forget that the battle is not over . . . we must persist so that a constant flow of role models can be supplied for the next generation and the next until the question of "*¿Dónde están las mujeres; las mujeres cafecitas, hermosas y fuertes?*" is no longer necessary.

## Notes

1. Kurly Tlapoyawa, *We Will Rise: Rebuilding the Mexika Nation* (Victoria, B.C.: Trafford Publishing, 2000).

2. Arturo Meza Gutiérrez, *Mosaico de Turquesas* (Mexico City: 1999).

3. The Náhuatl words for these energetic manifestations are often misinterpreted through a European, Christian lens, and misassigned a gender. *Tlalok*, for example, is interpreted as "Rain God," when in fact it is made up of two Náhuatl words, *Tlalli*, meaning earth, and *Okli*, meaning liquor, for a metaphoric representation of the rain, which nourishes the earth. Similarly, *Tonalteotl*, which is often translated at "Sun God," actually means hot (*tonali*) energy (*teotl*). Because *teotl* appears in many names of the natural elements, and because it is similar in pronunciation to the Greek *theos*, it has been used interchangeably for the word "God." Source for this is Irene Dominguez, a native Náhuatl speaker who deciphers Náhuatl texts and codices for

the Museum of Anthropology in Mexico City. She gave Náhuatl language workshops at Kalpulli Izkalli in Albuquerque in January, 1999.

4. Tlapoyawa, *We Will Rise*.

5. Meza Gutiérrez, *Mosaico de Turquesas*.

6. Richard F. Townsend, *The Aztecs* (New York: Thames and Hudson Ltd, 1992).

7. Tlapoyawa, *We Will Rise*.

8. Tlapoyawa, *We Will Rise*.

9. Ce Acatl, No. 6, 1991.

10. See also Jacqueline M. Martínez, "Radical Ambiguities and the Chicana Lesbian: Body Topographies on Contested Lands," in *Spoils of War: Women of Color, Cultures, and Revolutions*, ed. T. Denean Sharpley-Whiting and Renee T. White, 127–50 (Lanham, MD: Rowman and Littlefield, 1997). On page 132 Martínez has a paragraph captioned "Mother of the Mestizo People" in which she describes Malintzin Tenepal "as the interpreter, guide, and mistress for Cortez, La Malinche facilitated the conquest. For that, she is considered both the 'mother of the Mexican people' (mestizos), and 'La Chingada,' the fucked-one, a traitor to her people." See also S. Cypress, *La Malinche in Mexican Literature* (Austin: University of Texas Press, 1991).

11. Bernal Díaz del Castillo, *Historia de Conquista de la Nueva España* (Madrid: Espasa, 1997), p. 101. Printed almost a century after his death in 1682.

12. Henry Ramos, *The American G.I. Forum: In Pursuit of the Dream, 1948–1983* (Houston, TX: Arte Publico Press, 1999). See also *Justice for My People: The Dr. Hector P. Garcia Story*, a documentary available at www.justiceformypeople.org; Ignacio García, *Hector Garcia: In Relentless Pursuit of Justice* (Houston, TX: Arte Publico Press, 2002).

13. Armando Navarro, *The Cristal Experiment: A Chicano Struggle for Community Control* (Madison: University of Wisconsin Press, 1998); José Angel Gutiérrez, *The Making of a Chicano Militant: Lessons from Cristal*, Wisconsin Studies in American Autobiography (Madison: University of Wisconsin Press, 1999); Armando Navarro, *Mexican American Youth Organization: Avant-Garde of the Chicano Movement in Texas* (Austin: University of Texas Press, 2000).

14. See Margaret Sayers Peden, trans., *A Woman of Genius: The Intellectual Autobiography of Sor Juana Ines de la Cruz* (Salisbury, CT: Lime Rock Press); O. Paz, *Sor Juana Inés de la Cruz: Las trampas de la fe* (México, DF: Fondo de Cultura Económica, 1997); P. Kirt, *Sor Juana Inés de la Cruz: Religion, Art, and Feminism* (New York: Continuum Publishing Co, 1998); Jacqueline Nanfito, *El Sueno: Cartographies of Knowledge and the Self* (New York: Peter Lang Publishing, 2000).

15. Anna Macias, "Women and the Mexican Revolution 1910–1920," *Americas (Acad. of Am. Franciscan Hist.)* 37(1): 53–82. Shirlene Soto, *Emergence of Modern Mexican Woman: Her Participation in Revolution and Struggle for Equality, 1910–1940* (Denver, CO: Ardern Press, Inc., 1990) depicts the harsh reality of life as a Mexican woman (from forced rape to the backdrop of slavery). It provides the reader with a picture of how women during this time (prerevolutionary) were required to live under the constant scrutiny and shadow of a male-dominated society. Women were rel-

egated to thinking only about marriage, their husbands, their family, and the Church. We see why the women had no choice but to rebel against these conditions. Alicia Arrizon, "Soldaderas and the Staging of the Mexican Revolution," *The Drama Review* 42(1): 90–113. See also Elizabeth Salas, *Soldaderas in the Mexican Military* (Austin: University of Texas Press, 1990); and Doris E. Perlin, *Eight Bright Candles: Courageous Women of Mexico* (Plano, TX: Republic of Texas Press, 1995) for mini-biographies of Mexican women, including Francisca Alvarez of Goliad, Texas, and Andrea Castanon, aka Madam Candelaria of San Antonio (Alamo mission). For an earlier work on Andrea Castanon, see Maurice Elfer, *Madam Candelaria: Unsung Heroine of the Alamo* (Houston, TX: The Rein Company, 1933).

16. K. Klenke, *Women and Leadership: A Contextual Perspective* (New York: Springer Publishing, 1996).

17. Eden E. Torres, *Chicana without Apology: The New Chicana Cultural Studies* (New York: Routledge, 2003).

18. N. J. Adler, "Global Leadership: Women Leaders," in *Advances in Global Leadership*, vol. 1, ed. W. H. Mobley et al., pp. 49–73 (Stamford, CT: JAI Press Inc., 1999). This piece looks at issues that are specific to women on a global scale. It provides a discussion on shifting features of global leadership in the twenty-first century.

19. Martha P. Cotera, *Diosa y Hembra: The History and Heritage of Chicanas in the U.S.* (Austin, TX: Information Systems Development, 1976); Marta Cotera, *The Chicana Feminist* (Austin, TX: Information Systems Development, 1977).

20. Cotera, *Diosa y Hembra*.

21. Cotera, *The Chicana Feminist*.

22. Peggy McIntosh, *White Privilege and Male Privilege: A Personal Account of Coming to See Correspondences through Work in Women's Studies*, Working Paper No. 189. Wellesley, MA: Wellesley College, Center for Research on Women, 1988; Robert Jensen, "Fighting the Power at UT," *Texas Observer*, November 20, 1998, pp.12–14.

23. Alfredo Mirande and Evangelina Enriquez, *La Chicana: The Mexican American Woman* (Chicago: University of Chicago Press, 1979); Teresa Cordova et al., *Chicana Voices: Intersections of Class, Race and Gender* (Austin: University of Texas Press, 1986); Mirta Vidal, *Chicanas Speak Out Women: New Voice of La Raza* (New York: Pathfinder Press, 1971). The books delve into the contribution that Chicanas have made to the Chicano movement and explains why their actions, when trying to form their own organizations or trying to find their own voice, should not be seen as Chicanas turning their backs on "*La Causa*" but instead a way of showing that Chicanas need to be heard and they will no longer stand for the oppression that faces them from inside or outside of the movement.

24. Mirande and Enriquez, *La Chicana*; Irene I. Blea, *La Chicana and the Intersection of Race, Class, and Gender* (New York: Praeger Press, 1992). Blea discusses the contributions of Chicanas from the colonial period to the modern era. Her book details the struggle that many Chicanas have faced as they have tried to create their own space in a world that discriminates against them because of their race, their social class, and their gender. The book details some of the overlooked efforts made by

Chicana activists and academics during the Chicano movement; Marguerite V. Marin, *Social Protest in an Urban Barrio: A Study of the Chicano Movement, 1966–1974*, Vol. 1 of *Class, Ethnicity, Gender, and the Democratic Nation* (Lanham, MD: University Press of America, 1991).

25. Some Chicanas also are unable to grasp or experience the "Triple Oppression," for example Cherie Moraga writes in 1986, "I was not a part of La Causa. I never went to one meeting of MECHA on campus. *No soy tonta.* I would have been murdered in El Movimiento—light skinned, unable to speak Spanish well enough to hang; miserably attracted to women and fighting it; and constantly questioning all authority, including men's. I felt I did not belong there." See her "From a Long Line of Vendidas: Chicanas and Feminism," in *Feminist Studies/Critical Studies*, ed. Teresa de Laurentis (Bloomington: Indiana University Press, 1986), p. 183.

26. Cordova et al., *Chicana Voices*. Gilbert Gonzalez, *Mexican Consuls and Labor Organizing: Imperial Politics in the American Southwest* (Austin: University of Texas Press, 1999).

27. Mary Pardo, *Mexican American Women Activists: Identity and Resistance in Two Los Angeles Communities* (Philadelphia: Temple University Press, 1998); Christine Sierra, "From Activist to Mayor: The Controversial Politics of Debbie Jaramillo in Santa Fe, New Mexico," Presented at the annual meeting of the Western Political Science Association, Tucson, AZ, 1997; William V. Flores, "Mujeres en Huelga: Cultural Citizenship and Gender Empowerment in a Cannery Strike," in *Latino Cultural Citizenship: Claiming Identity, Space, and Rights*, ed. William V. Flores and Rina Benmayor, pp. 210–54 (Boston: Beacon, 1997).

28. Marisela Marquez, "Redefining Politics: Survey on Chicano and Latina Political Actors," Presented at the annual meeting of the Western Political Science Association, Tucson, AZ, 1997; Alma García, *Chicana Feminist Thought: The Basic Historical Writings* (New York: Routledge, 1997).

29. Yolanda Flores Niemann, Susan H. Armitage, Patricia Hart, and Karen Weathermon, *Chicana Leadership* (Lincoln: University of Nebraska Press, 2002); Kay Barbara Warren and Susan C. Bourque, "Gender, Power, and Communication: Women's Responses to Political Muting in the Andes," in *Women Living Change*, ed. Susan C. Bourque and Donna Robinson Divine (Philadelphia: Temple University Press, 1985).

30. Louis Mendoza, *Historia: The Literary Making of Chicana and Chicano History* (College Station: Texas A&M University Press, 2001).

# PART I

# *ADELITAS:* THE WARRIOR TRAILBLAZERS

The 1960s was an era of tremendous political advancement by Chicanos. The Viva Kennedy Clubs, organized in Texas largely by Bexar County Commissioner Albert A. Peña Jr. with state codirectors Hector P. Garcia of the American GI Forum and Texas state senator Henry B. González (D-San Antonio), helped elect John F. Kennedy president of the United States.[1] Chicanas played a central role in both the national growth of the American GI Forum (AGIF), the Viva Kennedy Clubs (VK), and in Texas politics.

For example, Olga Peña organized Chicanas into the Bexar County Democratic Women's Club and built the local network to elect and continue reelecting her husband, Albert A. Peña Jr. while he was traveling across the state organizing VK clubs and being commissioner. Olga Peña was the real organizer at the local level. During her marriage to Albert, Olga helped support the family while he completed law school. She gave birth to seven children. She managed home and family while maintaining the political machine that sustained her husband in public office. The Peñas divorced after his electoral defeat as county commissioner. Olga never remarried. She continued to work in the San Antonio community with the Mexican American Unity Council (MAUC) and was active in political campaigns of others. She is now retired.

Hector P. Garcia, a medical doctor in Corpus Christi, Texas, could not have organized the AGIF as easily had his sister Cleotilde Garcia, also a medical doctor, not taken over his client load while he also traveled the state and country, attending meetings and making speeches. She was his best lieutenant.

After the presidential election, the VK clubs did not vanish, rather, Peña and others reorganized themselves into the Political Association of Spanish Speaking Organizations (PASO).[2] Local PASO leaders such as Virginia Muzquiz helped elect the first Chicano city council slate, *Los Cinco Candidatos*, in Crystal City, Texas, in 1963.[3] PASO opened the first doors of equal representation for Chicanas within the political organization. Chicanas in every PASO chapter began to exercise public leadership and get credit for their contributions. Ms. Muzquiz became a local PASO officer; she attended state conventions and became a candidate for the Crystal City Council in 1964. The entire PASO-backed slate of Chicanos lost. She then sought the Democratic nomination as state representative; the first Chicana to do so in Texas, also in 1964. She lost that race but helped increase the number of Chicanos that paid the poll tax and registered to vote in significant numbers throughout the area of the district.

During the rise of the Raza Unida Party in 1970, she helped found the local party in Zavala County and later became a candidate. Ms. Muzquiz with all this organizing and election experience became an expert on the intricacies of the Texas Election Code. Ms. Muzquiz was the first Chicana elected in Zavala County as county clerk in 1974. She passed away in the late 1990s.

Alicia Chacón of El Paso had a similar path to power. She learned politics at an early age from her father and as a young woman worked for the local Democratic Party chairman. She worked as a volunteer and paid staff on many local campaigns, electing others and also getting herself, the lone woman, elected to the school board. In later years she worked on the presidential campaigns of Jimmy Carter, Walter Mondale, Michael Dukakis, and Bill Clinton, offering advice on transition teams to the winners. She headed the Small Business Administration regional office in Dallas and returned to El Paso for semiretirement. The lure of public office was hard to resist. She sought and won election to the city council. Eventually, she became the first Chicana elected as county judge in El Paso County. After her defeat in a reelection bid, she became the chief executive officer for the local United Way. She is now retired but highly sought after for endorsement by those seeking public office.

Lastly, electoral politics was not the only public activity of the Chicano community; grassroots leaders emerged, such as Reies López Tijerina, originally from Falls City, Texas. In the late 1950s and through the 1960s, he became the international leader of the Chicano Land Recovery Movement.[4]

His wife, María Escobar, often worked two jobs to support the family and Reies during all his travels in Texas, Arizona, New Mexico, California, Colorado, New York, Spain, and Mexico. During all his periods in jail or as a fugitive and during all his travels across the United States organizing and proselytizing, she not only supported Reies but also single-handedly raised the growing family, all six of them. After the first two children were born in Texas and the Tijerinas became itinerant preachers across the country, she was pregnant every other year.

Given Tijerina's notoriety and bold challenges to the government of New Mexico and the United States, María suffered physical harm, such as bombings, shootings, kidnappings and rapes of her children, and constant police surveillance and harassment. Rosa, the oldest daughter, was a frequent companion to her father in his travels to Mexico. Rosa also was the office administrator in Albuquerque, New Mexico, of the Land Recovery Movement organization. During the raid on the courthouse in Tierra Amarilla, New Mexico, Rosa was the reconnaissance figure. She was the first one on the front line and also the first one arrested when the men took to the mountains for escape. For that act she spent time in jail and also endured, like her mother, the physical danger that accrued to being Tijerina's daughter. To this day she fights depression and suicidal ideation stemming from personal abuse and terror dating to the late 1960s.

These five *Adelita* Warriors were among the first Chicana trailblazers in the public arena in Texas and the nation. They were trailblazers for others that followed in their footsteps.

## Notes

1. See Ignacio Garcia's seminal works *Hector Garcia: In Relentless Pursuit of Justice* (Houston, TX: Arte Publico Press, 2002) and *Viva Kennedy: Mexican Americans in Search of Camelot* (College Station: Texas A&M University Press, 2000).

2. The California VK clubs opted for the name of Mexican American Political Association (MAPA).

3. See John Shockley and Armando Navarro for incisive description and analysis of the politics in this community during this time frame.

4. See my translation and editing of his autobiography, *They Called Me "King Tiger": My Struggle for the Land and Our Rights* (Houston, TX: Arte Publico Press, 2000).

# CHAPTER ONE

~

# Olga Ramos Peña

"My maiden name is Ramos, of course, and I was born here in San Antonio, Texas. My parents came from Mexico. My father is from Salinas Hidalgo, Nuevo León. My mother is from Monterrey, Mexico, and they came to the United States when they were very young. They had third-grade education, both of them. They became citizens of the United States, I believe in 1937, and I grew up in the West Side on Leona Street right in the heart of San Antonio. I went to Navarro School for elementary school and then I went to Joel Chandler Harris and then to San Antonio Tech. While growing up we lived in a *vecindad* (neighborhood) and, of course, we didn't have plumbing facilities inside." That is how Olga Peña began her interview, speaking directly to the question of her family background and not stopping until an interruption gave opportunity to get names, dates, places, and the like.

Olga grew up in a segregated neighborhood. At age eighteen, she graduated from a segregated high school in 1943. She was born in 1925 to Guadalupe Gutierrez Ramos, her father, and Francis Navarro Diaz, her mother. Her mom stayed at home. Her dad worked delivering soda pop to retailers. He worked for a *Mexicano*-owned soda pop manufacturer. Olga, the oldest child, had two bothers, Guadalupe, whose nickname was Wally, and Hugo, both veterans of wars.

Her experience in the segregated public schools remains vivid in her mind. "I had a hard time. All I knew was Spanish when I went to school. I had a very bad accent when I spoke English. I didn't know any English when I went there, but I was very lucky that I got one of the teachers who was

17

bilingual, so she would teach us in both languages . . . if they heard us speaking Spanish from the office, you know, the Anglo people were the ones that were running the schools, of course, they would take a ruler and start hitting us. They would tell you to put out your hands and they would hit us with the ruler. And I don't mean just a little tap. I mean hard. And we didn't want to speak, so we would get away from the teachers and everybody to talk our lingo you know."

Her dad would drive her to school in his delivery truck. They had no family automobile. Olga's favorite thing to do since she was eight years old was dancing. Lydia Magon from the neighborhood taught the young kids how to dance the typical *folklórico* dances from Mexico. At the San Antonio recreation department, Berta Almaguer was the instructor. Olga learned the "*jarabe tapatío, Espuelas, Chapaneca* . . . I know about a hundred dances."

"Because of my dancing and being in the Spanish Club and I spoke to everybody. I was very friendly. Everybody knew me at school and any time there were any assemblies, I always danced. I got to be political because . . . I wanted to help. When I was about fourteen. While I was living in the *vecindad* a lot of the people were illiterate and I was, ever since I was small, I was always trying to help people. Some of the elderly and things like that and if they needed translation or something, they would come to me. For example, there was a man, a gentleman that had gotten hit by a taxicab and the lawyer, they had hired a lawyer, and then he came to the home and they were right next door, so they called me to go and do the interpretation and I did. I call myself a natural born advocate for people that are in need."

Olga's mom would not come and defend or protect her at school. She had to fend for herself. "I had to fight my own way. When my brothers got into trouble and they wanted Mom to come, it was Olga. When my cousins got in trouble and they would call for their mother, my cousins would send me. Tell Olga to go. *Háblenle a la prima* (call the cousin), and then call me."

Dancing became Olga's first paying job. She danced at various events for pay and even traveled to other cites to perform. After high school she attended Daughn's Business College. "I wanted to be a secretary. What a big deal, you know." She took a job with Perez Manufacturing Company, a dress making factory. They made an exclusive line of dresses for the department stores of the era, Joske's, Sakowitz, and Foley's in Houston. She worked there long enough to see the company go out of business. But before she left, she met her future husband, Albert Peña Jr. "OK, I was working at Perez and that was right across from the *San Antonio Express News*. The factory was right there and I was walking to lunch, to go get my lunch at lunchtime and I saw a friend of mine coming out of one of the buildings there and he says, 'Olga,

I am so happy to see you,' and this and that. He told me he was marrying this girl that I went to school with and he says, 'I want you to stand at my wedding.'" Olga agreed. Her friend asked her upstairs to meet someone. It was her escort for the wedding. "And it was Albert." But Olga had a boyfriend who she wanted to stand with, but her friend was adamant that it had to be Albert. So, Olga reluctantly agreed. "I just stood with him at the wedding. There was nothing, you know. I wasn't interested in him or anything like that. But Albert Peña, Jr. was persistent. He was *terco* (determined)." Within six months, they were married in September of 1947. "He had just come back from the war, World War II, and he was a veteran. He had very, very recently gotten out of the service. He was in the navy and he has just gotten out of the service and he was at St. Mary's. He was going to St. Mary's. [This was] about February of '47. Albert didn't finish there. There was discrimination at St. Mary's. He dropped out because of the discrimination. Or something happened that he got out. He is real smart, so I don't think that it was whether grades were the reason or what. And he was gonna quit because his father was going to open a pawn shop right there where that big courthouse is in the center of San Antonio. And Albert says, 'Well, honey, you know, Dad says that he can put us up and he can help me start a business and it's a very good business.' And I said, 'No. Albert. You wanted law. Don't you want to be a lawyer?'" Olga herself became the *terca* (determined) to move to Houston so Albert could finish his law degree. He did. "And, of course we were struggling. Albert going to school, and then I had Bill, my son, my first born, who was Bill Peña [William Albert] and we were . . . and he was a baby when we moved out to Houston. And there was a lot of discrimination in Houston. Worse. They didn't even have Spanish, Mexican food. We couldn't find Mexican food. No Spanish music. *Casi nada* (almost nothing), *y yo estaba acostumbrada* (and I was accustomed to) that I would turn my radio on to the Mexican music, you know."

While in Houston, the couple lived in Pasadena. They could not afford the rents in Houston, so they lived in subsidized housing in Pasadena. The local mayor had befriended Albert. No Mexicans were allowed to rent and live in the housing project but "Mayor Sam" got them in anyway. Olga gave birth to their daughter, Sandy, in Pasadena.

Friends and law classmates wanted Albert to remain and practice law in Pasadena, but he and Olga wanted to come home to San Antonio. Albert told Pasadena folks that he wanted to come home to help his people. Those words made Olga more convinced than ever that she had married the right man. "Because we had the same thoughts. Because remember I said earlier that I helped people in the neighborhood and there were other things that I did." The Peña family did not come back to San Antonio right after Albert's graduation; they stayed in Pasadena another year or two. Albert passed the bar exam and obtained his license to practice law. Again, Olga got *terca* and reminded Albert regularly about his promise to come home and help the people. "You said you were going to go back and help the people, so we are going to go back and help the people. I don't want to stay here."

They moved to San Antonio and Albert began to practice law with his father and brother, Richard. The law firm was named Peña, Peña and Peña. The couple first moved into a duplex off Palmetto, then to an apartment off West Avenue on Hermine. And Olga began to have more babies, all girls: Sandra Francis, Mary Magdalena, Olga, and Roxanne. She also started voting and attending precinct conventions. Olga and Albert started in politics together. "We would go to conventions, both of us, and we liked what we

saw, both of us. I loved it. I still do. So, I started getting into clubs. I was the first Mexican to get into the Democratic Women. I was treasurer and this and that. I never strived for it or anything. I just wanted to be loose. I didn't want to be committed by the *bolillas* (white women) to follow a certain candidate. I began to learn the issues and so I got very interested in it and I said, 'My God, this is a new world. This is how we help the *Mexicano*. This is how we do things.' And I started teaching myself because I was interested in it."

Olga accompanied Albert to Mathis and Hondo, two Texas communities with a history of school segregation and discrimination against Mexicans. Albert did the lawyer work while Olga visited with children and parents, asking questions, gathering evidence, and identifying potential witnesses. In Mathis, Olga was furious to find an overgrown boy purposely retained in the third grade by the Anglo teacher so he could translate for her what the Spanish-speaking children were saying. They traveled at their own expense, and Albert did the legal work for free on behalf of the American GI Forum and the League of United Latin American Citizens (LULAC).

Olga continued recruiting other *Mexicanas* into the Democratic Women's Club. "We would win at conventions because, of course, we had majority. We knew everything. I was very active in that. Now that I want to take a lot of credit for, because I got the people organized in that area in the conventions." Olga developed a roster of potential votes. She maintained her roster by calling people, visiting them in person, at church, in the street, and at stores while shopping. "I got all my church people involved in politics, even the Anglos that had the same thinking as myself. They were liberals and they wanted to go this way. I would get them involved. A mixture there. I mean, we couldn't win by ourselves. Now we have a lot of *Mexicanos* voting, but we had to pull them out to get them to the polls."

This was the era of the poll tax when a person had to pay $1.75 to register to vote. And *Mexicanos* were not deputized to collect the poll taxes. During the Dwight D. Eisenhower presidential campaign in 1952, Albert ran for the state legislature. Olga opposed that decision but it had been made. She helped in the campaign but not centrally. Albert made the runoff but ultimately lost. "In 1952, I ran our first West Side Headquarters for any presidential nominee or any political thing. I believe they didn't even have areas where they had a campaign headquarters in those days. This was the beginning of that era. And I was in charge and I was already in Democratic Women. But because we started at the precinct convention, we got very involved with the Democratic Party and, of course, I learned. But I could never have been one of those wives that sat in the background that said, 'No, I don't like it. You just go do it.' I loved it and I still do."

Soon after the national election, Albert announced he was going to run for the legislature again in 1954. This time Olga was adamant that he not seek a position that did not pay well. "I had two kids or three kids at that time, three babies. And I said, 'Let me work and go to it.'" But Albert had a *machismo* attack. His wife was not going to work. He was the breadwinner. He was the man. He had to work and support the family, not Olga. He loved her role as an organizer and her involvement with politics but would not have her working for money. Olga asked, "Why don't you run for something else that provides like a job, you know? Something that provides your funds, your money, you can support the family, and you can do what you want to. We can still do what we are doing, your organizing and, you can be the bread winner, and support us, the family support." Albert agreed. He ran for Bexar County Commissioner. Each Texas county has four commissioners and a county judge. County commissioners in Texas are elected from four different districts, in essence, single member districts. Bexar County in 1956 had many potential Mexican American voters in one county commissioner precinct. Olga called on her *compadres*, couples that had baptized her babies, Lalo Solis and Rubén Mungia, to help in the campaign. They would come over to her house, or she and Albert would go over to theirs. "I wouldn't stay in the kitchen, you know. I sat there and I heard everything that went on." Olga ran the campaign headquarters despite Albert's objections. He would tell her to call people to help, and she did. She knew them and Albert did not. He would ask her to run interference with the county Democratic Executive Committee on this or that issue. Olga would do just that. She knew them by first name. Albert did not. Olga had the list and roster of voters. Albert did not. Slowly, Albert realized that Olga was the organizer and without her, he was a doomed candidate. He let her loose. Olga ran with the organizing leadership mantle, "I would just call and call and just hit the bushes, hit the bushes, hit the bushes. Door knocking, door knocking, and by meeting in the church and this and that. All the time. I belonged to the auxiliary, the American GI Forum . . . your natural groups." Olga got them all involved in the campaign and voting. She called her friends at KCOR, the Raul Cortez family, and Manuel Leal at the other radio station. The Spanish-language media provided campaign support for Albert's race. It does not get clearer than this. Women do most of the electoral work in campaigns but seldom get the credit.

Peña got elected the first *Mexicano* commissioner in Bexar County. He now had a good salary. He was going to be paid to help the people. Olga was going to be able to keep organizing voters. She could afford childcare and didn't have to take the kids out every time she had a meeting or leave them with family. She did not have to get a paying job. Everyone won.

The newly elected county clerk, Jimmy Knight, a liberal, deputized additional voter registrars. For the first time, Mexican Americans were deputized. Olga was among the first Mexican Americans to be able to collect the poll tax and register people to vote. The number of registered *Mexicano* voters began to climb dramatically in Bexar County. "We were educating the people to vote. And sometimes they could pay it. You have to buy it, *para que voten por alguien que nos va a ayudar* (so that they would vote for someone who will help us), and things like that."

Between the first election in 1956 and the reelection campaign in 1960, Olga was busy building an organization in the commissioner precinct and across Bexar County. She recruited more women into the Democratic Women's Club, including Minnie Garcia, Esther Bernal, Carmen Villegas, Ana Esparza, Elvira Carbajal, and others. She also reached out to black women such as Ruth Jones, now McLendon, and Mrs. Howard. Olga became more active with the American GI Forum. She invited and organized their national convention to be held in San Antonio. She got involved in LULAC. During the same time period, she also had more babies.

The men in LULAC and the American GI Forum decided to join the John F. Kennedy presidential campaign under the organizational name of "Viva Kennedy Clubs."[1] The women, like Olga, knew the organizing and grassroots work would fall on their lap. The men talked, the women organized. "And we were organizing all the time, all this time, organizing, organizing, organizing through the executive committee, through the *barrio*, through Democratic Women, through GI Forum, throughout the state with the GI Forum. And anytime we needed something *le llamabas a fulano*, a Bob Sanchez in McAllen, Ed Peña in Laredo, and so on and so forth." The Mexican American community across the state and the nation organized themselves under the Viva Kennedy Clubs. Albert became a delegate to the National Democratic Convention held in Los Angeles, California; Olga did not. "I became a delegate several times to state conventions. I never got to the national." Olga accompanied him to Los Angeles and observed and learned from the proceedings. She was pregnant again. "As a matter of fact, Mrs. Kennedy was also pregnant at that time, and my baby, Roxie, was born about an hour [earlier than hers]. We made the front page, when our baby was born, that we had beat the Kennedy baby by . . . about an hour."

Lyndon Johnson was nominated for president as the favorite son from Texas in 1960. Albert was pledged to Johnson, but released on the subsequent ballots. He pledged to John F. Kennedy. Immediately, Olga got Albert on the telephone to Hector Garcia, the national leader of the American GI Forum, and the national LULAC president. "He called them too and said, 'Hey, I am at the convention and, what do you want? I am here. Will you, can we go with the clubs?'" They gave him the green light to join the Kennedy campaign as Viva Kennedy Clubs. Albert also cemented his relationship with the Kennedy bothers, particularly Robert and to a lesser extent, Ted.

These campaign clubs did not fade away after the election, as is the custom for political campaign organizations and groups whose sole purpose is to support the candidate. Viva Kennedy Clubs became the foundation for the Political Association of Spanish-Speaking Organizations (PASO) in Texas and the Mexican American Political Association (MAPA) in California. At the Houston, Texas, gathering of PASO, Henry B. González in his speech to those assembled took credit for the establishment of the Viva Kennedy Clubs, the formation of PASO, and other accomplishments. Olga was livid. "*Me pisas el cayo y respingó.* (You step on my corn and I'll rise up.) And so Henry got up there and he was talking about 'I, I, I, I, I.' He wasn't even at the convention in 1960. But then, Henry, at that point, he says, 'I, I, I, I, and Albert doesn't represent the *Mexicano*,' and all that . . . he says, 'I did this and that and that.' I was so angry and then, I wanted to jump up and say, 'Hey, you weren't in Los Angeles. Hey, you weren't this.'"

Olga did not say anything publicly about Henry B's gross exaggerations of contribution and accomplishment. As she explains, "Albert, you know, he was a spokesman, I was just to sit, I was the organizer, but I couldn't speak. I couldn't on an individual basis, I could not, you know." This may have been the beginning of the political rupture between Henry B. González and Albert Peña Jr. If not, the co-opting of the Peña *compadres*, Lalo Solis and Rubén Mungia, to the González camp may have been. In any event, it certainly added to the strain, tension, and bad blood between the two emerging political leaders.

Olga had tagged along to many meetings, but the growing family made it next to impossible for her to travel. Better Albert be absent than Olga and Albert be absent parents. "I sacrificed my family, and I don't think there was a need to do that. Because I could have taken care of both, but I was so involved in politics that somehow *no pude hacer a Bill que fuera al colegio, no-mas un rato.* (I couldn't make Bill go to college, just a little bit.) I think I raised my kids by myself, because he was always gone to Washington, this and that. As a matter of fact, that's what defeated him. Albert traveled too much to Washington. Albert got too complacent. They were calling Albert a communist."

There were other events that complicated the political life of the Peñas. In 1963 PASO supported and backed an all-*Mexicano* slate of candidates for control of the city council in Crystal City. That victory gave *Mexicanos* a big boost in political confidence but cost Albert Peña the organizational leadership role in PASO. Labor and white liberals backed away from the emerging Chicano nationalism. They dropped out of PASO and, more importantly, these two groups began to drop out of the Democratic coalition in the state. PASO attempted to repeat their electoral victory in Mathis, and that effort like Crystal City succeeded but only for one term. In both cities the *Mexicanos* held on to power for one term and were replaced by mixed slates of Anglos and Mexican Americans.

Olga ran Albert's campaigns for county commissioner four times until 1972 when they divorced. During that time the Chicano movement was in full swing. The Peñas were solidly behind the Chicano youth staging walkouts in the public schools; the farmworkers march from the Rio Grande Valley to Austin; the Palm Sunday March in Del Rio protesting Governor Preston Smith's removal of the VISTA volunteers from that county; and, in support of free speech rights and right to bail for Angela Davis, then a strong advocate for the Black Panther Party and a Communist. Albert and Olga began calling themselves national democrats, distancing themselves from the state Democratic Party headed by conservatives. Olga and Albert were solidly in the corner of the emerging Raza Unida Party. Olga hosted a fundraiser for the RUP at their home, one of the last events at that location.

Ernie Cortez became the Peña campaign manager for the 1972 election. He was no Olga. She was busy with another campaign, that of George McGovern for president. Albert Peña lost the race to Albert Bustamante, the congressional aide to Henry B. González. Olga, no longer the wife, had to find a job to support herself. "I have continued to work and in a different manner. I decided I needed a degree because I had to work for someone else. So, I started school and I started working. I took some classes. My English was bad so I started going to St. Mary's University. I got employment with the Unity Council [Mexican American Unity Council (MAUC)], with mental health. I was still political. Because we still, through MAUC, not to MAUC, as a—aside from MAUC—we got people together. And we did voter registration and stuff like that. Weekends we would meet and we would go voter registration. I even broke my hip going to a hospital, taking one of the kids that was having a baby and she was from Beeville. And she had gestation diabetes—babies having babies—and I fell and broke my hip." Olga continued working with MAUC in mental health, youth programs, housing, and counseling, but she had to be careful to keep separate her political work from that of MAUC, the nonprofit organization. She did less and less direct, hands-on political work and more just talking about the issues and making suggestions, offering her opinion to those that would listen.

Olga retired from full-time employment in 1996 to care for her mother and father. She moved her mother and father into her house. Her dad passed away during that time. But she still managed to volunteer to help in the Clinton presidential campaign. "OK, I am going to retire. I am going to help in a campaign. I am going to help in the Democratic Party. I am going to help there and I am going to do this and that. And as soon as I got Mom, I fell outside and broke my arm, so I was in a cast for about two or three months." Olga also contracted cancer. In 1974, two young *Mexicano* thugs broke into her house and mugged her. "I got injured badly."

Olga never regained complete control of her physical abilities. She has a hard time getting about, but she still drives herself everywhere. Her children and grandchildren come to visit. She has memorabilia galore around her home and in boxes. She is most lucid with the memories contained in the photographs, news clippings, political buttons, posters, telegrams, and programs of conventions and meetings. She is a walking historian of that era in San Antonio and Chicano politics in Bexar County, the state, and nationally. At this writing she is seventy-eight years young and looking forward to organizing her political mementoes into an exhibit. Olga has trouble using her arm, even for writing, but she hopes to write about her life someday soon.

# Note

Albert A. Peña Jr. passed away July 3, 2006.

1. See Ignacio García, *Viva Kennedy* (Austin: University of Texas Press, 2002) for the first comprehensive study on the role of Mexican Americans, particularly members of LULAC and the American GI Forum, in the Kennedy campaign.

# CHAPTER TWO

~

# Anita N. Martínez

Anita's grandparents came to Dallas in the late 1800s. On the maternal side were the Mongarras, "and they came from the Hill Country in San Antonio. And my grandmother was Trevino. On my father's side of the family, they came from Abilene and San Angelo and they were sheep shearers (*tasinques*)." The grandparents settled in what became known as Little Mexico, a *barrio* north of downtown Dallas that is now landmarked by a giant skyscraper, City Place. The Mongarras clan may have come from *Coahuila* into Texas. "I was able to go back to the Hill Country, to Bandera, and found out that we had been given land grants in 1854, in Bandera . . . in Privilege Creek, Texas." The migration to the Dallas area would suggest that perhaps the family lost the land at the time Texas seceded from the Union to join the Confederacy.

Anita was born in 1925, the fifth of six children to Anita Mongarras and Francisco Náñez. "My father would, would take people to the cotton fields and the onion fields, *las pizcas*. I would ride in the front of the cab with him . . . seven, six, seven, eight years old, and then, I'd get out there and I'd pick onions and I picked cotton just like the rest of them."

Anita's family included sisters Norita, Olivia, Tomasa, Beatrice, and a brother, Jose. Her older sister Norita was born in 1917. Jose, a twin to Olivia, was the only son. A sniper killed him during World War II while serving with General Patton in the 101st Infantry. Little Mexico was a thriving community, and Anita's mother was a beautician who had her salon in the front room of their home. This was the first beauty salon in Dallas for Mexican

American women. The Little Mexico neighborhood had seamstresses, tai-
lors, shoe shops, a bakery, and grocery store. At the heart of this community
was a Catholic school, St. Ann's. Anita longed to attend St. Ann's. She was
drawn to the clothing of the Sisters of Charity, their habits, particularly the
white, white, heavily starched wings on the headpiece. "We called them Angel Wings . . . just strolling from the school . . . to the convent . . . I was just
fascinated by it. They just looked so serene and so tranquil. I was curious to
see what they did." Her family couldn't afford the cost of the Catholic school
that also required school uniforms, so she attended public school. She attended Cumberland School through third grade. However, she did not give
up her dream of attending St. Ann's and became determined to find a way to
attend that school. Anita says, "I enrolled myself. I crossed Turney Avenue,
which is now Harry Hines Avenue, and went up to this nun, Sister of Charity, who worked at the Catholic School. I asked her 'What do you all do
here?' The nun replied, 'We teach here. Where do you go to school? Why
don't you come, to school here?' Anita replied, 'My mother said, "No, you
have to buy a uniform and we can't afford uniforms."' The nun told her they
could find a uniform for her. "They found a uniform that fit me and I went
to school there." That was the beginning of a love for St. Ann's that would
carry Anita through life. The nuns called her "Little Flower," and she was
their helper. She carried packages and accompanied them on errands. She
went to St. Ann's from the fourth through the seventh grade. Anita had to
attend the public vocational school, Crozier Technical High School, because
her dad had died and her mother suffered a heart attack, a stroke. At Crozier,
Anita would skip study hall; instead "I enrolled myself under the National
Youth Program and you got like six dollars a month. And then, with that I
was able to get my, my school supplies without having to ask my mother for
them."

Anita always seemed to have a goal and strategy for achievement. "So I
knew that, that I was, that I was going to have to be the breadwinner of the
family. So I had to take a course, I took a noncollege business course; you
know where they taught you shorthand and typing and computer now. And
then when I graduated I, my first job was at the Owen Beer Company." She
also took a civil service exam and moved on to a better job with the Aide
Service Command. At night she enrolled in night classes at Dallas College
on Ackard Street, which became Southern Methodist University (SMU).
"And I would go to SMU because I wanted to get college credits because I
decided then that I wanted to be an airline hostess." She recalls those family
experiences and history fondly. Anita did have a childhood.

As a child, Anita became involved in Mexican folkloric dancing, and it became a passion with her. Her youngest sister, Beatrice, "Bebe," had polio and that illness demanded much of her parents' attention. Her other sister, Tomasa, contracted tuberculosis. Her mother constantly was preoccupied with their illnesses and needs. She neglected Anita. But Anita found a way of getting attention elsewhere.

A lady in the neighborhood, Rosita Rosales, took her under her wing along with other neighborhood children and taught them Mexican folkloric dances. The lady's mother made the traditional Mexican dresses out of crepe paper. And the children would prepare the *patio* (yard) for a performance by sweeping the ground and wetting it down. They put sheets up for curtains and would perform for the people passing by. People would watch and applaud. "That gave me a lot of pride and confidence. . . . I learned to do something that people appreciated." Later on in life, this experience would lead to the formation of a Dallas legend, the Anita N. Martínez Ballet Folklórico.

Anita helped her mother make ends meet, but she never made it to flight training school for airline hostesses. She fell in love. She married Alfredo Martínez on January 27, 1946. They had four children in four years: Al Joseph, Steve Dan, Priscilla Ann, and René. Her husband is one of the Martínez brothers that owned a chain of family-owned Mexican restaurants, called El Fenix. Her husband's father started El Fenix restaurant in 1918 in Dallas. It was the first family-owned Mexican restaurant in Dallas, and "it's the oldest chain of Mexican food restaurants in the United States." Elder Martínez was a dishwasher at the Baker Hotel in downtown Dallas. "One day the cook didn't show up. . . . So he said, 'I think I can . . . do what that cook was doing.' And from then on, he got the confidence . . . to run and open his own restaurant."

Once her children had grown Anita became active in volunteer work. She was involved with schools like Ursuline Academy, St. Monica Catholic School, and Jesuit School and was president of the Dallas Restaurant Association Women's Auxiliary. She was destined to serve on numerous boards and commissions later on in life.

One day in 1969, Anita received a telephone call that was to change her life. A woman, Mrs. Candy Estrada, called her and asked that she run for the city council, "I think that the people that are out there will not represent us like you will. I went to Bill Alexander and he said, 'Do you know Anita Martínez? Well, if you can get her to run she will win.'" Connie Stathakos Condos, "she was on the selection committee of the Citizen's Charter Association. She was the only woman that was on the selection committee to select the eleven people that were going to be running under the banner of the Citizen's Charter Association."[1] Anita had served with Condos on the board of directors for the YWCA. Condos pushed her name for the eleven nominees, and Anita was chosen. The Citizen's Charter Association called and asked her to consider running for the Dallas City Council under their banner. There were eleven council seats up for election that year and twenty-eight persons filed, with four challenging for place nine, Anita's race. The Citizen's Charter Association would be endorsing a candidate for each of those seats. Anita was asked to run in place nine. All the seats were citywide elections, at-large, and the association promised to shoulder the full financial responsibilities for the campaign. All she had to do was say yes, and they would see to it that she got elected. After consulting with her family and figuring she was a mature woman at age forty-four, she agreed to run for the position. The fact that money for campaigning was not an issue did not keep Anita from going to "coffees for me and receptions, and then, I, I campaigned from seven to eleven, I'd go to the, to the breakfast, Optimist Club, the, the Lions Clubs, the, there, there wasn't one organization that I didn't go and talk to about, you know, what, what my goals were. And, you know, that I wanted their support."

She received much assistance from the Dallas Restaurant Association Women's Auxiliary. The organizations that she had volunteered and worked for also assisted her with her campaign. She won without a runoff, pulling down 23,000-plus votes citywide against three opponents, one of which had been endorsed by the North Dallas Chamber of Commerce and another Mexican American lawyer that was in the race. It was significant and highly symbolic that the first Mexican American on the Dallas City Council was sworn in as member on *Cinco de Mayo*, 1969. That night she invited her colleagues and their wives to a *fiesta* celebration in honor of the holiday and her swearing in as council member at Pike's Park. They all came. "The park was in shambles, dim lights, no working water fountains or hinges on the bathroom doors, the commodes didn't work, the swings were broken. . . . It was just a scandal." Anita was embarrassed, ashamed, downhearted, and brokenhearted. The next day she tracked down the park superintendent and marched up to him and said, "I was so embarrassed with all my colleagues there to see the state that this predominantly Mexican American park is. Why has it been allowed to get in such shambles?" The response shocked her into action. "He said, 'Mrs. Martínez, we're going to do away with that park because it's too valuable commercial property and so we are going to do, we're, we're phasing it out.'" Anita pledged that in her lifetime that would never happen. It hasn't.

As a council member, she was responsible for major improvements in the West Dallas area, which had a very neglected constituency of Mexican Americans. She pushed for the bond issue that funded additional recreational centers throughout the city and insisted that two of them be in the West Dallas area. When the city manager, Scott MacDonald, and the superintendent of parks announced that they needed an additional $300,000 added to the bond package being prepared for "these other parks." Anita pointed to the large blank spot on the city map, West Dallas and Little Mexico. She told them in no uncertain terms, "I will not work with this bond program." She got up and walked out. It was Friday. On Monday following not only were her items included in the bond package for city council action but also another of her projects, a recreation center for Reverchon Park. One of them was later named the Anita Martínez Recreation Center. The mayor at that time was Eric Jonsson.

When reelection time came, she was the second-highest vote getter, after Jonsson. Anita served two terms on the Dallas City Council. She truly enjoyed being on the city council. "You could get things done faster." She was responsible for improvements made to Pike's Park, in the middle of Little Mexico. She held town council meetings and took staff with her to these meetings. She involved grassroots people like Pete Martínez and John Zapata Gonzales, and service organizations like *Los Barrios Unidos* in West Dallas were created. With her insistence and persistence, together with grassroots community leaders, West Dallas and Little Mexico began to receive attention and facilities. More recreation centers were built, streetlights were installed, indoor plumbing was installed at Pike's Park in Little Mexico, and streets were improved with the installation of curbs and gutters. A freestanding library in West Dallas was built and a much-needed clinic in the West Dallas area was also established. She relied on volunteers and community leaders to help her get these services and would often treat the volunteers to "enchilada dinners" at her family's restaurant, El Fenix. She was the only woman on the city council during her tenure. She was voted mayor pro tempore by her peers but declined due to her existing time commitment to the city council and to her family. The Citizen's Charter Association imposed informal term limits on their candidates, so she was not asked to run for a third term. Her African American colleague on the city council, George Allen, also was not asked to run, but he did anyway and won without endorsement from the Citizen's Charter Association.

Anita moved on to volunteerism at the national level as well. While on the city council, she was appointed by President Richard Nixon before resigning the presidency to serve on the Voluntary Action Council. She was one of six persons appointed by the president to evaluate the strengths and weaknesses of the Peace Corps overseas, which had volunteers in sixty-eight countries at the time. She went to Ecuador, Honduras, Santo Domingo, Nepal, Malaysia, and the West Indies. Because of her investigatory work in Santo Domingo and subsequent report, the U.S. Attorney General's office sent a follow-up team, which resulted in the dismissal of the Peace Corps country director. The committee formulated forty recommendations that were delivered to incoming president Gerald Ford on how to strengthen the Peace Corps.

She also received a commission from President George Bush Sr. to serve on the Women and Minority Business Administration. Her task was to make sure "minorities and women got their fair share of . . . contracts for . . . highways that were being built."

Anita never forgot her youthful experiences with Mexican folkloric dancing, and in 1975 she founded the Anita Martínez Ballet Folklórico Dance Company. She started the Ballet Folklórico as a vehicle for Mexican American youth to know and appreciate their heritage, but more importantly, so that they could actively participate at the Recreation Center, the first built in the Mexican *barrio* of West Dallas. She said too often she saw the Mexican American youngsters hugging the walls of the recreation center while the "other ethnic-group kids" dominated the basketball court. The center was almost adjacent to the public housing project predominantly occupied by African Americans.

She described the difficulties of maintaining the Ballet Folklórico for the last twenty-five years. While still in operation, the group has seen some difficult financial times. It depends solely on contributions for operations. The children's dance group was started, and the parents began to support the dance group to a much greater extent. The folkloric dance group accepts interested people from ages 5 to 105 and has a professional company in addition. To keep the Ballet Folklórico afloat has required persistence, perseverance, and passion from many people. On one occasion, the Ballet Folklórico was in need of $5,000 to meet payroll. Anita called Ross Perot and convinced him to contribute and continue the dance group. Several times the Ballet Folklórico has been close to shutting down due to lack of funds, but she continued to lean on her citywide contacts for contributions to keep it going. She had met Charlie and Sadie Seay at the height of her community work. They have contributed $8,000 and $17,000 to keep the Ballet Folklórico alive. She approached the Meadows Foundation for a grant, and they gave the group $25,000 on another occasion. All throughout, Anita has watched over the Ballet Folklórico and has fought for its survival. At times, she would even have fundraising events at community centers doing what her family knew best . . . selling *tostadas* and *enchiladas* and having the mayor and council members participate. She laments that the Ballet Folklórico does not receive that level of support needed from Hispanic businesses.

Today she has institutionalized an annual fundraising event where they highlight a state in Mexico. The thematic approach has worked very well. Dallas is full of Mexican immigrants from many Mexican states, particularly Guanajuato, San Luis Potosi, and Jalisco. Carnaval Veracruzano was a recently featured state as was Carnaval Oaxaca. The state for the event is showcased with a typical meal from that state, which is served to all in attendance. Mexican artifacts, textiles, and music from the featured state are the décor and ambiance. Distinguished guests from both the Mexican state and Texas are also in attendance at these events. The event is high class, Anita's style.

Anita's civic duties continued long after her term on the city council. She was on a first-name basis with many Dallasites due to her involvement in civic organizations such as the Dallas Children's Medical Center. These people would later help her with her projects. She approached people, particularly Mexican Americans, to serve on boards and commissions. She was involved in getting Trinidad Garza to consider a seat on the Dallas Independent School District school board. According to a study done by Southern Methodist University, the number of Hispanics appointed to boards and commissions went up 600 percent during her era of volunteerism. She appointed a Blue Ribbon committee of Hispanics to recommend Hispanics who could serve on boards and commissions, in political office, and in programs. Anita Martínez has certainly been a power wielder to be reckoned with all through the 1960s to the 1990s. And just when the Dallas community thought Anita Martínez was enjoying life at her full age, she made front-page headlines again, leading protests and demonstrations.

The Catholic archdiocese was reported in the news to be selling the St. Ann's School property to a developer. The church argued that they lamented the news, but they needed to sell the property to pay for lawsuit settlements. The liability to the Catholic Church for wrongdoing by parish priests ran into the millions of dollars. Anita the mover and shaker organized a committee to stop the archdiocese from selling St. Ann's. She was going to try to save her beloved childhood Catholic school, St. Ann's, from being sold, even make a counterbid for the property, if necessary. The Save St Ann's Committee had demonstrations, protest marches, candlelight vigils, and special Mass services, and even made a bid for the property. The archdiocese did not budge. After much politicking and attempts by the committee to have the school declared a historical landmark, they failed. The reason St. Ann's failed, Anita believes, was because members of the city council went against them and their recommendations. They moved to compromise too quickly. Anita felt that compromise was a "mortal wound to the legacy of the . . . Hispanic historical landmark in Dallas." Her group together with the Dallas Children's Theatre offered the Catholic archdiocese $6.1 million, but the offer was rejected. Anita in defeat reminisced among the old warriors joining her in the protests and the fight to Save St. Ann's. People who had not seen each other in years came together for this cause, and to support Anita Martínez.

Anita Martínez has had a full life, one that is punctuated with dedicated community service. Her childhood experiences catapulted her to Dallas City Councilwoman, presidential appointee, founder of the Anita Martínez Ballet Folklórico, initiator of infrastructure repair in West Dallas, and tragic savior of St. Ann's Catholic School. She has left an indelible mark in providing leadership. She effectively instigated change and brought much needed services to a sizeable neglected constituency. Anita Martínez is a prime example of one who has loved her people and has given back to her Dallas community time and time again. She has a legacy that includes volunteerism and staying true to your roots at the same time.

She has never forgotten her beginnings and continues to work at making Dallas a better place for all citizens—particularly the Mexican American community. Her legacy lives on.[2]

## Notes

1. Mrs. Martínez refers to this group as the Dallas Charter Association but there is another group called the Dallas Citizen's Council. See Patricia Everidge Hill, *Dallas: The Making of a Modern City* (Austin: University of Texas Press, 1996), pp. 109–27 for an explanation of the role of each organization.

2. The public papers of Anita N. Martínez are placed with Southern Methodist University, Dallas, Texas. The University of Texas, Special Collections Department, in Arlington, Texas, has a small amount of archival material donated by Mrs. Martínez in the course of this interview.

~

# CHAPTER THREE

# Virginia Muzquiz

Virginia Aguirre never knew her father, Juan Aguirre, while growing up in Southeast Texas. She was born in Nordheim near Cuero, Texas, on December 13, 1925. Her mother, Anita Vega, was from Starr County in the Rio Grande Valley. Anita married young and raised a large family. Virginia was one of seven children, five sisters and two brothers. As a single parent and in order to make ends meet, Virginia's mother traveled the in-state migrant stream to such places as Big Springs in West Texas, Rock Springs in the Hill Country, and Victoria and Robstown near the Gulf Coast in search of seasonal agricultural work while the children were young. Once the older children could handle an adult load of migrant work, including Virginia as a preteenager, the family began traveling out of state, particularly Wyoming, to weed and thin sugar beets.

As a migrant worker, Virginia's formal schooling was frequently interrupted. Virginia recalls attending the first grade in Nordheim and the third and fourth grade in Wyoming. And that was the extent of her formal education. As a child Virginia was thin, anemic, gaunt, and sickly, with the beginnings of her lifelong bout with tuberculosis. Early medical attention and diagnosis was not only unaffordable but also unheard of among migrant families such as the Aguirre's. The family thought she was just frail and a sickly child. Most children do experience frequent earaches, fevers, stomach ailments, and the like, particularly the children of impoverished seasonal, agricultural workers.

The life of a migrant family is an ordeal. Women bear the brunt of hardship while on the road in search of work, making them more vulnerable and susceptible to illness. Migrant women rise earlier than all family members to make breakfast and tortillas, making and packing the noon meal, working all day alongside the men and children in the fields; then they continue working at home after the field work into the night, washing dishes from breakfast, cooking the dinner, washing and ironing clothes, cleaning house, and many other assorted tasks regarded in those times as a woman's job. Although females are more prone to illness than males, they tend to live longer.

Many a young person trapped in poverty, sickly, and with adultlike responsibilities to the family, views any other option outside the family as heaven sent. The proverbial greener pasture looks really good. Virginia's greener pasture option was marrying someone named García. [Ms. Muzquiz did not provide the first name or further details.]

Ms. Aguirre, the teenager, became Mrs. García and soon was pregnant with Luz Elena. The marriage, however, did not solve any of Virginia's problems. In fact her life got worse. She remained a migrant, poor, and even sicker given that the early pregnancy as a teenager debilitated her frail body even more. Wisely, she left the relationship and returned to her nuclear family, now living in La Pryor, Texas. Her older brothers, Juan and Miguel, also lived nearby.

Virginia had been diagnosed with tuberculosis during the birthing process and was soon interned in a hospital in San Angelo at age seventeen. Later, she was interned in another facility in Mission, Texas. Her baby child, Luz Elena, taken from her right after birth, was raised by her mother, Anita, and sisters, Jesusa, Anita, and Trinidad. Virginia was in and out of sanatoriums until she was twenty-two. When she was not interned in a tubercular facility, Virginia worked in and around La Pryor, but work was scarce. A family friend recommended that the young sisters look for work in nearby Crystal City. Virginia took the advice and went to Crystal City, a mere seventeen miles south down Highway 83 looking for work. She quickly found a job at a restaurant. Health permits were not required in that era.

She also quickly found another husband, "*Bueno yo lo conoci a el aqui* [Crystal City]. *Yo vivía en La Pryor, entonces allí vivíamos nosotros como siete años cuando yo tenía como . . . andaba en viente años. Cuando no había nada de trabajo en La Pryor entonces una señora dijo que en Cristal tenia una hermana de ella un restaurante y así fue como conocí al Sr. Muzquiz.*" The owner of the building where the restaurant leased was Jesus Muzquiz, a young arrival from Mexico. Many families caught in the Mexican Revolution of 1910 fled into the United States and settled temporarily along the U.S.-Mexico border area. In the case of Jesus Muzquiz, his father was a general in the Mexican federal army of Francisco Madero and could not desert. Instead, he sent Jesus, the youngest male child at age fourteen, to the United States. Additionally, Jesus Muzquiz suffered a childhood injury to his right leg that caused him to walk with a pronounced limp his entire life. The Muzquiz family was wealthy, socially and politically connected, as well as well educated and prestigious. They were related to a previous Mexican president, Melchor Muzquiz.

Jesus, unlike many other political refugees of the Mexican Revolution, came with money and formal education. He immediately began making investments in real estate and started several businesses. Not only did young Muzquiz own properties but he also began a thriving business in *pianolas* (Rock-Ola, aka jukebox). *Pianolas* were the popular coin-operated, music boxes of the era. Wurlitzer Rock-Olas were found in bars, restaurants, and emerging fast food businesses everywhere. Mr. Muzquiz for decades had a virtual monopoly of *pianolas* in Crystal City, La Pryor, and Carrizo Springs in adjacent Dimmit County, another thirteen miles south on Highway 83.

Mr. Muzquiz, the bachelor, frequently ate out and patronized the restaurants that housed his *pianolas*. He eyed Virginia, the new hire at one of these restaurants, and found her attractive. Virginia had gained some of her health and appearance back with the treatments for tuberculosis. She was a strikingly attractive young woman of nineteen going on twenty years of age. Virginia was tall, slim, well developed, with long auburn hair, and hazel, brownish eyes. "*Sr. Muzquiz*" as she always referred to him, never by his first name, soon proposed marriage to Virginia. She told *Sr. Muzquiz* about her daughter, Luz Elena, from that early marriage. Mr. Muzquiz must not have been concerned with that past history because he repeated his proposal of marriage. The arrangement also must have included that Luz Elena continue to live with Virginia's family in La Pryor.

The marriage to Mr. Muzquiz soon brought another child into the world, Elda. A third child was born, but she died in infancy. The back-to-back pregnancies must have weakened Virginia immensely because the tuberculosis came back. Elda was only three years old. Mrs. Muzquiz was interned again in the hospital for tuberculosis patients in Mission, Texas, until Elda was seven. "*Elda tendría ya como tres años cuando me interné en Mission, Texas y hasta cuando ella ya tenía como siete años entonces la vine recogiendo allí.*"

During her internment at this tubercular hospital, Virginia wrote to *Sr. Muzquiz* asking him for permission and money to take a correspondence course to learn English. Evidently, he also thought this was a good idea because Virginia enrolled and successfully completed several English and business courses offered by the Hemphill Correspondence School. Upon release from the Mission hospital, Virginia, Jesus, and Elda set up their household across from the *Panaderia de Canela* (Canela's Bakery) in Crystal City, Texas, his base of business operations.

Mr. Muzquiz had also bought that property and made it into a hotel and restaurant. This location was the only lodging place for Mexicans coming into or through *Cristal* during the 1940s and 1950s. The downtown hotels and restaurants were segregated and did not allow Mexicans as renters or patrons. There were other Mexican restaurants in town, but they were located in or near the *cantinas* in the *Mexico Grande barrio*, the largest Mexican business district area of Crystal City. There was another smaller, similar area in *Mexico Chico*, another Mexican neighborhood, but it did not have a hotel. The Muzquiz property was the only hotel with a restaurant facility, and it was away from the loud and sometimes dangerous area of Mexican bars, pool halls, and theatres. Moreover, the Muzquiz family did not have to pay rent for their quarters. And the mortgage payment was made by the jukebox business and restaurant.

Jesus made his daily rounds collecting coins from his jukeboxes, rent from tenants, and making bank deposits. Virginia, with her newfound expertise in English and business acumen in bookkeeping and accounting, helped Jesus, Elda with school work, and friends and neighbors with English-language interpretations. These friends and neighbors, including tenants and business associates of Mr. Muzquiz, soon were calling on Virginia to translate documents, fill out applications for the Food Commodities Program (later Food Stamps), and decipher notes written in English from teachers. At times, Mrs. Muzquiz would accompany these friends, neighbors, tenants, business associates, and other persons to Anglo businesses or schools to interpret and even advocate for them. She became a notary public and that added another dimension to her expertise and a stream of separate income. Virginia did not like the bother of having to ask her husband for money for all the necessaries of family life, much less the minor luxuries women want and need. He never denied her any request, just counted out the exact amount she needed, not a penny more or a penny less, and insisted on receipts.

Mr. Muzquiz was most frugal. He didn't even own a car. He preferred to travel by taxi, either the Jesus Salas taxi or the Salvador Trevino taxi. At times he would ask friends who owned automobiles for a ride. He would always be seen standing on some corner, invariably waiting in Carrizo Springs, La Pryor, and Crystal City, sometimes Eagle Pass, the border town with Piedras Negras, Coahuila, Mexico, for someone to stop and ask if he needed a ride. Because of his labored walking due to the limp, someone always stopped.

Mr. Muzquiz was born in Mexico and raised a Catholic, but like many such persons, was not a devout practitioner of the faith. Mrs. Muzquiz on the other hand was a devout Methodist, having converted while in the first tubercular sanatorium. Her circle of church friends associated with the Mexican Methodist Church also increased her social capital. The Protestant churches in *Cristal* were segregated. The Catholic church, being the only one in town, instead had segregated services. The cemeteries in *Cristal* were also segregated. It was the Mexican Methodist churchgoers that first brought her into the electoral arena. They were abuzz with talk about "*Los Cinco Candidatos y PASO.*"

The San Antonio–based Political Association of Spanish-Speaking Organizations (PASO), led by Bexar County Commissioner Alberto Peña Jr. in alliance with the Teamster's Union that had a union local at the Del Monte plant, were organizing a slate of Mexican American candidates to run for the Crystal City Council seats open in April 1963. During this time voter registration was most difficult and expensive. Voting definitely was not seen as a right in Texas, but mainly a white privilege. From 1903 until 1945 the state of Texas had primary elections in which only white persons, after taking an oath swearing they were of the white race, could register and vote if they paid $1.75 for a poll tax. The poll tax was instituted on June 12, 1837, and was made a prerequisite for voting in 1902. This special tax was not eliminated until 1966.[1] Voter registration was open only from October 1 to January 31 of the year preceding the elections for city council, school board, community college, county, state, and national elections. The federal courts did not strike down this highly restrictive process until 1971. Virginia took an interest in these developments in *Cristal* and discussed them with her husband.[2]

Jesus encouraged his wife to attend the political rallies being held across town at *La Placita*. This barren square of land with a circular concrete slab in the center and no toilet facilities was the only park in town available to Mexicans and was located in the furthermost southeast corner of the city. Not one of the streets in *Mexico Chico* was paved or had sidewalks. *La Placita* in *Mexico Chico* was five miles from the Muzquiz home. The *Mexico Grande barrio* where they lived was located in the west side of the city. To get from one end of town to the other, a person had to cross the railroad tracks downtown, which delineated Anglo neighborhoods and businesses from Mexican *barrios*. A Mexican person however could not walk diagonally across the city taking the shortest route. The Anglo community did not allow Mexicans in their neighborhoods, particularly after sundown. A Mexican person had to walk to the furthermost southern edge of the Anglo business district, then cross the tracks and walk east skirting the edge of the city into *Mexico Chico*. The one-way distance was just less than two miles. Mr. and Mrs. Muzquiz with Elda in hand would walk to the rallies but usually got a ride back from someone. The winters in *Cristal* are not frigid, except for a couple of weeks in January. The area is known for its mild, temperate climate, hence its name the Winter Garden. But it does rain in the winter months and the chill at night is often frosty. After the first couple rallies in mid-February 1963, Mr. Muzquiz suggested to Virginia that she speak publicly on behalf of *Los Cinco Candidatos* because their public speech making was atrocious. "*Me decía mi esposo, 'No saben expresarse Virginia.'*"

A speech was all it took for Virginia to get bitten by the political bug. She was introduced at one of the political rallies in early 1963 by the campaign organizer, Moy Falcon, for *Los Cinco Candidatos*: Juan Cornejo, Manuel Maldonado, Antonio Cárdenas, Reynaldo Mendoza, and Oscar Martínez. Her oratorical skills, compared to those of the male candidates, were superior. She was most articulate in Spanish, in fact she was eloquent. Her poise, appearance, clarity, and passion before a crowd became legendary. Mrs. Virginia Muzquiz spoke at every political rally on behalf of Chicano candidates beginning in 1963 and continued with her own candidacy in 1964, 1965, and 1974. She continued speech making until the end of La Raza Unida Party in Zavala County with the 1980 elections. She was highly sought after by Chicano groups engaged in electoral efforts in their communities across the area, statewide, and even nationally. Raza Unida women, a caucus within the political party, looked up to her as mentor and role model. They too constantly asked her to attend and speak at *Mujeres de la Raza Unida* meetings.

Her role within the local electoral effort was not limited to making speeches. Mrs. Muzquiz together with other women such as Enriqueta Palacios, Rita Yanas, Pura Mendoza, Elena Díaz, Gregoria Delgado, and Eva Castillo began selling poll taxes. Mrs. Muzquiz became a poll watcher in the 1963 election and subsequent elections in which she was not a candidate herself. She became an expert on election laws. Her power of recall and memory was incredibly exact. She could quote the Texas Election Code as accurately as she could quote scripture from the Bible. Every year for years, she would walk to the Zavala county clerk's office and purchase an Election Code book. Later she would order it by mail from the Steck Publishing Company in Austin, Texas. She was among the few nonlawyers that would study the Election Code diligently. She not only would debate fine points of the election laws with election judges but also would frequently call the secretary of state to complain of wrongdoing and erroneous interpretation of the laws by local officials. Mark White, when he was Texas secretary of state, from time to time would call Mrs. Muzquiz for her opinion on voter provisions contained in the election laws.

Virginia Muzquiz's efforts on behalf of *Los Cinco Candidatos* paid off for them. They won every position, the first for a Mexican American slate of candidates. In 1964 when the incumbent state representative for the Winter Garden (Dimmit, Zavala, Medina, and Uvalde counties) H. O. Niemeyer, a rancher from Knippa in Medina County, chose not to seek reelection, the owner of the Rexall Drug Store in Crystal City, Dave Howard, announced his candidacy for the post. The Zavala County Chicano effort to expand the political foothold tenuously held in the county seat to the county level needed candidates in partisan elections. Since Reconstruction, the Democratic Party had held a one-party stranglehold on all positions across the state from the lowest rung to the highest offices of U.S. senator and governor. Election as the party nominee in the May primary was tantamount to victory, barring an exceptional write-in campaign in the November general election. Virginia Muzquiz filed against Howard. She was the first Chicana in Texas to run for this position.

Without help from PASO, the Teamsters Union, or *Los Cinco Candidatos*, who had considerable political troubles of their own fighting a recall petition drive and City Charter amendment election, she traveled the length and breadth of District Sixty-seven in borrowed cars. Jesus Muzquiz, the dutiful husband, again supported his wife in her valiant and pioneering effort. He paid for the voter lists for each of the four counties. The cost was fifty dollars per county, not a small sum in 1964. He paid for the gasoline to travel. He paid for lunch money. He paid for the printing of her push cards to hand out to voters.

Mrs. Muzquiz, the orator with a microphone in *Cristal's La Placita*, was out of place in *cantinas*, *billares* (pool halls), by the roadside of agricultural fields, *tienditas* (small grocery stores), and church halls in the various cities of the district without a microphone or megaphone. She had to struggle with all her might to be heard. By nighttime and on the road back home, Mrs. Muzquiz would collapse with exhaustion into a stupor of sleep. Mrs. Muzquiz, since her days after tuberculosis, lived with one lung. She gasped for air and tightened her stomach muscles to project her voice. She coughed phlegm from the dust of the unpaved *barrio* streets and the stench of chemicals in the fields, both pesticides and herbicides. But she went out day after day in pursuit of votes.

Most Mexican Americans outside of Crystal City did not buy the poll tax. What for? It was better to pay $1.75 for a sack of russet potatoes from Idaho, Pioneer Wings flour from San Antonio to make *tortillas*, or *frijoles pintos* (pinto beans) from Colorado than for the privilege of voting for the lesser evil between two white males. She lost badly. But so did Albert Fuentes Jr., another PASO leader from San Antonio seeking the nomination for lieutenant governor at the same time. He lost to Preston Smith, the segregationist from Lubbock, Texas, that later became governor of Texas. George Bush, running for the U.S. Senate on the Republican Party ticket in 1964 also lost in the general election.

Why would such an astute and intelligent woman run against such odds in an unwinnable race? "*Abrir brecha, exactamante! Entonces yo sabía mi secreto y yo me lo sabía, verdad.*" She knew she was going to lose but never uttered those words. Her campaign would increase voter participation and interest among Mexican Americans and make the public aware that women could run for such positions. She was opening doors for future generations. She relates how she scolded another candidate, Erasmo Andrade, when running for a state senate seat, because of his campaign rhetoric. Supposedly Andrade would tell audiences that he knew he could not win but wanted them vote for him anyway to show Mexican strength and unity. According to Mrs. Muzquiz, the voting public does not want to hear that because they feel as if they are throwing their vote away in voting for such a candidate.

In 1964, one Mexican American woman held the highest public office available, which was the county level in Texas: Mrs. R. R. Anaya. She was the county treasurer for Hidalgo County in the Rio Grande Valley. A second Mexican American woman, in Brooks County, joined Mrs. Anaya after the 1964 general election: Zulema Garza. Many Anglo women held that position across the state at that time. The clerical offices in county government were considered suitable for Anglo women, but not the executive or judicial posts until the 1970s.

Undaunted from defeat in 1964, Mrs. Muzquiz joined the PASO slate for the city council race in Crystal City in 1965. She was the first Chicana and woman to run for such a position in the city. The PASO slate, *Los Cinco Candidatos*, had barely survived their first term. The white power structure did not sit back and watch the Mexicans govern. The backlash unleashed by the white community was tremendous. The local weekly newspaper, the *Sentinel*, editorialized against them. The San Antonio newspapers, both of them, *Light* and *Express News*, would also regularly lambaste the Mexican-run city council. The media character assassination campaign against the "unqualified former migrant field hands" running Crystal City made allies and friends duck for cover. Nobody wanted to say they had supported Juan Cornejo and the others.

The Anglo community made overtures to moderate Mexican Americans and formed a counter-organization, the Citizens Association Serving All

Americans (CASAA). On the 1965 election ballot was also the City Charter amendment instituting stronger residency requirements for officeholders and setting up staggered terms for the city council. CASAA also recruited a Mexican American of their choice to run and become mayor, Carlos Avila, a local electrician whose bread and butter came from servicing air conditioning units in Anglo homes and businesses. Chicanos could barely afford the utilities let alone air conditioning, besides most families left town in the summer months in search of agricultural work in the northern states. The PASO slate, including Virginia, lost badly. The Chicano electoral movement in *Cristal* came to a halt for the remainder of the decade.

On December 9, 1969, the Chicano students of Crystal City High School walked out of school protesting the unequal education and treatment they were receiving at the hand of Anglo teachers and administrators. At one of the student rallies, Armando Trevino, a former student, spotted her in the audience. They called her to the microphone. Mrs. Muzquiz eagerly came up to the microphone and once again became the Chicano community's voice in support of the student protest. Regardless of the weather and location, Mrs. Muzquiz was there for the students. The cold was particularly hard on her. When she spoke at these student rallies, even with a microphone, the audience could hear her gasp for air between statements, laboring with her one lung. Nevertheless, she moved her audience with her words. She was the best orator in the region, if not the state.

By January 7, 1970, the students had forced the school board to capitulate to their demands. The following weekend on January 10, 1970, the Raza Unida Party of Texas was organized in Zavala County and three other counties: Dimmit, La Salle, and Hidalgo. The party was not given ballot status that year, and their first candidates were removed from the 1970 general election ballot. By 1972, however, the fledgling political party achieved ballot status and won some races, including some in Zavala County for county attorney, county commissioner, and justice of the peace. Her friend Elena Díaz from *Mexico Chico* had won as the first Chicana county commissioner for Zavala County under the banner of the new political party. Virginia Muzquiz had joined the Raza Unida Party effort in 1970 and was elected the county chairperson in 1972.

In 1974, she filed as a candidate for county clerk under the new Chicano political party. She won her first race handily this time and served in that capacity for one term. After the election victory and before taking the oath of office, she visited the defeated county clerk, Georgia Price, and was refused entry to the office, a public place. Mrs. Muzquiz walked down the hall calmly and spoke with the new county attorney, Rey Perez, who in turn called Mrs.

Price and reminded her of the law concerning citizen rights to public offices and records. Mrs. Muzquiz leisurely toured the office suite and inspected records, furnishings, and layout while Mrs. Price fumed.

In 1978 Mrs. Muzquiz did not seek reelection. The Raza Unida Party had term limits, and she still believed her primary role was to open doors. During the organizing of the Raza Unida Party across the state Mrs. Muzquiz trained countless volunteers on how to obtain voter signatures on the ballot petition and on election laws governing poll watchers. She also advised the Raza Unida Party officials, county and statewide, on the intricacies of election laws governing the conduct of primary elections. Once the Raza Unida Party obtained ballot status, they were entitled to receive state funding to run their own primary elections. Mrs. Muzquiz virtually and single-handedly trained personnel in every Texas county holding a primary election. Maria Elena Martinez, Evey Chapa, Gloria Garza, Marta Cotera, Alma Canales, Irma Mireles, among others to this day still recall her detailed lessons on the Election Code and advice on Chicana feminism.

On other occasions she would travel to speak at conferences sponsored by *Mujeres de la Raza Unida* or to public events held by opponents of the Raza Unida Party. A former Crystal City resident, Ramon Montemayor, had left the city after the Cornejo election of 1963 and resettled in Pearsall, Frio County, Texas. The Raza Unida Party was organizing a grassroots effort there under the organizational direction of Modesto Rodríguez. He called Mrs. Muzquiz for help because Mr. Montemayor was publicly on the air via local radio blasting the lack of accomplishment by candidates of the Chicano political party. The local newspaper was carrying his diatribes weekly and creating doubt and hesitancy among Chicanos being recruited into the new political effort. Mrs. Muzquiz rounded up the girlfriends, Elena Díaz, Gregoria Delgado, Enriqueta Palacios, Marta Cotera, and others to travel to Pearsall and attend a public meeting of the *contras* at which Ramon Montemayor was to speak. They arrived early and sat in the front row. Ramon Montemayor was so intimidated by their presence that he left without speaking and the event was a disaster. The Raza Unida women from Zavala County stayed for the entire meeting, then introduced themselves and mixed with the audience lauding the Chicano efforts in the area.

On another occasion when local farmworkers went on strike at the Wagner Farms by River Spur, a *colonia* south of Crystal City, the local sheriff, C. L. Sweeten, arrested them. The sheriff had arrested hundreds of farmworkers and could not transport them all to the jail. He decided to make them walk into town, approximately seven miles. Some of those arrested slipped away and came into town to alert their friends and neighbors. Mrs. Muzquiz got word and quickly got money from Jesus Muzquiz. She walked up the street and paid Ignacio Luna, owner of the Luna Theatre, one of two Mexican movie houses in *Cristal* to go street by street announcing the arrests and urging folks to gather at the courthouse to protest. She also called the new Chicano school superintendent, Angel Noe Gonzalez, urging him to declare a field day at the high school and bus the students to the courthouse to learn firsthand about the administration of justice. Within hours the courthouse area and adjacent streets were filled with thousands of Chicanos protesting the sheriff's actions. All the farmworkers were released and no charges were ever filed.

As county clerk she hired young, competent Chicanas to staff the office, such as Diana Palacios García and Oralia Guzmán Trevino. The county clerk in Texas is the office for official postings of notices, filing of legal instruments, and conducting absentee balloting (now called early voting). The county clerk also serves as the recording secretary of the minutes for the commissioner's court, the executive body in county government. When her term ended in 1978, she stepped aside and endorsed Diana Palacios García, a former student protester and activist, for her position. "*Les dije, yo no voy a querer morirme en el asiento como se medio murió la viejita que estaba allí, no. Yo nomas quiero entrar para abrir la puerta para otras personas.*" Diana won the 1978 election by a landslide and served her term. Today, she is the city manager for Crystal City, the first Chicana and woman to hold that position. Oralia Guzmán Trevino at this writing is the Zavala County Clerk.

Mrs. Muzquiz semiretired in 1978 and would on occasion visit the county offices, but they were across town and walking such distances was beginning to be a problem. Moreover, her husband Jesus and brother Miguel were sickly, and she was the primary caregiver to both. When Severita Lara, the first Chicana and woman to seek the position of county judge, filed in 1986, Mrs. Muzquiz walked across town to the campaign headquarters. She told Ms. Lara personally that she could no longer help out with election duties as poll watcher or advisor given her health and that of her husband and brother. She pledged her vote and left a money donation. That was the last public act of Mrs. Virginia Muzquiz. Her husband died, and then her brother's and her own health deteriorated tremendously. She stayed indoors near her oxygen tank and television at her brother's house. Virginia was a rabid fan of baseball. She even videotaped games so she could replay them after the season. She admired Fidel Castro and lamented that she was not among those chosen by the Raza Unida Party when the delegation visited the island country in 1975. She proudly showed visitors photographs of her five grandchildren from her daughters, Luz Elena with three and Elda with two. Additionally, she had eight great-grandchildren from Luz Elena.

Virginia Muzquiz opened many doors for others in her lifetime. She was in so many respects the first Chicana feminist and nationalist among many who emerged in the late 1950s and stayed the course into the twenty-first century. Virginia Muzquiz opened her last door when she passed away on February 12, 2002, in Crystal City, Texas.

## Notes

1. Even though the Twenty-fourth Amendment to the U.S. Constitution eliminated the poll tax entirely, Texas continued to require it for state and local elections until 1966.

2. For an ample discussion of politics in Crystal City, Texas, in 1963 and later see John Staples Shockley, *Chicano Revolt in a Texas Town* (Notre Dame, IN: Notre Dame University Press,1974); and José Angel Gutiérrez, *The Making of a Chicano Militant: Lessons from Cristal* (Madison: University of Wisconsin Press, 1998), pp. 62–77. See also Ignacio García, *United We Win: The Rise and Fall of the Raza Unida Party* (Tucson: Mexican American Studies Center, University of Arizona Press, 1989); Armando Navarro, *The Cristal Experiment: A Chicano Struggle in Community Control*, (Madison: University of Wisconsin Press, 1998); and his larger work on the political party that Virginia Muzquiz was very instrumental in organizing and building, *La Raza Unida Party: A Chicano Challenge to the U.S. Two-Party Dictatorship* (Philadelphia: Temple University Press, 2000). For a brief mention of Virginia Muzquiz, see also Teresa Palomo and Ruthe Winegarten, *Las Tejanas: 300 Years of History* (Austin: University of Texas Press, 2003), pp. 236–37, 329–30. Mrs. Muzquiz is incorrectly named as the national chair of the Raza Unida Party in this latter work (p. 330).

# CHAPTER FOUR

~

# Alicia Chacón

Alicia Chacón's road to becoming the first Mexican American female county judge in Texas was hard fought. The Anglo establishment in El Paso, Texas, did not give in easily to her initial electoral victory. But in the end of her one and only term as county judge, she became one of the most powerful politicians in El Paso.

Chacón had helped her dad work on winning Democratic campaigns since she was a young girl. She made her father proud in these early campaigns. Alicia also worked for years for the county Democratic Party leader as the paid staffer. Working campaigns is very different from working in your own campaign for election to public office. When Alicia's turn came to run for office, she had an uphill battle. First, she ran for school board seat in Ysleta, a *colonia* in those years just on the edge of El Paso, and won. Then she ran for a countywide position, county clerk, and won. Then she ran for a seat on the El Paso City Council. And then another countywide seat, county judge of El Paso County. Despite heavy opposition from the white establishment, Alicia won her race, the first for a Chicana and a woman. She was perceived as a radical Chicana by the white business community of El Paso and those living in its suburban environs because of her history of supporting Chicano students during a school walkout and of supporting labor unions during strikes. She wasn't seen as a "safe" Hispanic candidate that the white establishment could support as a token minority in spite of her long labor on behalf of the Democratic Party and her opposition to the Raza Unida Party. Alicia was among the founding members of the Mexican American Democrats of Texas (MAD).

Alicia had inherited her gumption and fighting spirit from her maternal grandfather, General Carlos Almeida, who served in Pancho Villa's army during the Mexican Revolution of 1910. Her mother, Jesusita, had also given her a revolutionary consciousness since birth. Her mother's favorite song as a child was "Jesusita de Chihuahua" a song of the revolution. Her grandfather was killed in the revolution. Her grandmother, Escolia, brought her mother Jesusita to live in the United States in 1916 when she was two years old. For a long time, they lived in south El Paso, and then later bought a house in Canutillo, where she met Alicia's father, Willie. Her father's parents were George Rosecrans, a German Jew, and Josefa Ordónez. They separated when Willie was a baby. He was raised by his maternal grandparents. After the 1930s Depression in the United States, the grandparents returned to Mexico. They left Willie in Canutillo when he was nineteen. Everybody in the town worked at the cannery, and that is where Alicia's parents met. Jesusita was sixteen and Willie was nineteen when they married. They moved in with Jesusita's mom because they could not afford to set up a household. Her mother never was legalized, much less naturalized, even though she lived in the United States for some thirty years. On one occasion, while returning to Canutillo from Chihuahua, the U.S. Border Patrol of the Immigration and Naturalization Service stopped her. They wouldn't let her cross into El Paso. Instead of fighting the immigration authorities, she decided to stay in Juarez with her sister. Her sister had contracted cancer and died within a year, leaving Jesusita and Willie her house. Willie started working with El Paso County and came to love politics. His first taste of politics was getting elected constable, which is the lowest rung of a law enforcement position. Even though he had a baby girl, he was conscripted into World War II by the U.S. Army and was gone for three years. During that time, Alicia's favorite memory was of being so close with her mother. She and all her siblings were so well behaved. Alicia thinks it was because their mother was raising them all by herself.

Alicia recalls going to the movies in downtown El Paso. The owner of the theater would announce the movie was starting by having a boy beat a drum really loudly. He would run the projector by hand. She also remembers the big celebrations and speeches they would have for the *Dieciséis de Septiembre*, which celebrates Mexico's Independence from Spain on September 15–16 each year. When her father returned from the war, he got a job in nearby Ysleta as a mechanic and moved the family. It was a small town with more Anglos. Consequently, the Mexicans were subjected to more segregation and discrimination than they had ever seen in their sheltered childhoods in Juárez, Mexico, and in Canutillo and El Paso. Since they were excluded from most of the extracurricular activities at school, the Chicano kids spent much of their free time at the Catholic church, which held dances and bazaars. The church had a very active Catholic Youth Organization (CYO). In high school, Alicia became involved in the 4-H club and focused on public speaking. She won many competitions, and the U.S. Department of Agricultural Extension agent, Elkie Mentor, took an interest in her. Ms. Mentor took Alicia around the state of Texas competing and seeing the sites as a regular tourist. She learned about Texas, its size and historical facts. Sometimes motels wouldn't let Alicia stay there because she was Mexican, and Ms. Mentor would just drive to another one.

"Miss Mentor was very good because she protected me from that and on all of the trips. And, I went to numerous competitions with her because she really encouraged you. I mean she just kept after me and so she was a very strong influence to me."

In high school, Alicia noticed that the *Mexicanos* didn't participate much in school activities, such as sports and cheerleading. They didn't have a single Mexican teacher or administrator as a role model. But Alicia remembers some very sensitive Anglo teachers, such as her third grade teacher Miss Chesser, who would recite poetry. She also remembered Christina Barron, who was a nurse that influenced her a lot. Alicia tutored Christina's children, and thought about becoming a nurse herself, but the nursing school in El Paso run by the Sisters of Charity didn't accept Mexican students. As far as other options, Alicia was never encouraged while in high school to attend college.

"There was never anyone that really said, 'Hey you all should go and get more education. You all ought to go to college.'" She says, "It was never even a consideration for most of us. I think all of us knew that when we got out of high school we would find jobs. And so we were kind of preparing ourselves. You know, I took all the clerical things." She said some *Mexicano* students didn't expect to even go beyond grade school. She said she believes the school system didn't expect them to go on either, and that is why they had these big, elaborate eighth-grade graduation ceremonies. Anyone who went on was just getting that much more preparation for work. Only about half the *Mexicanos* that started school ended up graduating with her, and of those twenty or thirty graduates, only two went to college, she said.

But she did get involved in politics while she was still in high school. Through her father, who was a Democratic Party election worker, she helped with Ralph Yarborough's campaign for governor in 1957 by passing out cards in front of the polling places.

"I couldn't vote then because the voting age was still twenty-one, but I was involved. I stayed at the poll for him. It was a special election giving his cards, and my dad had been bringing people to vote."

She then volunteered in the Viva Kennedy Club of 1960, which campaigned for John F. Kennedy for president. This led her to become a delegate to the state Democratic Party Convention. She and the group from El Paso would go to the conventions usually held in Austin. They'd be the only Mexicans at the fancy receptions. She was the first *Chicana* elected to the state Democratic Party Executive Committee. Soon after that, the County Democratic Party chairman, George McAlman, hired her. She went to work for the Democratic Party as his assistant. She became an expert of the Texas Election Code. At the same time, she also became involved, like her mother had, in the school's PTA. They tried requesting that the school board improve the Ysleta schools, but they didn't even receive the courtesy of a reply. *"Nos dio mucho coraje."* (It made us very mad.) There had never been a Mexican American school board member in Ysleta's history. She decided to run. She started going door-to-door, registering people to vote and telling them how the schools were being run. She found out that the children of *Mexicanos* south of the freeway from where she lived were experiencing the same problems in their schools. There also was a need for bilingual education, but the Anglo teachers weren't willing to provide it and were unqualified for that method of instruction.

On election night, she won by fifty votes. The school board and superintendent, however, wouldn't declare her the winner. They called for an investigation and said the voting machine had been tampered with by fifty votes. They recounted the ballots and obtained sworn affidavits from the people who had set up the machine and witnessed the set up saying it had started at zero and that it was not malfunctioning. So there was no explanation. The school board then did all sorts of unprecedented, and possibly illegal things, including calling for another election for just those people who had voted in the first election. They wanted to require people to vote again the exact same way they had voted the first time.

Alicia accused the board of racism and of conducting an illegal election. The local state court of appeals and federal court would not render a decision either way, which in effect, allowed the incumbent to stay in office. More importantly, the nondecision was a decision that allowed the school board to conduct a second election. Alicia was represented by MALDEF, the Mexican-American Legal Defense and Educational Fund, which had just been organized in 1968. But the election came before the case could be litigated, and Alicia and her supporters worked at getting out the vote from sun up to sun down daily, Monday through Sunday, with no respite. The hard work paid off. The Chicano community had galvanized and was acting in concert behind Alicia's candidacy. After the second election and voter fraud scandal, Alicia won by a larger margin and became the first Chicana on the Ysleta school board. All she could accomplish as the only Mexican on the school board, however, was to cramp their style, which had been to conduct all their business in secret. She would tell her constituents what they had decided. The sole victory she had was in getting a first Mexican American principal appointed. Challenging the superintendent's recommendations, she asked why there was no qualified Mexican American faculty for that position. The superintendent had to admit there was at least one such person, C. V. Domínguez.

Twenty years later, the superintendent is Mexican, 70 percent of the administrative staff are Mexican, and at least 50 percent of the principals are Mexicans and women. The greatest resistance was against Mexicans, and not so much against women, she said. But she fought for women also.

"I would support the women's movement and I supported the affirmative actions on their behalf. But my real interest and my work has been the advancement of Mexican Americans." Alicia became an asset to the Chicano movement because of her elected position, her knowledge of the Election Code, and her experience. About two hundred students from Ysleta High School walked out in 1973 over allegations of discrimination and bad treatment. All the students were expelled. Each one had to have a private hearing with the school board in order to be reinstated. During these hearings, the students described all the things they had been through, all the names they had been called by teachers. What came out of that was a requirement that all the faculty, staff, and administrators undergo sensitivity training.

In 1976, Alicia and another Chicano, Oton Medina, ran for school board, campaigning door-to-door again. They both won by large margins. The *Raza* voters had learned the electoral system quickly and became very active. In the 1978 election *Raza* voters elected a third *Mexicano* to the school board. In 1980, shortly after the census enumeration took place Alicia began to fight for the creation of single-member districts from which to elect members to the school board. Single-member districts would give *Mexicanos* the ability to elect representatives from political districts reflecting the geography of their neighborhoods. At-large elections had kept the Anglos in power, and now single-member districts would keep the Chicanos in power. After single-member districts were established, only one Anglo board member was elected. *Mexicanos* had become not only the majority of the population but also of the voters in their districts.

Mulling her options, Alicia decided on a quantum leap from the rural-based school board. Her next political move was to run for El Paso county clerk, an at-large election because it was countywide. The campaign got ugly immediately.

"I guess that was the first time that people started saying that I was a communist. That was the next thing. . . . Before I had always just been divisive and racist, now I was a communist." Her father became very active in politics again, this time to help his daughter win. She also had the support of labor unions, the Democratic Party, the Catholic Church, and of grassroots Chicanos. Alicia had always been a strong supporter of labor, first because of her father's affiliation with the International Machinists Union and later because of the Farah garment workers strike in El Paso.

"Farah had a very paternalistic attitude towards the employee and he knew what was better for them. I mean—if they were sick . . . well, he had a doctor there for them. He didn't want them going to their own doctor. . . . *Les dan un turkey pa [para] Thanksgiving. Les dan . . .* (They give them a turkey for Thanksgiving. They give . . .) you know, all these little things that Farah had . . . I mean . . . well, are these people free or are these people, you know, Louie Farah's slaves?

"So, when I combined the garment workers with the grass roots Chicano movement, which, independently . . . was not that cohesive. But on my behalf they would both work. It came together, you know, that I had a lot of votes."

Again, she went door-to-door campaigning, rather than buy radio or television ads, and put up hundreds of yard signs and posters. On the day of the election, she drove a huge truck through the neighborhoods, holding up traffic, to remind people to vote.

"It takes a lot longer to manipulate a truck and a cop can't really do much about a truck. And so we would get a large truck—the largest vehicle that was still legal to have in all of these neighborhoods and then maybe five or six cars, decorated, pickups. *Y hacíamos borlote.* (And we made a lot of ruckus.) Because the whole thing was getting—is to motivate voters."

She also called on precinct chairs that were her friends. She approached the leaders of the small black community in El Paso. She also counted on Raza Unida Party members to support her, or at least to not oppose her. The loose-knit coalition held neighborhood rallies and parades on her behalf. "Well, I was very close to the Raza Unida here in El Paso. It was never that viable, but the people that were active in Raza Unida were close friends of mine."

Raza Unida represented a challenge to the Democratic Party, which Alicia was a part of. But she didn't feel threatened, she said. The challenge was healthy at the statewide level, but was not necessary at the El Paso County level, she said, because the Mexicans had already taken over the Democratic Party locally. In fact, Alicia became one of the organizers of MAD, the Mexican American Democrats organization. She brought several ex-Raza Unida members back into the Democratic Party at that time in 1976.

She decided not to seek reelection as county clerk. Instead she worked for the Carter campaign on behalf of the Texas team from the Hispanic Advisory Council, an affiliated arm of the National Association of Latino Democratic Officials. President-elect Jimmy Carter then asked her to help with his transition team. Carter had included Chicanos during his campaign when he needed their votes, but after he won the election, he was hard to access. Alicia thought twice about going to work for him. Eventually President Carter asked her to stay on as the regional director of the Small Business Administration (SBA) in Dallas, Texas. But she didn't get the job easily. U.S. Senator Lloyd Bentsen, the senior senator and Democrat from Texas didn't want her to get that job. But she finally took it, for two reasons. "If he don't want me to have it, I will just show him that I can have it. And you know, the other thing that I wanted to show? I wanted to show other *Mexicanos* that they don't have to kiss *gringo's* asses to get something." Senator Bentsen challenged her qualifications for the appointment, but he lost. The whole thing embarrassed her, but she stood with her head held high during the whole nomination and confirmation process.

Even after she accepted the political appointment, she had trouble. President Carter wouldn't fire the former SBA regional director. And he refused to leave. So she waited around for five months, hanging out in temporary offices and hallways looking for things to do until she finally got fed up. She organized a retirement party for him, asked him for a report, and just moved into the office during the going-away party. He had no choice but to leave, right then and there.

As the regional director of the Small Business Administration, she helped fulfill many entrepreneurial dreams of people. She made it a priority of her administration to loan lots of money with which to open small businesses to eligible women and *Mexicanos*. "Oh, we gave breaks to many, and it was exciting to meet them and to see how they were progressing and what great potential they had that hadn't ever been given the opportunity to develop." She also helped a lot of minority businesses get government contracts and grants to help them buy the equipment they needed to be viable.

While she may have had little influence on Carter's administration and a lot more helping Chicanos as the SBA regional director, working for the president was actually a big sacrifice for her. Once Carter was out of office, Alicia Chacón and all other political appointees had to come back home and start all over again. Alicia drove back to El Paso from Dallas via San Antonio. In San Antonio she attended the annual St. Mary's University Clam Bake and bought some raffle tickets for a brand new Cadillac. She won it. Once in El Paso she bought a tortilla factory with the cash proceeds from the sale of the Cadillac.

She didn't get back into El Paso County politics right away, partly because some of her old supporters were unhappy that she had left them after they worked so hard to get her elected in a countywide race. They had gone on to other candidates, campaigns, and other interesting things. By 1982 she had decided to run for a city council spot. She ran against an incumbent city council member, David Escobar. Alicia had a favorable opinion of him at first; he seemed to be a good person. After watching him for a term in office, Alicia and many others concluded he was a Hispanic sellout. According to Alicia, Escobar relished doing the bidding of the white mayor and establishment.

The campaign pitched Chicano against Hispanic, and she won, two to one. "Y *somos Chicanos o no* (and we were Chicanos or not) period. Y *este vato no es Chicano*. (And this guy is not a Chicano.) And that was it. And so I defeated him."

David Escobar may have had signed his own electoral death certificate when he insulted a Mexican priest in public. Alicia served as city council member for two terms, but gave up after that. She felt like the city council was not the place to effect real change. "They wind up doing nothing but potholes and trash. And, so I didn't feel particularly satisfying period during that time. And I decided that I would not seek reelection." She took a few years off to spend with her father, who was getting sickly. Her mother had passed away a few years back, and Alicia feared her father would soon follow. She began to observe national politics from an El Paso vantage point. She reflects on presidential comparisons: "Clinton reached out for safe Hispanics. Carter reached out to Chicanos who were philosophically Chicanos. And to others, that maybe aren't familiar with the *movimientos* (movements), there is a world of difference. And, I compare it sometimes with women's groups that say that you reach for a woman instead of a feminist."

In her spare time Alicia helped a Catholic nun organize El PISO, an organization that represented poor people, including those living in *colonias* outside of El Paso. These residents have no running water, sewer, electricity, gas, paved streets or sidewalks, and no garbage pickup. They are almost exclusively persons recently arrived from Mexico or of Mexican ancestry.

In 1990, she decided it was time to run for public office once again. It had been 100 years since El Paso County had had a *Mexicano* county judge. The time had come for both a woman and *Mexicana* to hold the position. Alicia said, "'How much more are we going to wait?' And so, we mounted a magnificent effort. We were able to get every *Mexicano* group that was activists and probably every prominent *Mexicano* or economically prominent *Mexicanos* to agree that if they didn't support me, they would not support anybody else."

She won. In winning she made Chicana history, as the first to become a county judge of a major urban county in the state. As county judge-elect, she had a very difficult time. She was watching the incumbent county commissioners and county judge spend and spend, month after month, every penny in the budget before she could be sworn into office. When she was sworn into office in January 1993 one of her first priorities was to cut services and raise taxes, both very unpopular initiatives. After the budget crisis passed, she was able to bring in millions of dollars from both state and federal governments for water systems in the *colonias*. She built community centers for the elderly. She lobbied Texas lieutenant governor Bob Bullock to get a state prison established in El Paso. The location made it easier for family members to visit with inmates in prison. The prison also became a source of jobs. Alicia had ample social capital, in large part, from her longstanding relationships with people in state and federal government, which she had developed over twenty-five years. County Judge Chacón could marshal resources for needy constituents out of thin air it seemed. But the other members of the commissioner's court were not impressed with the newcomer to their bailiwick.

County Judge Chacón was a woman leading a group of men on the commissioner's court. The only woman. "It was difficult because one of the things . . . and I don't . . . sometimes I don't know if it was just because I was a woman or it is because of the type of woman that I am and my lifestyle. One of the things that I don't do is that I don't drink. I am a teetotaler and so I don't go to . . . to happy hours and those types of activities that the commissioners would many times do with each other. And they would go, after the session or after discussions or after any meetings, they would maybe go to a local bar or a drinking hole and have the opportunity to give and take in discussion. And many times when they came to the court, well they had already had a discussion, either over drinks or over a golf game or something that I was not privy to. And that my own lifestyle doesn't lend itself to that. *No ando compadreando/comadreando con gentes.* (I was not socializing with those people.) So, that hurt me. That they had a different relationship with each other, not just a working relationship and that my relationship was strictly a working relationship. And sometimes they would agree with me in discussions about the need and the validity of a cause or of a particular matter, but they would vote against it because they had made an informal agreement over beers."

A person can build social capital in many different ways, but politicians have a routine. They make appearances at events. That is an aspect of her personality that doesn't lend itself to politics and the building of social capital. Alicia is reluctant to make public appearances just for the sake of being seen. "I don't like that thing that people do, even office holders do what they call cameo appearances. I don't do that. If I agree to go to a function, that is what I am going to and I am going because I see the validity and the value of helping them or because I support their cause; I support what they are doing. I don't go to things to be seen. And that is a very different, I think, you know . . . from others."

Alicia Chacón lost her reelection bid. At that time, no Chicana had ever managed to win reelection as county judge in Texas.[1] "I think that a lot of people were discouraged with my loss and felt a real sense of loss when . . . in the Chicano community, and felt that it was a setback and a disappointment. And, I have tried to say, well, you know, this is one person, you know, *se cayo un chango, sigue el circo* (a monkey fell, the circus goes on); that that has to be our attitude in that we have to continue."

During her brief four years in office as county judge, she helped a lot of other people get elected and appointed to judgeships and different offices in El Paso County and the state. She also prevented other people from getting elected. The Alicia Chacón blessing in El Paso politics is coveted, and her curse is avoided.

After local and county government service and presidential appointment, Alicia Chacón still continues to have an influence over El Paso politics and human services. She became the executive director of El Paso's United Way, another first for a Chicana.

## Note

1. José Angel Gutiérrez, "Experiences of Chicana County Judges in Texas Politics: In Their Own Words," *Frontiers: A Journal for Women* 20:1 (Spring 1999).

~

# CHAPTER FIVE

# Rosa Tijerina and María Escobar

This mother and daughter duo has not held public office, but they have been in the public arena most of their adult life. María Escobar is the first wife of Reies López Tijerina,[1] the leader of the Land Recovery Movement. She was born in April 1927. Rosa is the oldest daughter of that union. Rosa was born February 2, 1949, in Victoria, Texas. The Tijerina family is from Texas, but like many migrant families they traveled to many states before settling out of the migrant stream. In the case of María and Reies, they were children of migrants themselves. As young newlyweds, they also continued in the migrant stream, toiling in the fields and pursuing a spiritual ministry with the Assemblies of God. María and Reies both attended Bible school in Saspanko, near San Antonio. They met while studying the Bible. María finished divinity school at the Latin American Bible Institute, but women were not permitted ordination as ministers. Instead, María taught Sunday Bible school, sang in the choir, cared for children during services, and generally assisted Reies. Reies did not graduate in 1944, but began his ministry as an itinerant preacher nevertheless.

María married Reies in San Antonio, Texas, in 1946. Her sister, Esther, had married one of Reies's brothers, Ramón, a couple of years earlier. Reies pastored three churches before he quit the Assemblies of God. "They didn't agree with him because some things or he didn't agree with them in some beliefs. So, he was out. Somewhere in some convention in Houston, I guess, that's where they put him out. So, he was a pastor in a church in Eden, Texas. That's where he was the pastor of the church, Assemblies of God organization," María recalled.

The Tijerina family began a life of summer work in the fields and spiritual ministry the balance of the year. They traveled across the United States saving souls as far up as New York State and across the Southwest. It was during one of these sojourns that the family made friends with others that shared similar religious beliefs in Colorado, California, and New Mexico. These families banded together and formed a commune in the Arizona desert. They pooled their monies and bought 160 acres of land. Without money to spare, the families dug into the desert floor and made underground caves, *subterraneos*, for their homes. "We started this organization of brothers and sisters. . . . So, we got united and we went in Fruta, Colorado. Some family went with us and then some families from California. They went and bought a piece of land over there in Casa Grande, Arizona, near Eloy. They called it Valle de Paz (Valley of Peace). So, we all lived there and they built little houses. Some . . . we lived in tents first. They, they . . . *Como se dice 'subterrano'?* (How do you say 'subterrain'?) That is where Irabella was born, in a basement, or *subterrano*." [Note Irabella's birth name is *Ira de Ala* (Ire of Allah).]

The idyllic location in the Arizona desert quickly turned into a nightmare. An eight-year-old daughter of one of the families was raped and murdered. The roofs covering their underground homes were burned and destroyed. The children were afraid to walk three miles across the desert to wait for the school bus in order to attend school. A U.S. government airplane crashed on their land and scores of investigators trampled all over the area. The one-room school the commune had managed to build for their children was burned to the ground. The local police would not investigate these crimes; however, they did investigate the families. Reies, Zebedeo and his wife Veroniz, from Monero, New Mexico, and Margarito, another of Reies's brothers, were arrested and jailed. After many days in jail they were released, except for Margarito, who was charged with violation of parole. He was subsequently transferred to Michigan to serve his remaining sentence.

María meanwhile taught the children, hers and those of the others. "I taught them the basics, you know, like how to read and . . . that's about all I could teach them. The ABC's and starting from the ABC's to help them to learn to read. I guess *mi problema financiero* (my financial problem) was very bad, you know. Circumstances were so rough for me and the kids, I just couldn't think that it was worth it for us to be going through so much. That's what I thought at the time. I used to tell him lots of times. He would get mad. Then we'd start arguing. I would tell him that the kids needed to go to school. We should settle down somewhere and send the kids to school. They're growing up. He didn't believe that. He thought he would just . . . we could teach them at home and whatever they would learn in school, I guess, wasn't too much necessary at that time. So, the struggle started worse and worse." David, the oldest child, was eleven at this time and Rosa, the oldest daughter, was nine. Rosa recalls, "My parents moved around a lot. I remember that my dad never allowed me to go to school. Me and my brothers and sisters didn't go to school. He didn't view it . . . very unhappy and always had been with the system. You know, it destroys the family. He was worried about what would happen to us out there. We didn't learn English. But I do remember that we used to move from city to city, you know, working in the fields. That was the only kind of work he could hold being that he was a fugitive. As a family we suffered a lot. They were always catching up with him, the FBI. So, we would stampede out of wherever we were at. And here we are going again. One time we even ended up in Mexico City. We stayed there I don't remember how many months." María and Reies had six children in ten years. Childbirth was almost an annual affair for María. Rosa also had to help her mother with providing care for the little ones, she being the second oldest in the family.

During one of the times Reies was in jail, he befriended another inmate, an Anglo, and he asked this person's wife to go to the commune to help María. This woman went to the commune and was welcomed by the group even though she was not of their religious persuasion or nationality. Another time, Reies went to see his brother, Margarito, and was rearrested on other charges of possessing stolen government property. His court-appointed attorney told him he and his group were not welcome in Arizona and that he should consider leaving. The alternative was to be sentenced to a long prison term. Reies took his advice. During a recess, he walked out the courthouse door into the world of being a fugitive. He was now wanted on the original charges, plus jumping bail. Reies fled to Mexico leaving María and the children penniless and alone in the desert. María left the Valle de Paz and made it to Tierra Amarilla, New Mexico, to be near Zebedeo and Veroniz Martínez who had left the commune earlier. She enrolled the kids in the public schools for the first time in their lives. She had some money saved from prior summer work, "picking peaches, cotton, potatoes. We canned a lot of peaches and he killed deer and we packed the meat. We canned the meat in jars." María also dropped the Tijerina name and began using Escobar. It made things easier for her than to have to answer questions about her husband and his whereabouts. Reies always managed to return and cause the family grief. He couldn't hold a steady job or work too long in any given place. He couldn't preach. He had to hide most of the time for fear of apprehension. María always had to support the family in all their needs, clothes, food, medicine, school supplies, rent, toiletries, and the like. Her husband was usually absent, but when around had no money for the family.

Rosa recalls how life changed in Tierra Amarilla. "I don't remember having a really neat, enjoyable childhood. It was a very, very hard childhood, you know. We were always I fear, you know . . . . for the first time, my dad allowed us to go to school here in the United States. I was already nine. It was really hard because I didn't know English. I couldn't communicate with the other kids and the teachers. I always felt very isolated."

María and Rosa have stories of being pursued and hunted by the police because of Reies. Rosa said to her mother during their interviews, "Remember when the police raided the house over there in . . . . up north in New Mexico. We all had to run from that house 'cause they found out that he was hiding there. Don't you remember? We all had to run. That's when he took us to Texas. With grandma and then he ended up in Mexico." María needed Rosa's prompting because she does not remember all too clearly now or maybe does not want to remember. She said, *Es un history terrible que todo el tiempo* (terrible in that all the time) worried and . . ."

On that occasion Reies and María's brother, Efraín Escobar, fled into the mountains when the police cars where approaching. David, the oldest son, had been riding a horse and sounded the warning when he spotted the line of vehicles making their way up the road. María was pregnant with her last child, Noe. As soon as the police left empty handed, the Tijerina's fled to Texas. Reies delivered his son, Noe, as he had done with Ira de Ala at the Valle de Paz. Reies could not take his wife to any hospital because he had no money and he was a fugitive. After the birth, Reies left for Mexico again. And returned again.

On another occasion in Plainview, Texas, Rosa was bathing in the kitchen when police cars drove up. Again David sounded the alarm. Reies and his oldest brother, Anselmo, crawled into the kitchen where Rosa was bathing in a tub. María was sitting on her bed when the police barged in with guns drawn. They pointed a gun to her chest and demanded to know the whereabouts of Reies. The police told her "that they would lock me up if I wouldn't tell where they were. I said, 'Well, I don't know.'" The police looked around and headed for the kitchen because the door was closed. "'My daughter is taking a shower in there,' *les dije*" (I told them). And Rosa adds to this story by quoting her father, "'Rosa, if they open the door you stand up naked in front of the door so they won't dare come in.' I could understand what my dad wanted me to do and why, you know. I was shaking in the water. It was a tin tub." Reies and Anselmo tore a screen off the window and jumped out. And away they went, Reies to Mexico and Anselmo elsewhere. Again, María was left penniless and alone with the kids. María eventually heard from her husband and joined him in Mexico in 1958. They lived in Mexico for eight months, and the children were able to attend Mexican schools briefly. María returned to Texas in May to pick cotton. Anselmo, the oldest brother, attempted to cross into the United States at El Paso and was apprehended. He served two and one half years in prison for an assault charge pending in New Mexico. Reies stayed in Mexico that summer and returned under a false name through Laredo, Texas. He rejoined his family. They picked cotton from Texas to Tucumcari, New Mexico. Because their car had a burned engine, María and the teenage kids plus little ones had to stay behind and continue picking cotton while Reies went to Albuquerque to rent a house: two rooms for thirty dollars a month for a family of eight.

In 1959, Margarito Tijerina was released from prison in Michigan. He went to live with his sister Josefina in Chicago. Reies took his family to Chicago for that partial family reunion and arranged to meet with Elijah Muhammad of the Nation of Islam. They discussed the struggles of Africans and Indo Hispanos[2] in the United States. Reies had been a subject of investigation in state police records for some years, particularly Colorado and New Mexico; now he was targeted for surveillance by the Federal Bureau of Investigation for associating with these black Muslims. Reies had evolved in his thinking and had found a new religion, the land recovery movement. This was now his cause. His travels to Mexico were not only to avoid capture but also to research land titles in archives there. During his travels to Mexico, he would take Rosa, now a young woman. His travels to Spain in the mid-1960s also were to research land titles and study land grant laws. In the United States he could not freely walk into libraries and national archives for fear of apprehension. He still considered himself a wanted man. He was mistaken, but did not know at the time that he was no longer wanted in the states.

The Tijerinas received a windfall in 1961. The Valle de Paz land had not been forfeited when Reies jumped bail. A buyer came forward and Reies sold the land. He was the agent for the commune, and its members had dispersed, while others joined Reies in the new cause for New Mexico's land grant heirs. The proceeds from the sale of the land were used to buy a large building on Third Street in Albuquerque. The building became the headquarters for La Alianza Federal de Mercedes y Pueblos Libres (The Alliance of Land Grants and Free City States). The family moved into the roomy headquarters. Rosa and David, primarily, began working closely with their father. Rosa became a secretary and clerk. She kept notes of meetings, handled correspondence and telephone messages, booked and scheduled events, filed membership cards, staffed the office, and did whatever her father asked of her. David worked security details and gathered intelligence information for his father.

Reies wrote in his autobiography, *They Called Me "King Tiger"*:

During 1962, I would go in and out of Albuquerque. Cristobal and his family returned to Texas. The economic difficulties for my family got worse. My wife suffered and struggled for many years. She was tired of all of this. I always told her, "One day all of these things will change. Be Patient." But that day would not arrive. She, like me, was getting up in age and was thinking of life at age forty and fifty. When she began studying how to be a secretary, our difficulties multiplied. She mentioned divorce for the first time, and it seemed to me like I had been hit by a car. The difficulties between us began the first days of 1962. Because I had been a fugitive, any time there was a knock on the door, I'd run out the back. One time, some men drove up and I disappeared. It turned out to be a pastor and his assistants from a church who were dispensing gifts to people in need. As 1963 entered, my wife and I discussed divorce as a solution to our problems. Over the previous eighteen months I had reconciled myself to that reality more and more. I knew I loved her very much and that she loved me. I knew that we had both been faithful to each other. But the toll that my life as a fugitive had taken on our relationship was too great. My children were going hungry and doing without the necessities of life because of my life. Many times my wife asked me to abandon the cause of the struggle for the land to attend to the needs of my family. I tried working at ranches. I tried getting odd jobs, but within days my wife would see my spirit decline, as if I were a prisoner. My wife would tell me "Your heart is not in this. It is better that you continue your mission." Finally, my wife went before Judge Paul Larazolo and obtained a divorce. I did not appear. I still feared the power of the judges over my liberty. My wife took custody of the six children, our three boys and three girls. My wife continued helping a lot in the Alianza, and my sons and daughters did not go far away from me.[3]

María and Rosa have a different version. Rosa claims the divorce was a ploy. She admonished her mother during the interview, "Tell the truth. Daddy told you to for the cause. So, that they [the state] could support the family cause he couldn't work." Reies didn't work or couldn't work; his job was leading the land recovery movement. The Alianza paid all his travel and personal expenses, lodging and meals were free at the headquarters, and his older children worked on Alianza business without pay. Moreover, he did not pay child support.

María had the six children, and she had to vacate the Alianza headquarters once the divorce decree was final. She now had to pay rent and utilities and groceries and clothes and medicine for the kids. He remarried shortly after that.

María got a job at Bernalillo County Medical Center, now the University Hospital, as a file clerk. However, as the Alianza and Reies gained notoriety, María suffered job retaliation and terminations. She lost the job at the medical center. "I think I lost that job because of that. They wouldn't give me the job back. So, I kept doing other jobs, sewing, the stores, salesclerk, house work." And the violence directed at her ex-husband followed her as well. "At my house we lived on Lead Street and they threw a bomb there. We don't know who did it. But that bomb they threw it through the alley. And there, my brother was here. Efraín was in here. They had the little girl, two-year-old little girl, Madelyn. She was sleeping in the bed by the window. She flew all the way to the kitchen when they threw the bomb. It was after the raid" [Tierra Amarilla Courthouse raid].

María was always concerned about the danger the Alianza activities placed her children in. "I thought at that time it was very sad for them to help because it was a real true history of our people. So, I never complained. I never told them not to. When there was times . . . I sometimes I would think it was dangerous . . . I would kind of feel bad about it. You know, like marches, when they threw bombs it scared me. I didn't want my children hurt. I was there the night before the raid happened, no? I was there. I went to see because Danny was gone and you [Rosa] were gone and David. So, I got the rest of the kids and went all the way over there to see how they were doing. 'Cause they said they were going to a picnic. That's what they told me. Reies never told me anything."

On June 5, 1967, Alianza members with Reies in charge drove to the courthouse in Tierra Amarilla to make a citizen's arrest of Alfonso Sánchez, the district attorney. He had been harassing the Alianza members for some time. He had sued to obtain their membership records. He had arrested some members for trespassing on government land. They were being held in the jail at the courthouse in Tierra Amarilla. Reies had David and Rosa with him as part of the Alianza group. Reies, David, and other *Alianzistas* were armed. Rosa was instructed to be the reconnoitering advance person. The assumption being that as a young woman of eighteen she would not attract attention or be seen as suspicious while walking around the various floors of the courthouse. She was to enter the courthouse alone, scope out the location of persons, especially armed police officers, look out for D.A. Sánchez, and come back and report.

My Dad says, "You're going with them." I didn't know what was going on yet. So, I sat in front of this pick up with Fabian and Juan. Fabian Durán and Juan Valdez. I noticed they were armed. So, we got in the truck and we drove to

Tierra Amarilla. Fabian and I and Juan got off the pickup and we went inside. I, you know, I was supposed to look for my uncle cause he was having . . . they were having a hearing on my uncle and Felix Martínez at the courthouse in Tierra Amarilla. I went up the stairs and I didn't see any people or reporters or nothing. In fact, that was weird. Then, I was looking around, and then, I heard somebody say, *"Dame tu pistola"* (Give me your gun). He said it in Spanish. I didn't even want to look. I just made a u-turn and started running down the stairs. When I was running down the stairs I heard a shot. I just ran even faster. I ran to the back of the pickup that we were driving cause I knew my dad was back there. Sure enough, I opened the . . . there was like a huge canopy thing. I pulled it and I said, "Hurry, hurry." I didn't know what to say because I didn't know what was happening. I remember my dad saying, "What happened? What happened?" I said, "I don't know, just hurry, hurry." So, I remember all the men jumping out of their pickups. And, my brother David, pulled me to one side and said, "You go back inside the pickup. Lay on the floor. And no matter what happens, don't come out of there." So, I did that, you know. When I was lying like that I could hear all this shooting, you know, screams, men. Men's voices. So, I was scared for my brothers, 'cause David was there and Danny. Danny was fifteen. David was twenty. So, I ran back in there. When I opened the door I saw blood on the floor on the stairs. I saw Nick Saiz, the policeman, on the ground, on the floor bleeding. He was crying. He was begging, telling them that he was bleeding and that he needed help. But I remember my brother Danny putting a rifle to his head and making him pray. He made him pray, "Say the Our Father." Then, my boyfriend, Fabian says, "You shouldn't have gone for your gun. Why did you do that? Why didn't you give me your gun?" Then, I went into this other room. I saw all this, you know . . . the staff people, members. They were all sitting in a room, you know, like this. Their hands behind their . . . up in their neck. Baltaazar Martínez was in charge of everything in that room. Larry Calloway was on the floor of the telephone booth. He had attempted to call, I guess, you know. He's the reporter. My brother caught him and tore off the phone line. Pulled him out of there. I remember Benny. I think he was Benny Naranjo telling my dad, "What did I ever do to you Reies? Why are you doing this to me?" I remember my dad just beating him . . . somebody came in and yelled, "There's a bunch of police on their way. There's a line of cars coming down the road." So, we all started to run outside. Then, my brother said . . . he pulled me back in, my older brother, and he said, "Rosa, I don't want you to go out here." He goes, "You go back in there and hide in the closet. Don't you come out until everything is over, until it's quiet." He started pulling me. And I turned and said, "No, no. I don't want to die in a closet. I want to be out here with you." So, we went outside. I remember seeing the line of white cars. They looked like white cars to me with the lights on flashing. They were headed this way to us, to the courthouse. I remember that our men shot out all the tires. They just turned around and left.

The boys . . . they just made a u-turn, and all of them left. I don't know how many cars there was but they all ran. They left. I felt really relieved 'cause I thought we were going to die there. I was so sure we were gonna die.

Rosa made it back to the starting point, Canjilón, and saw her dad consoling his new wife, Patsy, because "it was already all over the news that the National Guard and everything was on its way. So, she knew my dad had to flee. I was in shock. I couldn't cry. I don't remember what I felt. I remember being scared but I was in such horrible shock. I was numb. I couldn't cry." Then her dad motioned her over and said, "I'm gonna go to the mountains to hide. Your brother is going with me. I leave you here. You have been so brave. I leave you here. Just be brave and don't be afraid. Everything is going to be fine." Reies, David, and others ran into the mountains. Some were caught quickly, but not the Tijerinas: Reies, David, or Danny. Juan Valdez, Baltazar Martínez, and others also remained at large for days.

Everything did not turn out fine in Canjilón. The National Guard and state police decided on a strategy. They held all the Alianza membership, women, children, and old men in a cattle pen. They put the news on the radio in case the fugitives had a radio and could hear the news. This would compel them to return and spare their loved ones the ordeal of being held hostage prisoners. The fugitives did have a radio and did hear the reports but did not return.

The hostages were made to sit in the mud. Rosa remembers, "A really tall *gringo*. He was so angry with us, so furious. He had this huge long arm, you know, rifle. He said, "And don't move from there because I'll shoot you. And nobody, but nobody's gonna get away with shooting a policeman. Nobody!" The police set up a camera to photograph the prisoners. One by one they made each person face the camera. "They forced us to face the camera. I remember I wouldn't turn but they forced me. So, by force they took my picture. I guess that's how Nick Saiz identified me."

The National Guard decided to haul them off the Canjilón campsite and began packing the prisoners into paddy wagons. "They put us all in paddy wagons, Oh, my God, I couldn't breathe cause they shoved us in there like sardines, you know. It was horrible. I was getting phobic, you know." Before they were moved, Governor David Cargo called and rescinded the relocation. He wanted them to remain in the area until the police and military personnel had more information about what was going on. "The National Guard was all around us. They had us in this *corral* (pen), you know, where you keep animals, . . . I needed to go to the bathroom so I walked up to one of the guards and I said, 'I need to go to the ladies room.' He said, 'You're not going anywhere.' I said, 'I need to go.' He says, 'Well, there's the ground.' I said, 'I'm not going to use it there.' He says, 'I'm sorry.'"

Rosa decided to face the consequences and began walking away from the *corral* to an outhouse up the hill. "They all put their rifles to me. A bunch of guards. I cannot believe these, you know, these . . . a teenage girl. Then, I went in the house, you know, in the little outhouse. It had a lot of *rendijas* (cracks), you know, cause it's wood and it's old. They put this huge light, strong light into the house. Into the outhouse. I said, 'Oh well. What can I do? I have to go.' So, I went."

The next morning Rosa was singled out of the crowd. "You! You!" these two police *gringo*s yelled at her. "So, I started walking towards them. Fabian called out to me, 'Rosa . . .' I turned around. And he just got whatever rifle he was holding and he stabbed me in the back with it. So they took me in. Yeah, they always handcuffed me. They took me to jail in Santa Fe. I had never been in jail in all my life."

At Santa Fe before booking her, the police interrogated her by threatening to kill her father if she did not tell them where he was hiding. "'You know we have the right to kill him on sight?' I wouldn't answer. 'I don't know where he is. All I know is that he's not here.'" Frustrated, they took her for photographing, fingerprinting, and the intake process. "They made me stand there . . . where they took my picture there was cells. Right here next to me on my left side. There were prisoners there. These prisoners were sticking their hands on me. It was like they did it on purpose. They took it right where they knew I would feel horrible abuse. I still couldn't cry. I was angry, scared, but no tears. Stripped me, yeah. There was a male guy. I asked for a woman. He said, 'You can tell me whatever you need to. Needs. I have whatever you need. You need a Kotex?' It was really insulting."

The next morning Rosa had a preliminary hearing. María had brought her clothes but the guards kept them from her. Rosa was still wearing the wet, mud-stained clothes from the raid. Her clothes and her shoes were also soiled on her bottom and down her legs. She was on her menstrual cycle. When she heard her mother yelling out for her in the hallway, Rosa broke down and began to cry uncontrollably and fainted. María began screaming and the judge evicted her from the proceedings. Rosa was remanded to the state penitentiary. The judge said, "You get that woman out of my courtroom. Get her out of here. I don't think she understands what being taken to the state penitentiary for safekeeping means." Rosa was transferred to the penitentiary with nineteen Alianza men. She was held in solitary confinement. Only the first day in prison was she allowed contact with the other inmates. After that she spent her time alone, isolated in a cell. Male guards would watch her bathe.

Often the guards would wake her at night just to shine their flashlight in her face and see her reaction. Rosa has always been a very beautiful woman.

Some inmates threw rocks at her window and yelled out messages to her. The inmates were so proud of her and her role. They saw her as their heroine. About a month later other inmates let her know that her dad and others had been caught without incident. They were unharmed and in the same penitentiary. Rosa attempted to see her father but was denied. She often was told she was being released on bond, would pack and be ready, only to be disappointed. The ploy was to harass her, not release her. They would wake her in the middle of the night and escort her to the matron's office to wait. Sometimes they would ask her to sign papers so she could be released. Rosa signed and to this day does not know what she signed. "I think I felt very intimidated and scared. You know what? It's very spooky to be in a place like that when you're eighteen years old. And you know that all these people have you at their mercy. They can do with you what they want and nobody can hear you. And nobody can come to your aid. My mother couldn't come to my aid. My dad was next door locked up. So were my brothers. I don't remember everything that they would tell me, you know. I don't . . . to get me to sign. I was very naïve, too. We finally got out. They released us."

After only a few months of liberty, Rosa was back in the penitentiary. Eulogio Salazar, the jailer at the Tierra Amarilla courthouse, had been brutally beaten and murdered. He was a witness for the prosecution in the trial against Reies and the Alianza members, Rosa included, for the Tierra Amarilla courthouse raid. Rosa was arrested in connection with that murder. Again she was placed in solitary confinement. The male guards still watched her bathe. The guards still woke her up in the middle of the night for no reason. She spent another month in detention. Three times she was ordered to pack up and be ready to be released. Instead she was taken to the male side of the penitentiary and held there for hours while the guards discussed out loud if she should be released before her father or after and finally would take her back to her cell.

Rosa's legal ordeals did not subside for years. She never was tried for any offense in connection with the courthouse raid. Her dad was at first acquitted for the courthouse raid. Later, he was convicted and committed to prison for other federal property crimes.

In 1969, Rosa married her only boyfriend, Fabian Durán. They had two children, Esperanza and Gabriel. And she was still working free for her dad and the cause. "I used to get a lot of pressures from my husband, you know, 'Hey,' you know, 'you have a home and babies. And here you are giving your time to your dad when your dad pays other women to do his work. What is this? We have to pay doctor bills. We have to pay a house.'" Rosa still would accompany her dad on trips and meetings. During the Poor People's Campaign in Washington, D.C., her room at the school where they were staying was ransacked, and she barely avoided being raped. She was abducted on another occasion after receiving a phone call supposedly to attend an Alianza meeting. She called her mom to come babysit her babies and when the car drove up Rosa got in without hesitation. As the car sped off she realized that she did not know these men and noticed camera equipment in the car. Patricia, her dad's new wife, alleged she had been raped by police officers while Reies was in prison. Her brother Noe as a child endured an attempted raped by another police officer.

Rosa asked them who they were. They did not answer with identity. Instead, they said, "You see those cameras back there in the back seat? Those are for you. We need to send pictures to your dad to show him what rape really is. Accusing the police of raping his wife, we want to show him what rape really is." At the first opportunity, Rosa leaped out of the moving vehicle, tumbled onto the pavement, and ran as fast as she could into a bar, Chesterfield's, and the woman bartender called her mother, not the police.

Rosa went to Mexico with her dad to make movies. The Mexican government and the private sector made two movies about Reies and the land recovery movement. Rosa played bit parts in them. She had been with her dad in Mexico before when they met with President Luis Echevarria Alvarez and other dignitaries. Rosa was always the focus of attention. But in 1975 she had enough. Her marriage was breaking up. The last trip to Mexico for the movie had almost destroyed the marriage and her. She suffered a severe kidney infection and was hospitalized. She also began to realize that her father had used her for years. "I got very depressed because my dad didn't tell them anything about the role I played in the TA raid. He didn't say nothing about the role I played. I thought, I cannot believe this." She began to drink and overdosed on that occasion with pills and alcohol. That was her first suicide attempt.

Fabian, her children, and Rosa left for Washington State upon her return from Mexico. She began a singing career. In addition to her beauty, Rosa has an amazingly powerful, rich voice. She sang *mariachi*. Ironically, on a trip back to Albuquerque, former New Mexico governor, David Cargo, began dating Rosa. He had been the one that sent the state police and National Guard to hunt them down in Canjilón after the Tierra Amarilla raid. In 1985, he pressured Rosa to become his lover. He attempted to promote her *mariachi* cassette recording that he produced for her. During this brief fling, Rosa made it back to Dallas, Texas, as part of her attempt at a singing career. She

loved the singing, but hated the music business with the many lecherous pro-
moters, reeking of stale beer and cigarette dance halls, smoky bars, greasy
restaurant food, and cheap motels. She also tried living in San Antonio, but
her uncle Ramón and aunt, her mother's sister, were still too shell shocked
from the experience with the Alianza. Briefly, Ramón had taken the reins of
the organization while her dad was in prison. Now they were fanatically religious. She came back to New Mexico.

Between 1976 and 1987 Rosa divorced Fabian and later married Alfonso
Arandas. But that marriage did not last long—five years. Arandas died of a
heart attack while making love to Rosa. "So, that sent me into a horrible,
horrible depression, into a trauma, you know." She returned to Albuquerque
for help. Fabian and the children lived in Albuquerque also. "I was in and out
of hospitals for severe depression. You know everything from the past. It was
like when he died it's like a . . . this closet opened and all these skeletons just
covered me up and I couldn't get out of it. So, I was in depression until 1999.
Eleven years." Rosa attempted suicide twenty-three times during this period.
She claims that she hears this little girl screaming inside her, begging for
help. Rosa knows this little girl is her in early childhood. She also has figured
out why the girl was begging for help.

Rosa had remarried Fabian. He had convinced her that he would care for
her and she needed to live, if not for him and herself, for the children now
grown and in high school. In 1995, they moved out of Albuquerque and its
memories to Phoenix. But remarriages do not always work, and this one
didn't. By 2000 Rosa was spending more time with her grown and married
children in Albuquerque than with Fabian in Phoenix. María was caring for
grandchildren and Noe, the youngest son, in Albuquerque.

María, like Rosa, tried relocating back home to San Antonio, Texas, in
1982. María's mother was very ill and in need of constant care. She took Noe
and Bernadette, a grandchild, with her. They stayed in San Antonio for a
couple of years, but Bernadette missed her friends in Albuquerque. She
wanted to graduate from Del Norte High School, but that was not to be.
Bernadette ended up graduating from a high school in Truth or Consequences, New Mexico, because María moved in with Ira de Allah and her
husband.

Rosa was rehabilitated somewhat in 2001, so she returned from Phoenix
to Albuquerque for good and found a job with a health care agency. Her
brother David died from alcohol abuse. He drank himself to death.

She divorced Fabian again and began writing her autobiography. The
writing caused her pain and relapses into depression and suicidal ideation
again. The writing contains allegations of sexual abuse by her father in the

early years when she was a child and while in Valle de Paz. She believes the little girl child inside her is her and that she was begging for help, for the abuse to stop. "And I got to leave it alone for a week or two. I've been doing that, you know. So, it's like taking me long. And there's issues that I didn't mention here [interview] that really tear my guts apart."

Leaders, male and female, neglect family. The children of the leader are the first collateral damage in any social movement. Rosa is the partial price paid by her dad and the Alianza for the land recovery movement. María and Patricia, the former spouses, David, Danny, Noe, Patricia, Rachel, and the other grown Tijerina children also turned out to be collateral damage. The leader chooses the path, the family endures the journey.

## Notes

1. See Reies López Tijerina's autobiography, *They Called Me "King Tiger": My Struggle for the Land and Our Rights*, translated and edited by José Angel Gutiérrez

(Houston: Arte Publico Press, 2000). The original 575-page autobiography was entitled *Mi Lucha por la Tierra* and was published in Mexico City in 1978 by Fondo de Cultura Economica. There are many other publications on Tijerina: Michael Jenkinson, *Tijerina* (Albuquerque: Paisano Press, 1968); Peter Nobokov, *Tijerina and the Courthouse Raid* (Albuquerque: University of New Mexico Press, 1969); Richard Gardner, *Grito! Reies Tijerina and the New Mexico Land Grant War of 1967* (Indianapolis: Bobbs-Merrill, 1970); Patricia Bell Blawis, *Tijerina and the Land Grants: Mexican Americans in Struggle for their Heritage* (New York: International Publishers, 1971).

Dr. Gutiérrez also interviewed most of the members of the Tijerina-Escobar family, except Rachel and Ira de Ala. Daniel died on May 1, 1974. These interviews, video and transcription, are on file with the Center for Regional Studies, Zimmerman Library, University of New Mexico, Albuquerque, New Mexico. Since those interviews, done the summer of 2000, David Tijerina has died. Reies Tijerina is terminally ill with severe diabetes and hypertension, bedridden and living in Uruapan, Michoacan, Mexico, with his third wife. The widow of David Tijerina, Jo Ann, is attempting to relocate Reies and his spouse to Albuquerque. The second wife, Patricia, also lives in Albuquerque, as do some children from that marriage.

2. This is the term Reies López Tijerina employs as a self-descriptor and ethnic group label.

3. Tijerina, *They Called Me "King Tiger": My Struggle for the Land and Our Rights*, pp. 46–47. María states the year for the divorce as 1962. Rosa remembers she was thirteen years old at the time.

# PART II

# THE CHICANO
# MOVEMENT ACTIVISTS

Grassroots Chicano leaders in the 1960s captured the imagination of a new generation of Chicana leaders across the country. During the Vietnam era, Chicano youth, mostly students, took to the streets in protest of the war. They were concerned about the growing Chicano casualty list and rapidly depleting federal resources curtailing domestic programs, given burgeoning military spending. Chicano males were being drafted and volunteering at record numbers. Military recruiters hounded Chicanos in the *barrio*, schools, and college campuses. The youth and the poor were particularly vulnerable targets for the military. Chicanas experienced firsthand the loss of a relative, boyfriend, or husband during this time. Given their lack of political power, these Chicanas began to do something about the war, their poverty, unequal education opportunity, and social marginalization.

Chicano students, both high school and college, began hearing and reading about the exploits of César E. Chávez and Dolores Huerta in California; Reies López Tijerina and his daughter Rosa in New Mexico; Rodolfo "Corky" Gonzáles and his daughter Nita Jo in Denver, Colorado; and of the five young men in Texas forming the Mexican American Youth Organization (MAYO).[1] Every one of the Chicanas in part II began their public activism as members of MAYO, except Trini Gámez.[2] She began her involvement via employment with Texas Rural Legal Aid and as a plaintiff in redistricting litigation. When the farmworker movement from South Texas began organizing in her West Texas area, Trini began a support group. She turned to electoral politics and ran for local office; she lost, but others after her won utilizing the strategy and network she organized. She is retired now, but her daughter has continued as a local activist.

MAYO organizers engaged in fomenting school protests in Texas, as did others across the nation. MAYO members took trips to attend the Denver Chicano Youth Liberation Conferences; joined as pickets and security for the farmworker strikers in South Texas and led urban boycotts of grapes, lettuce, wine, and other products; and followed Tijerina's challenges to the government with great approval, particularly his citizen's arrest attempts of scientists at Los Alamos laboratory in New Mexico, the chief justice of the U.S. Supreme Court, and his coalition building with Rev. Martin Luther King Jr., the Black Panther Party of Oakland, California, the Nation of Islam, and the Student Non-Violent Coordinating Committee. Tijerina was laying claim to *Aztlán*, the Chicano homeland.

Alma Canales and Linda Reyna Yáñez became involved with MAYO activists in the Rio Grande Valley during the farmworker strikes and school boycotts of classes. Later when MAYO began developing the Raza Unida Party (RUP), Canales and Reyna Yáñez became organizers, leaders, and even candidates. In Alma's case, she was the first woman and Chicana to run for lieutenant governor in Texas.[3] Linda was fired from her teaching position because she displayed an RUP "Muniz for Governor" sticker on her car. She became a lawyer and championed immigrant rights. Later, she won election as appellate judge for several terms in the Rio Grande Valley's Thirteenth Court of Civil Appeals. In 2002, she became the first Chicana to run for the state supreme court bench. Regrettably, the statewide "Dream Team," comprised of male Democrats—an Anglo (John Sharp), Hispanic (Tony Sánchez), and African American (Ron Kirk)—did not include her in their campaigning. The Democrats lost all these races.

Irma Mireles was working with the Neighborhood Youth Corps in San Antonio while Rosie Castro was a student at Our Lady of the Lake University and active with the Young Democrats in the late 1960s. Both joined MAYO at the first opportunity and rose to become RUP leaders in San Antonio and Bexar County politics. Irma was the first Chicana to win a countywide election on a shoestring budget of ninety-eight dollars in the early 1970s. Rosie raised twin boys as a single mother and still managed to be involved in local politics. Now she continues her electoral and community activism but it is primarily on behalf of her sons, Joaquin, a state representative, and Julian, a former city councilman.[4]

Severita Lara was the walkout leader of the 1969 Crystal City high school protest. She also turned to electoral politics after a period of activism with MAYO and the Raza Unida Party. Severita won the Democratic primary election for county judge in 1986, only to lose the victory during litigation. She lost her case for lack of money to appeal a district judge's ruling in her election contest. In Texas among Chicanas only Dolores Briones (El Paso) has been reelected as county judge. In all other cases, Chicanas that have sought the county judge position lose, and if they win, they lose winning a subsequent term.[5] Later she was elected to the city council and then mayor of her hometown.[6]

Another remarkable woman was Representative Irma Rangel, who passed away in March of 2003. This amazing Chicana was described as a "Texas Trailblazer" in MALDEF's (Mexican American Legal and Educational Fund) Winter 2003 newsletter for her incredible role as an advocate for higher education and her twenty-five years of public service. Irma was the first Mexican American woman elected to the Texas House of Representatives in 1976. Later in her legislative career she became the first woman to chair a major committee. Representative Rangel was the key for allocating almost half a billion dollars for South Texas universities, including the school of pharmacy at Texas A&M–Kingsville.[7]

These Chicanas, almost a generation removed from the *Adelita* Warrior Trailblazers, pushed completely open the door for women. They grew into adulthood as MAYO activists and RUP players in the public arena, competing with and besting men—Chicanos, blacks, and Anglo—at the podium, election box, protests, and in effecting public policy.

## Notes

1. Mario Compeán, Ignacio Perez, Juan Patlan, Willie Velasquez, and José Angel Gutiérrez.

2. See Zamora et al., *Mexican Americans in Texas History*, and chapter 17 of this book.

3. Maria Alvarado became the second Chicana to seek this office in the 2006 Democratic primary.

4. "Twins Peak," in *Texas Monthly*.

5. See José Angel Gutiérrez, "Experiences of Chicana County Judges in Texas Politics: In Their Own Words," in *Frontiers: A Journal of Women's Studies* 20, Spring 1999:1 and also with Rebecca E. Deen, see "Chicanas in Texas Politics," Occasional Paper No. 66, Julian Samora Research Institute, Michigan State University, East Lansing, MI., October 2000.

6. See José Angel Gutiérrez, *We Won't Back Down! Severita Lara's Rise from Student Leader to Mayor* (Houston, TX: Arte Publico Press, 2005).

7. The school is named after her and is scheduled to open fall 2006.

# CHAPTER SIX

~

# Alma Canales

For years, Alma Canales lived a quiet life, active in her children's school and in her community of Waco, Texas. She didn't talk much about her past or the role she played in the Chicano movement. It wasn't until her oldest son, Raza, studying the Chicano movement in college started asking questions about that social protest movement. Once again she began to place herself in history. And Raza was reintroduced to his mother and the Raza Unida Party (RUP) of the 1970s.

He realized his mother had been an important leader of that movement. She and others had helped make it possible for Chicano/*Mexicano* students like him to attend college and learn their history. They had paved the way for progressive people to organize their communities for change, either through elected office, or through social protest movements, direct action, and nongovernmental organizations. When Raza was home from college, he asked his *mamá* to tell him about the *movimiento*. He wanted to know what had ignited the fire in her soul that transformed her from naïve Almita to a strong leader, willing to take on enormous odds. She remembered the moment she was transformed. It was a day in her freshman year at Pan American University in Edinburg, Texas, when she went to a rally to hear José Angel Gutiérrez, a leader of the Mexican American Youth Organization (MAYO) based out of San Antonio. He had been traveling around South Texas, educating and organizing *Raza* about the white, one-party power structure that dominated Texas politics. He advocated for a Chicano political party.

"What happened in that room that night has stood out in my mind," Alma told her son. She recalled that after the Gutiérrez's speech, the room's audience split in two during the questions and answers directed at the MAYO leader. Students disagreed with what Gutiérrez had said, about half of those present. Their questions were more self-serving statements. Some proclaimed they had never been discriminated against. Others placed blame on problems like the Chicano dropout rate and teen pregnancy rate on the victims themselves. They did not want to be associated with a Chicano movement. It offended and intimidated their white friends. They desperately wanted to be accepted by whites. Then there was the other half. They were sick and tired of the discrimination and were saying, "We've got to do something about it."

"I obviously went with the group that said 'Ya Basta!'" Not long after that fateful day, Alma Canales would rise to the challenge of becoming the first and only Chicana in Texas history to run for lieutenant governor. She was the candidate of the Raza Unida Party for that statewide office in 1972. The Raza Unida Party was the first Chicano effort and first challenge to the two-party dictatorial electoral system of the United States.

The lieutenant governor position in Texas is the most powerful state post, more powerful than the governor. The lieutenant governor presides over the state senate and controls legislation and budget.

Alma's political consciousness had been developing since a very early age. She was born in Starr County, in the town of Rosita, Texas, in 1947. Her parents are Zaragosa and Consuelo Canales, whose families had lived in Texas since before it became a state. She is the oldest of three sisters, all of whom grew up in Edinburg in South Texas. The family were migrant farmworkers during the summers, traveling to pick cotton in West Texas and cherries and sugar beets in Michigan.

In some ways, Alma remembers those days fondly. While on the migrant street within the state or out of state, she recalls they invariably lived in these little one-room shacks near the fields.

"It was amazing how my mother could pack everything for our annual trek to find work. A stove with a little gas tank on the side, the ironing board, the broom, the mop, all our work clothes, clothes to go out on weekends." She remembers how her father often asked her to deal with the *patron* or boss on issues of money, because he didn't speak English. She believes that is when she first learned how to negotiate and how not to be intimidated by anybody, particularly white men. But during those trips, she also experienced discrimination for the first time. She saw signs in the windows of barbershops and restaurants that read, "No Mexicans allowed." She learned that Mexicans were only welcome at the local movie theater on certain nights.

"My first brush with the harsher, more overt racial discrimination at the hands of the *gringos* was of course in West Texas," she recalled. She had seen discrimination in Edinburg, in the form of lower wages and poor working conditions in the fields, including the lack of toilet facilities and no potable drinking water, and the fact that workers had to eat lunch under the hot sun amidst the pesticide- and herbicide-sprayed crops. As a young adult the discrimination seemed very obvious to her; it was patently clear.

Alma escaped from the harshness of farmwork by immersing herself in school. She remembers a few teachers who had high expectations of her and demanded excellence. They recommended her for Honor's classes. She felt out of place because none of the other students in the Honor's classes were migrant workers or Mexicans. The difference between them became apparent one summer when she was required to take algebra during summer school if she was to remain on the Honor's track. She couldn't. Her entire family had planned on leaving for the summer to work the crops in the fields, as usual. She begged and pleaded with her parents to let her stay behind. Finally, they let her stay home alone. It represented a huge sacrifice, since the family needed the money she would have earned from working. Hands in the field are a vital and necessary source of family income.

Her Honor's class teachers began encouraging her to go to college. She never thought it would be possible. During her senior year, her journalism teacher offered her a scholarship. He was the editor of the *Edinburg Daily Press*. The scholarship would come with an internship at the daily paper. Again, she had to beg her parents to let her stay behind and go to college. The family reluctantly, once again, relented on two conditions: She must remain living at home, and she must contribute her earnings from the newspaper to the family's income.

Like too many young Chicanas, particularly, but also Chicano young men, Alma was the first in her family to go to college. She became a student at Pan American University and began working at the local newspaper. It didn't take her long to start writing controversial stories. The United States was in the throes of the Vietnam War. Young people opposed to the war were organizing antiwar demonstrations around the country. Alma hardly remained a detached observer like reporters were supposed to be. Young men who she had gone to high school with were getting killed and coming home to Texas in body bags. She wrote stories about who they were and how they had died. The estimates for Chicano casualties were pegged at 26 percent while the Chicano population in the country was a mere 6 percent. Chicano youth were dying fighting for a so-called democracy in South Vietnam while they had no such right in South Texas. In politics Chicano voters could vote for or against the white candidates of the Democratic Party. That was South

Texas democracy. She also started writing stories about city and county government. Her journalistic stance for the Chicano community made her more of an advocate than a detached reporter. Alma could not be detached; she was engaged with her *Raza*.

"I became a real advocate, you know, outspoken and pretty strong and pretty vocal. I made some demands and real statements," she recalled. "I became real assertive in questioning county officials and city officials. I wasn't gullible and naïve as I had been at the start when I was 'Almita' and a real pet, and kind of patronized. And all of a sudden, it was, 'Uh oh. She knows too much.'"

During her four years of college, while working at the newspaper, she became involved in Chicano student groups, including MAYO. She participated in protests and walkouts, vigils and meetings, *teatro* and other events all aimed at helping Chicanos get better education, health care, and jobs. One of the protest marches she helped organize in the Rio Grande Valley was an all-female protest against the police murder of a young man in Pharr who was an innocent bystander of an earlier march. The organizers believed the police wouldn't attack or arrest a group of female protesters and couldn't accuse the women of causing a riot like they had Efraín Fernández, the local MAYO leader.

Toward the end of her college days, she attended the national MAYO conference in December 1969 held nearby at La Lomita on the outskirts of Mission, Texas. The year prior she had attended the Chicano Youth Liberation Conference held in Denver, Colorado. At these conferences, organized and sponsored by Chicano youth just like her, Alma began learning more about the Chicano movement and its leaders such as Corky Gonzáles, Reies López Tijerina, and César Chávez. At the national MAYO conference, she attended a workshop on women as leaders in MAYO. After the conference and from then on, Alma felt that she could become a leader herself.

When she'd go back home to visit, however, she would have to explain her political activities to her parents. They were very conservative. They did not want her to get involved with the Chicano movement or MAYO. But it was too late. She was already a local leader and an organizer for MAYO and the Raza Unida Party. As part of her process of maturing and becoming independent, she moved to Austin, Texas. It was in Austin that she met her future husband, Steve Espinosa.

At the time, there were two major factions in the statewide Raza Unida Party. Those who wanted to turn the party into a statewide party, with candidates for governor, lieutenant governor, and the legislature. And those who wanted to keep Raza Unida a local regional party, such as José Angel Gutiérrez, running candidates in city, county, and school district elections, where they had been successful before. Alma believed it should be a statewide party. Her faction prevailed at the statewide nominating convention of the Raza Unida Party. Now the task facing the party and those in favor of a statewide strategy was finding candidates to fill the ballot, top to bottom.

"I remember thinking, 'Well somebody has to do it, and I'm here and I'm willing to do it,' and I did," she said. "And one of the considerations that I had was women that had trusted in me and had placed some sort of faith in my being able to maybe be a candidate and representing women on the ballot." She accepted the nomination to become the first and only woman, and Mexican American, to this present day, to run for lieutenant governor in Texas. And she also became the first and only female statewide candidate running on the Raza Unida Party ticket. Later, the Texas Raza Unida Party would be headed by a Chicana as well.

She was twenty-four years of age, not yet legally old enough to be elected to the second-highest office in the state. But she ran anyway. There were no qualifications required to run, only to hold the office. She was on the statewide ticket with Ramsey Muniz, the Raza Unida Party's candidate for governor. Across the state, first in the primary election and later in the November General Election of 1972, the name ALMA CANALES was on the ballot for voters to see and decide with their vote the outcome of that race.

Alma traveled around the state trying to find voters for her race and the other Raza Unida Party candidates also running for statewide offices. She gave speeches at all her stops, often ad-libbing since she had no previous experience speaking in front of groups. She recalls feeling most comfortable and confident in small towns like the one where she was born. She felt more comfortable talking with rural people in their backyards and *Placitas* than she did with the city-educated Mexican Americans that held receptions and coffees for her. At these stops, she would emphasize how she related to the townspeople. She too had worked in the fields and had felt the discrimination. She drove miles by herself in a borrowed car. At each stop, she'd pass the hat in order to collect enough gas money to get to the next town. Her campaign was worse than shoestring. She had no literature to hand out. She had no bumper stickers to paste on cars. She did not even have push cards with her name on them to give to voters. But she had lots of *ganas*, passion, and commitment to the cause of the *Partido*.

Both groups of Chicano voters, rural and urban, however could relate to her speeches about *Mexicanos* lacking opportunities, facing economic discrimination, suffering police brutality, and exclusion from the political process. "We were basically showing the strength and courage to come out and say what people were already thinking and knew to be true."

In the 1972 election, 80,000 people voted for her. Ramsey Muniz got 214,000 votes. The difference, she believes, was that only women voted for her and possibly the hard-core Raza Unida Party members. It did not help her cause any for Muniz not to campaign with her or invite her to join him at podiums where he spoke. Alma ran her own solo campaign. Muniz also may have picked up a few borderline and protest votes from Anglo voters against the Republican and Democratic parties. Overall, the failed statewide campaign signaled the difficulties ahead for the Raza Unida Party in Texas. Muniz ran again in 1974 and Mario Compeán also tried to win the governorship in 1978, but it was clearly the beginning of the end. The Raza Unida Party was doomed to repeat history as an alternative political party and fail. Moreover, Ramsey Muniz after his second electoral defeat had been indicted on drug charges and became a fugitive from justice having jumped bail on the eve of his trial. His arrest, indictment, and bail jumping were a death blow to the political party. And some say a deliberate setup by police authorities.

But to Alma, 80,000 votes was a victory, certainly not a defeat, in many ways. Every time the thought of one person voting for her entered her mind, she was humbled. Her campaign had organized at least 80,000 persons for the next campaign. She had found new volunteers for the campaign effort and recruited them into the *Partido*. She had made history for women generally and Chicanas specifically. But in the final analysis, the loss was personally devastating. She felt inadequate and that she had not measured up to the rigors and demands of a statewide campaign. She second-guessed her decision and vote to push for the Raza Unida Party to compete statewide. People within the party believed outside forces beyond their control had sabotaged the campaigns. Police regularly harassed Raza Unida Party supporters. Employers threatened workers with firing if they were seen with *Partido* paraphernalia or were found to have voted for La Raza Unida candidates. The opponents, usually entrenched Mexican American *politicos*, after the election would say things like, "I told you so." The anti-Raza Unida Party forces incessantly preached that things weren't all that bad for Mexican Americans and that the group wasn't as powerless and disenfranchised as Raza Unida made them out to be. They pointed to themselves as living proof that the Democratic Party was open to *Raza*. Alma began to believe that the Raza Unida Party had pushed too soon, too hard, and had alienated mainstream Mexican Americans. And now in defeat it seemed that the Raza Unida Party candidates and leadership had upset the white establishment, and Ramsey's folly had made them all look bad and potentially guilty of drug trafficking.

"It was a feeling that we had gone a step beyond the comfort zone. It was a feeling that Raza Unida Party embarrassed us. I remember a comment, '*La Raza Runida*,' or 'the gnawed people.' It was sort of like we were the whipping boys or the punching bags for anybody that wanted to hold us up as the example of what not to be," Alma recalled.

The internalized negative energy took months to reject and recover from after the unsuccessful campaign. A lot of people had said, "*No se vayan con La Raza Unida*," she said, because they didn't think it was a viable political party. Others had said Canales wasn't qualified to run. "But I got just as many people saying they know it was a good thing." That made her feel the effort was at least worthwhile. "I had always felt like it was a necessary thing. I had a natural love for politics. I felt like it was a winnable, doable proposal—that what we proposed to the people, had we had the resources and the time, that eventually we would have been quite successful." Alma also took the name Raza from the *Partido* and gave it to her firstborn child. A memory for a lifetime.

The result of all the Raza Unida Party work in the 1970s has been the election of more Chicanos to state and local offices, and the downfall, in some cases, of *patrones* who had used public office for personal gain. It also led to the establishment in 1976 of the Mexican American Democrats in Texas (MAD), as a component of the Democratic Party. MAD was the first time Mexican American Democrats had leverage within the Democratic Party; previously they were taken for granted. MAD originally was set up in direct competition with the Raza Unida Party. Since the demise of the *Partido* and loss of ballot status, MAD has basically absorbed all the original Raza Unida Party members. MAD members call the ex-Raza Unida Party members, BADies for Born Again Democrats. Some disillusioned *Partido* people also got involved in other third-party campaigns, such as Jesse Jackson's Rainbow Coalition, Ross Perot's Reform Party, and even the Republican Party. Many just quit electoral politics for years.

A most significant gain from the experience in the Raza Unida Party was more equality between Chicano men and women, Alma says. Chicanas also became seasoned, experienced political workers and leaders in countless local communities across the state. While Alma and Ramsey and other statewide candidates lost their elections, many down ballot RUP candidates won, and they were often Chicanas. The Chicano movement and the Raza Unida Party effort opened the doors wide for Chicanas to enter the public arena.

For Alma her activism continued after the unsuccessful run for lieutenant governor. She opened a daycare center in Wisconsin and went out to the field to sign up children to attend. She found them staying under trailers and trucks while their parents worked in the fields. She also started a newspaper for the United Farm Workers union in the Rio Grande Valley. She volunteered in programs of the Vista Minority Mobilization program and the Southwest Council of La Raza (now the National Council of La Raza), as well as MAYO. She was a reporter for the *Ya Mero* newspaper. While she was a student at the Chicano-led Colegio Jacinto Trevino in the Rio Grande Valley, she developed a curriculum for high school "dropouts" who wished to graduate. She taught classes herself.

In Waco, Texas, married and settled down, she became a mother. This began a new phase of her life, in which she became involved in local community affairs through the League of United Latin American Citizens (LULAC), the Parent Teacher Association, and even the Mexican American Democrats and other organizations.

"I continued, and I proved my commitment to community involvement in many ways since then. And I continue to command some respect and have continued to hear from some people who still believe in me," she said.

Now, she is involved in trying to restart the Raza Unida social movement in Texas, perhaps through the Mexican American Democrats as they become disenchanted with the two-party system. "If we can reach a consensus and if there is a viable avenue to take, then I probably will be the first one to join," she said. She says she may even run for office again one day. "As big a thing as I think it is, and as much as I think that other people would do a much better job, and as inadequate and hesitating that I have been, I think that if somebody said, 'You gotta do it,' then I probably would say, 'Well, it's got to be done.'" Alma still has *ganas*, passion, and commitment to *La Causa de la Raza*.

~

# CHAPTER SEVEN

# Linda Reyna Yáñez

Linda's father, David Reyna, must have had an extraordinary sense of humor. He learned on November 30, 1948, that his wife had given birth to a daughter. Linda was born at her grandparent's house in Rio Hondo, a little South Texas town. In fact she was born on the same bed in which her father had been born. Her father proudly named his first born, Soila Linda Reyna. Phonetically and in Spanish, Soila is pronounced *Soy La*, which means "I Am." *Linda* means beautiful. And *Reyna* is pronounced like *Reina*, for queen. *Soy La Linda Reina*, aka Soila Linda Reyna, means "I Am The Beautiful Queen." Yáñez is a married name. She dropped Soila for Linda early in childhood and always uses both surnames in her professional capacity. She is Linda Reyna Yáñez, now Justice Reyna Yáñez of the Thirteenth Court of Appeals for the State of Texas.

The Beautiful Queen was raised in South Texas by her grandparents, Victor Reyna and Petra Guerra, from age five to her graduation from high school. Her parents were poor and the family was large, four brothers and sisters. The family left her behind with the grandparents while they worked in factories and lived in and around St. Charles, Illinois.[1] Linda grew up in Rio Hondo "in the midst of poverty and attended segregated schools." Reyna recalls, "that they [her parents] left me with my grandparents when I was still five; I was still in the first grade. And my mother [Angela Zavala Reyna] didn't want me to miss out, as I had already started school and she felt that I had all of the skills to be a good first grader. So, she changed my birth certificate date of birth so that I could get into school. I probably should have been in kindergarten. My mom did the kindergarten teaching at home. The reason I think this is significant is because when I was placed in school we had a segregated system."

Even though she didn't grow up with her parents directly, they were still coming to visit. She was always in touch with them. When her parents were with her, they constantly reassured her about how much they cared about her. She does remember picking cotton with her parents in South Texas.

Her father always told her that she was going to college. It was a good thing he kept the pressure of achievement on Linda, because she wasn't that focused. Reyna Yáñez remembers thinking about going to college, little else. When the thought crossed her mind, she imagined herself as an engineer, maybe a lawyer or a teacher. In junior high school Linda became a social butterfly and got elected class president and cheerleader. But she also was a solid academic achiever. Her grades were consistently good. In high school she basically continued her social trajectory from junior high. During her last years in high school she was nominated and selected to serve as vice president of the National Honor Society. Linda Reyna was also very active as a member of the band and earned a spot on the cheerleading squad for the football team. Her classmates elected her class representative on the student governing board. And a triumphant moment was being chosen queen of the high school, truly *Linda Reina* at school. She was popular and enjoyed lots of support from all of her classmates. Her high school years were happy years.

She applied for admission to the local university and was accepted to Pan American University[2] in Edinburg, Texas, just a few miles from where she grew up. For her major she didn't choose any of the childhood dreams. Instead she earned a major in Inter-American Studies. She wanted to become a diplomat. She wanted to work for the OAS (Organization of American States). "Pan Am," as the local population refers to the university, had a Model Organization of American States (OAS) program in which students study the member countries and role-play international relations. The Model OAS at Pan Am and other institutions competes regionally and nationally in an academic contest. While at Pan Am, Linda traveled to Washington, D.C., to compete and visit the headquarters of the OAS. Her involvement with the Model OAS program got her interested in the Pre-Law Society and the Young Democrats of Texas. She joined these campus organizations.

She also joined the Newman Club, a campus-based, Catholic student organization. Linda and her grandparents always went to church. Linda was very profoundly religious since childhood. The activities at the Newman Club and going to church regularly began to affect Linda in a significant way. Her life changed dramatically her sophomore year at Pan Am University when she decided to become a nun. She had always been very active in her church. She volunteered as a catechism teacher. She was at the local Catholic church three or four days a week doing many different things. "It was all around me—a strong Catholic upbringing. The Church was major in my childhood, a major part of my growing up. I was just thinking how I could be a good person."

She says, "I had a very strong spiritual base and I thought I had a calling. I decided that's what I wanted to do for the rest of my life. My father thought I was nuts, and my mother also thought I was crazy. They convinced me to finish at Pan Am and then make the decision of where to go with my life." That was very savvy and experienced advice. Linda took her parent's advice and admonishment to heart and focused on graduation. And she graduated within a couple of years in 1970.

Richard Millhouse Nixon had been elected president of the country. In response to growing Chicano voter strength in the Democratic Party, Nixon devised a strategy to compete for those Chicano votes and support. Trying to be inclusive of all Latino groups in the nation, Nixon formed the Cabinet Committee on Opportunity for the Spanish Speaking with Martín Castillo as head. Linda Reyna was invited to come to Washington to be a part of the committee's staff. She accepted and worked on Spanish-speaking affairs for Mr. Castillo a year. While in D.C. she met Ben Hernández, who later became the first Hispanic Republican to seek the presidential nomination. He encouraged her to return to the childhood dream of becoming a lawyer.

That dream was not to be for a number of years because her ex-boyfriend from Pleasanton, Texas, Eusebio Compián, came to Washington looking for her. Soon, they renewed the relationship, married, and Linda got pregnant. She kept the baby, Regina, and dropped the husband. She returned to South Texas, baby in tow, thinking she had become a failure.

Linda needed a job in South Texas to provide for her baby daughter and herself. She said, "I made up my mind at that time. Number one, that I was going to get away from this horrible relationship and this terrible person, you know my, my first husband. I now had to grow up. I had a responsibility for another human being and I had to stop being so self-centered and frivolous and I needed to get on with things. By this time I'm already twenty-two. The, the wonderful thing was that I had a degree. I had a piece of paper that was going to at least give me some mark, you know, put me in the job market." She decided to teach elementary school in Weslaco. She also decided that she needed to get politically involved in back-home politics.

She volunteered to work for the George McGovern presidential campaign in the Rio Grande Valley and the Ramsey Muniz gubernatorial campaign

(Raza Unida Party). At the same time she got very involved with the local farmworkers unionization efforts (UFW) going on in Rio Grande City over in Starr County. Linda was also attracted to the work of the Raza Unida Party upon meeting some of the organizers and local leadership, including Ramsey Muniz. As was the custom then, less so today, supporters of causes, candidates, and campaigns would display stickers, logos, emblems, and the like on car bumpers primarily. Linda had her car plastered with bumper stickers announcing her support for McGovern, the UFW, and the Raza Unida Party. A problem quickly arose and became an altering moment in her life.

During some political activity, a local television station interviewed her about her politics. She came out and on strong with her views during the evening news broadcast. Linda was also very, very photogenic and vivacious and still is, ideal for television. The following Monday, her school principal, Bill Clements, informed her that the school superintendent had terminated her teaching contract. She no longer had a teaching job. Being the fighter for the underdog that she had become, Linda sought out the local legal services program for a civil rights attorney. Someone reminded her that the McGovern campaign coordinator was David Hall, director of the Texas Rural Legal Aid (TRLA) in Weslaco. The battle over her teaching job because of the bumper stickers and political work changed her life. Over the next few months David Hall convinced her to apply and attempt a law school career.

Linda Reyna eventually applied and was admitted to one of Houston's law schools, Texas Southern University (TSU), the historically black college. Her freshman law class had the first Chicanas at TSU: Irene Canales, Thelma García, and Linda. She moved to Houston, Texas, and fell right into a larger milieu of activists and activism with the urban support group for the Texas Farm Workers Union. The farmworkers, at the direction of their national leaders, César Chávez and Dolores Huerta, had called for a boycott against grapes. Linda was adamant that all would hear her yell, "Boycott Grapes!" She helped boycott neighborhood grocery stores carrying nonunion grapes and even organized a protest march downtown to the Tenneco building. Linda joined the local TSU chapter of the Chicano Law Students Association and ultimately became their delegate to the state and national conventions.

She managed to apply for and obtain an internship with the Legal Assistance Foundation of Chicago, Illinois. She not only got to visit with her parents regularly during that brief period, but also got law course credit for her time. Linda graduated from law school in 1976. But before she graduated, she had married again during her second year of law school, this time to Emilio Yáñez. Upon graduation, the couple moved to Chicago, and Linda was soon pregnant and without a job or a bar license to practice law in Illinois. Linda got a job working full-time with the same folks that gave her the internship, the Legal Assistance Foundation. She was eight and a half months pregnant and studying for the February bar examination, plus working full-time. She passed the bar and she gave birth to Amparo in Chicago. She also gave birth to a stellar immigration law career. Linda worked on the precedent-setting case of *Silva v. Levy* (1977), which legalized more than 450,000 persons of Mexican ancestry.

By 1977 after Amparo was born and with Regina in hand, the Yáñez family, Linda and Emilio, decided to relocate to South Texas. Linda took another legal aid job with David Hall, working immigration cases. She and Emilio began studying to take the Texas bar. She passed and he didn't. One of the immigration cases she worked on and litigated in federal court in Brownsville, Texas, ultimately was joined with *Plylar v Doe* (1981), another precedent-setting case, in which the U.S. Supreme Court ruled on equal protection grounds that all children regardless of citizenship had a right to educational opportunity in the United States. Within days, Linda was on *Good Morning America* explaining the significance of this ruling to the country.

During the Reagan presidency, the national legal assistance programs came under severe budgetary and programmatic attack. The legal aid programs were gutted of their class action litigation capability. They could not sue government entities among many other prohibitions. Linda's immigration practice in TRLA came to an end. She opened her own legal practice and began a private immigration law service without her husband. They had divorced in 1981.

Within a short time, the Reyna Yáñez law firm was filled to the brim with immigration cases, including ones beginning to challenge the U.S. policy on political asylum. The government in El Salvador was killing thousands of Salvadorans, with the complicity of the Reagan administration. Those that fled and managed to enter South Texas faced deportation by the U.S. Immigration and Naturalization Service (INS), and deportation meant guaranteed death upon arrival. Deportation was the death sentence being imposed on Salvadoran refugees by INS.

Linda put on her legal battle dress and went to Washington, D.C., to testify before the Organization of American States (OAS). The prestigious law firm of Steptoe and Johnson was her ally. She had the evidence to link deportation based on denial of political asylum to subsequent murder of deportees by the Salvadoran government. Some disembarking deportees never even made it out of the San Salvador international airport. Linda's reputation as an expert on immigration matters got her an invitation to join Welch and Black, a Rio Grande Valley law firm, and head their immigration practice. She accepted.

With the influx of additional political refugees into South Texas, the INS opened a new detention facility in Los Fresnos, called *El Corralón* by the detainees and local folks. Nicaraguan refugees were now coming into South Texas in addition to other Central Americans. The Reagan military interventions in Central America produced political refugees by the hundreds of thousands. Walking to the United States was their only option. Linda Reyna Yáñez was their legal savior. She defended the establishment of *Casa Romero* in Brownsville, the first sanctuary home in Texas, and also began to take on drug-related court cases. She was burned out by 1990.

Linda left her hefty six-figure salary and moved to Chicago again. She took a job with the Mexican American Legal Defense and Education Fund (MALDEF) as its regional counsel beginning in 1991, a legislative redistricting year. The MALDEF redistricting effort was aimed at establishing a Chicano congressional seat in Chicago, the first in the Midwest. The research and evidentiary materials developed by Linda to support a litigation challenge to the MALDEF congressional map held up. The Chicano district looked like a pair of lungs with the University of Illinois between the lungs. "I'm very proud of the fact that what won our case was the affidavit that I prepared from the people from the University of Illinois, who said that the only reason those communities are separated is because of the political decisions that were made to build the University of Illinois right smack in the middle of that community." The Chicano congressional seat became a Latino seat with the election of Puerto Rican Luis Gutiérrez to the U.S. House of Representatives.

During the whirlwind of legislative lobbying, political infighting for favorable political turf, candidate selection, and defensive legal maneuvering to keep the Chicano seat, Linda got burned out and homesick. Her baby Regina was finishing high school in Texas, her other baby, Amparo, was in a boarding school for academically gifted children in Newport, Rhode Island, and she was alone in Chicago. One morning while reading *Interpreter Releases*, a legal newsletter, "I see an ad for a position to run an immigration clinic at Harvard Law School. And I thought that sounds interesting and that's only an hour away from Amparo." At the last minute she submitted her resume by Fed Ex and was offered the position in November. By the following January, Linda relocated to Boston to head up Harvard's Immigration Law Clinic, earning more than MALDEF could pay and down the road from Amparo. But Regina was still out there in Texas.

In 1992, Bill Clinton won the presidency and began scouting for a transition team to help him put an administration together. Linda got a call from the MALDEF people inviting her to consider being part of that transition team because the infighting between those that got Clinton elected and those that were going to help him govern was intense. Chicanos were few in either camp. They needed help. Linda submitted her resume and Peter Edelman offered her the position of team leader to develop the presidential briefing book on immigration issues and policy for the administration. She jumped at the chance and took a leave of absence from Harvard.

Linda got a taste for the real power of governing. "Power is an amazing thing. Called up the U.S. Attorney's office and I said, 'I want the following files to be ready at three o'clock on Wednesday. And I want whatever lawyers you have assigned to those cases to be ready to talk settlement in these cases.'" Because the Clinton appointee for attorney general, Zoe Baird, was not approved and the subsequent nomination of Janet Reno took longer than expected, Linda continued to serve the president, "I was getting calls almost on a daily basis on immigration from the White House." During the following summer Linda returned to the Rio Grande Valley to assist Haitian detainees that had been relocated from the Northeast to Texas. Harvard gave her a summer leave, and she brought Amparo and collected Regina. They were finally a family.

Regina interviewed her for a college sociology class and asked, "Mom, when did you decide that you were going to work hard at being a strong Hispanic woman?" Linda said, "I never did that. I never consciously did that. I just wanted to be a good person. And being born a Hispanic female was what I was born into. That was inherently me." Her daughter also asked her about women's issues.

> I feel that a lot of the issues that the women's groups are concerned with, are white women's issues. And when I identify myself, I identify myself first as a Chicana, and secondly as a woman. Politically, therefore, I'm going to have to spend the time that I have working on Chicano issues rather than on woman's issues because you white women can do that and spend that time. I just relate more. That was a conscious decision that I made. My time was going to be spent on issues, on these other issues rather than on, than on women's issues even though I knew the women's issues were also very important, and there were so few of us, but there were so few of us, as Latinas than there were as white women.

While in South Texas the summer of 1993, Ann Richards, the newly elected governor, had a vacancy on the Thirteenth Court of Appeals, in the

Rio Grande Valley. Linda got a call to come interview with Fred Ellis with the governor's office for that position. She was appointed and became the first Chicana on that appellate court and won subsequent reelection campaigns to retain her judicial seat. In 1998 she received her master of law from the University of Virginia School of Law. That year she sought reelection and was unopposed. It is no wonder that she polled 149,236 votes in the general election.

An unusual election law quirk is that judicial candidates on the appellate court do not have to resign their position to run for a higher office. In Texas there are only two such higher offices, the supreme court and the other supreme court for criminal matters, the court of criminal appeals. Positions on both of these supreme courts and the appellate courts carry a whopping six-year term of office, and they are staggered terms. Justice Yáñez did not have to face reelection until 2004. And she has been the only justice that has not had to face opposition in her elections for that position.

In 2002, Justice Linda Reyna Yáñez decided that from her guaranteed seat on the Thirteenth Court of Appeals until 2004 why not give it a shot for higher office. In 2002, Justice Reyna Yáñez announced her candidacy for the Texas Supreme Court. She sought the position "because I feel very strongly that the reason why we have multiple members at the appellate level is because there's supposed to be a dialogue, a deliberation in the court, and I believe that is not taking place now. All of the members of the court are coming from the same place and have the same perspectives."[3]

Initially the race seemed to hold the promise of getting the first Chicana elected to that court. At the top of the Democratic Party column were the candidates referred to as the Dream Team: Ron Kirk, Tony Sánchez, and John Sharp. The Dream Team consisted of an African American seeking the U.S. Senate seat; a Mexican American running for governor; and an Anglo wanting to become the lieutenant governor of the state. The problem was they were all males. The Dream Team members never thought of inviting women candidates also running statewide races such as Justice Reyna Yáñez or another woman appellate court justice from Houston, Mirabal, to join them at any forum or campaign with them. Linda Reyna Yáñez had tough opposition in this race, and like most Democrats running in this election, the Dream Team was running without them. Campaign resource sharing and more importantly, get-out-the-vote efforts were not coordinated among the statewide Democratic Party candidates. The Republican candidates not only were more coordinated in their campaigns but also asked supporters to vote a straight Republican Party ticket. The various Republican candidates appeared together at many more functions than did Democrats. And the Republican Party column on the ballot contained more minorities as candidates than the Democratic Party column.

The entire Democratic Party slate of statewide candidates went down in defeat, Justice Linda Reyna Yáñez included. Four million-plus, 4,370,298, voters went to the polls and cast ballots in the race for supreme court, place 1 in the 2002 general election. Her opponent Mike Schneider received 56.01 percent of the vote, 2,451,791 votes. Linda received 41.54 percent of the vote, 1,815,581, the most votes any Chicana candidate had ever received in the state of Texas.[4]

Even though she ran an unsuccessful campaign to become a justice on the Texas Supreme Court there were many pluses. She had gained statewide experience at raising money, building a campaign organization, and getting her message out effectively to 1.8 million voters. This in itself is no small feat. She also had to manage her caseload on the court of appeals and campaign on weekends, basically. Various newspapers and other media outlets got to know her and she them. The *San Antonio Express-News* endorsed her candidacy, "Her nine years of experience as an appellate court justice will serve Texas well if voters elevate her to the state's highest court. In addition to her excellent credentials, if elected Yáñez will bring independence and a fresh perspective."[5] She kept her seat on the Rio Grande Valley appellate court. And she did make history as the first Chicana to run for the Texas Supreme Court. At this writing, she is unopposed in the 2004 Democratic Party primary election.

## Notes

1. J. Elliot, "Appellate Judge Launches Bid for State High Court," *Houston Chronicle*, November 12, 2001, p. 13.

2. Now a part of the University of Texas system and is called the University of Texas–Pan American at Edinburg.

3. *Texas Lawyer*, October 2002, p.17.

4. See www.sos.state.tx.us and go to Election Returns, 2002 General Election, Supreme Court Place 1. See also www.courts.state.tx.us for information about this supreme court in Texas.

5. *San Antonio Express-News*, October 10, 2002, p.5G.

# CHAPTER EIGHT

~

# Irma Mireles

Irma is a native-born Texan, fifth generation. Her parents were from around Seguin, Lockhart, and Martindale, and she was raised in Lockhart. Her parents are Trinidad and David Mireles. Her mother's maiden name was Martínez. Her paternal grandfather was from Abasado Nuevo León, Mexico, and became the only blacksmith in Seguin, Texas. When her paternal grandparents decided to marry it was with the condition they would give up their firstborn son to the grandparents. Among some Mexican families, it was customary to give up a child, usually a younger or the youngest female to the grandparents so that the child would become the caregiver to the aging grandparents, seldom a son. An Uncle to Irma, Juan, was the child given to the grandparents, but he was sent to seminary. And he didn't like it and left, but did not return to the grandparent's home. He wandered off elsewhere. It was generations and years later in San Antonio when Irma and her brothers were playing out front and a man was walking by. They mistakenly ran up to him thinking it was their dad. He wasn't and that is how they met *Tío* (Uncle) Juan. Amazingly enough, *Tío Juan* only lived two blocks from them.

Irma's maternal grandparents had moved to Lockhart, Texas, in the early 1900s. However, her grandmother became sick, which made it necessary for her grandfather to obtain some extra cash. He borrowed money from a German neighbor and signed a contract to pay him back. He didn't know how to read, though, and signed with an X. The collateral he pledged was the land and cattle. Unable to pay on time, he lost the land and livestock. He had to move his family. The family began a migration in reverse. They moved to

San Antonio then to Monterrey, Mexico and back to Seguin and up to Lock-hart and back to Monterrey. Times were hard. The family moved to where jobs were available. Irma's father was an avid baseball player, even played ball with a local league in Mexico and Texas. Her mother met him at a dance af-ter a baseball game. Her mother is from the Rio Grande Valley of Texas. But the family moved north to Lockhart and the Martindale area. Her mom loved to dance and her dad loved baseball. They married shortly after that chance encounter and began a family. Irma was born in Martindale, Texas, in 1947 followed by brother David in 1948 and Richard in 1949, followed by three others, one after another. But her immediate family had to move to Mexico when Irma was young.

Irma attended school in Monterrey until about the third grade. Then they came to live in San Antonio. She recalls discrimination in the public schools of San Antonio. She and her brothers were always in trouble for speaking Spanish. She recalls an incident when she was nine years old, "Being in class and my youngest brother, Richard, comes in and he wants to talk to me. And the teacher will not let him talk to me; he came into my classroom, until he asked for me in English. And she wouldn't let him. She just wouldn't let him. I finally got my stuff and I grabbed my brother and I got out of there. I really got into trouble. My brother was sick and he needed to go to the bathroom. And I remember I didn't want to go to school anymore after that. . . . To this day, he's had problems with the whole culture shock. He never got over that."

Her father didn't either. He told his kids stories of discrimination when he was growing up. "My father will tell us stories about in Seguin when he was a young man that if there was a *gringo* walking on the sidewalk, any *Mexicano* walking on the same side had to step down. He tells us about the Guadalupe River, that *Mexicanos* couldn't go swimming there." Irma also recalls that Seguin was physically a divided town, with Mexicans living on one side and Anglos on the other. As a child she also never understood why the homes of her friends were boarded up in the summer until she learned about migratory labor going to the northern states. Her family had not been migrants, so she never realized what was going on.

While attending junior high school she met her first Mexican American teacher, "A teacher that looked like us. And she made a big impact. Then in high school I remember that I had another real good teacher, the sponsor of the student council, who helped a lot when people tried to *hacernos menos* (make us feel less). But he was Anglo and he was a pretty good sponsor. I re-member being in the pep squad." Irma was also elected treasurer of the stu-dent council on one occasion at Breckenridge High School. Irma was in her senior year when the class was taken on a field trip. "I was real good in short-hand. And I was a real good typist. All those business courses that they give you in high school . . . they gear you to the most you can be is a secretary at Kelly Field or at USAA. And I remember doing the field trip to USAA and I swore I'd never work there. It was like desks full of people working *como hormigas* (working like ants). I don't know if they were all secretaries, but I do remember that all the males were white men in offices." Yet, as seniors about to graduate in 1966, no counselor ever discussed with her or her class-mates any career options. It was assumed they would graduate and become secretaries.

The Chicano movement and black civil rights movement were underway, but Irma felt she couldn't get deeply involved. Her compromise was to take a job at Fort Sam Houston, one of many military installations surrounding San Antonio, Texas. Jobs with federal installations and programs were good jobs to have in the San Antonio economy. President Lyndon Baines Johnson initiated the War on Poverty in 1964. Federal money flowed into communi-ties across the nation in the form of programs at the neighborhood level. These were more jobs. In Irma's community it was called the San Antonio Neighborhood Youth Organization (SANYO). She took a job there because it was closer to home, and she did not drive a car. Never has. "Not knowing how to drive has never kept me from what I really wanted to do. I always manage."

While working at SANYO she met some of the founders of the Mexican American Youth Organization (MAYO) who also worked there. Her child-hood friend and classmate since she first came into the public schools in San Antonio, Anna Rojas, had been telling her about MAYO. Irma was now con-necting the name and stories with the young men behind them. Her first real political involvement however had been through her mom when she was about sixteen. Her mom was really taken by John F. Kennedy and helped in his presidential campaign. Anna Rojas, her lifelong friend, invited her to be-come active in the Mexican American Youth Organization.

Initially Irma's work with MAYO was limited, but she met other young ac-tivist women such as Rosie Castro and Gloria Cabrera. She volunteered to be the secretary for the local MAYO group of activists. "But once I got in-volved and I guess I really got involved in late '68, early '69. To this day, I've never let go. Once I got involved I was in." And even though she hated the thought of being a secretary, she realized the position had power. "Because of what I heard and what I transcribed was very important to the history of what was happening. And I also realized that some of the people who had come before me or had held any kind of position as secretary in any organization outside of the *movimiento* (movement) were people that actually controlled what was being recorded. And so I thought I can do that and I can tell our story. I kept tapes. I have a lot of cassette tapes and I have some written notes." She has not decided what she will do with her treasure trove of historical data.

In 1969, MAYO decided to launch its first electoral challenge; heretofore MAYO had concentrated on making school reforms. MAYO organized many student boycotts of schools, including several in San Antonio schools: Lanier and Edgewood, for example. Irma was not too involved with the school walkouts as the boycotts were often called.

She became involved with the Committee for Barrio Betterment, the slate of Chicano candidates that sought seats on the city council. They challenged the political hegemony of the Good Government League (GGL), the Anglo political machine that ruled San Antonio. This electoral challenge was tantamount to climbing a mountain without gear or water. The San Antonio City Council members were elected at-large, in citywide contests for every district. There were more Anglo voters than Chicano voters, with some black voters in the city. The minority, brown and black, had no representation, except that permitted by the GGL establishment. They did include a

*From left to right: Rosie Castro, Mario Compean, José Angel Gutiérrez, and (standing) Irma Mireles*

black and brown face in their slates from time to time. Henry Cisneros became one of those handpicked and GGL-sponsored Hispanic candidates in 1975.

Irma contributed money and time to the effort. She was the only one of the core activists holding down a job. She helped run silkscreen campaign posters, conducted voter registration drives, organized political rallies, and attended the candidates' meetings. She was not only the secretary for the group but also the personal friend of two candidates, Mario Compeán, the MAYO leader, and Dario Chapa, a schoolteacher. While the slate lost the election, Mario Compeán, who ran for mayor, polled enough votes to force a runoff election with Walter McAllister, the GGL stalwart. In 1971 MAYO and Barrios Unidos tried again. This time the slate included two women: Rosie Castro and Gloria Cabrera, plus Willie Benavides and Mario Compeán, once again. Irma was even more involved this time; she was volunteering upward of sixty hours a week despite her regular job. She was single, not living at home, had a job, and her best friends were running for public office. They were out there for La Raza. So was Irma. These political races were Irma's equivalent of going to college, something she never got around to doing, although she since has taken some sixty hours of college courses at night.

While the courts and legislative bodies wrangled over how single-member districts would be established in order to comply with the Voting Rights Act, MAYO had moved on to form La Raza Unida Party (RUP) as a regional political party in 1970 and statewide in 1972. Irma was not directly involved with the regional party efforts because they had taken place in rural counties such as Hidalgo in the Rio Grande Valley, La Salle, Dimmit, and Zavala in the Winter Garden area of Southwest Texas. In 1972 however, the *partido* (party) delegates meeting in a statewide convention voted to form a statewide political organization. Irma and hundreds of other Chicano militants and activists previously involved with school walkouts and other protests including incipient electoral challenges jumped at the opportunity to work on a large goal. In order to qualify for ballot status, the Raza Unida Party had to gather sufficient numbers of signatures of voters on a petition. The numbers were in the tens of thousands. It was a difficult task. The party leadership assigned signature quotas to county chapters in order to get the job done in a timely fashion for the filing deadline.

Irma and other *partido* militants went to Mission County Park to collect signatures for the petitions to get Raza Unida on the ballot. *La Raza* frequented this park and a few others on the West Side of town. Cooking out, playing music, and dancing at the park are favorite weekend Chicano activities. While at the park the signature-gathering proved difficult, particularly in explaining to each individual what they wanted, why, and by when. Someone suggested the signature gatherers get up on the stage and speak to the people at the park through the microphone. The belief was that once the message got out, the people who were interested would come to up and sign the petitions.

This activity became a pivotal moment for Irma. No one wanted to take the stage and microphone, so Irma boldly stepped up. This was the first time she spoke in front of a large audience. She explained who the Raza Unida Party was and what their purpose was. She asked all 3,000 people in the parks to sign the RUP petition. It worked. Irma obtained more signatures than anyone else.

While attending the Raza Unida Convention in 1972, she accepted election to the position she thought she never wanted, that of secretary. By transcribing official speeches from events and taking minutes at meetings, she became keenly observant of the people present and their motives, political maneuvers, philosophies, and voting behavior. Irma began to discern the diversity of philosophies represented within RUP. She criticized some as being more *gringo* than Mexican in their philosophies. She lost respect for Rodolfo "Corky" González, the RUP in Colorado leader and head of the Crusade for Justice in Denver.[1] At one of the women's conferences she attended, Corky's men had walked in and one of them dropped something in her lap. She handed it back without thinking, but it turned out to be a gun. She met Reies López Tijerina at the *partido's* national convention in El Paso. He was the architect of the People's Constitutional Party and Alianza Federal de Pueblos Libres (Federal Alliance of Free People) in New Mexico. Tijerina was a fiery Pentecostal preacher whose militant approach culminated in a massive march to the state capitol of New Mexico, the occupation of the Echo Amphitheater in Northern New Mexico in 1966, and the courthouse raid in Tierra Amarilla, New Mexico, in 1967.

Irma became more politicized by Joe Castillo while attending meetings of the Federation for the Advancement of Mexican Americans (FAMA) and their training classes. Maps of a city displayed at these meetings showed that the white, more affluent areas of town had many parks, while the Chicano areas virtually had none. This meant that Chicano kids were forced onto the streets to play and hang out. This left an indelible mark on Irma.

During one election in which RUP candidates were running, Irma became an election clerk. Her involvement with the mechanics of running an election prompted her to learn more about the actual process. Most of her friends were former MAYO activists that now were involved in organizing and building the Raza Unida Party. During various elections she had received calls about people being prevented from voting. As an experienced election clerk she knew what to do. Once while working an election she heard that voters were being stopped by election judges and accused of being drunk and of electioneering near the polling places, both illegal acts. She could not get a hold of any statewide election officials to correct the injustice, so she transformed a light-skinned, Hispanic-looking guy, well versed in English and Spanish, and put him into a borrowed suit and tie to pretend to be from the Department of Justice. After rehearsing him on what to say and how to say it, he went to the polling place and put an end to the underhanded tactics.

In January of 1973, she and some other women leaders from the RUP met in Crystal City to discuss the formation of a Chicana caucus within the RUP. By the summer of 1974, they had formed a group called *Mujeres Por La Raza Unida* (Women for La Raza Unida). Irma and several other RUP women, including Evey Chapa, Rosie Castro, Marta Cotera, and Linda Valdez, had attended the Women's Political Caucus, which was comprised primarily of white, middle-class, professional women and feminist activists. The RUP Chicanas not only objected to the agenda, but also took these meetings over. According to Irma, there is a double standard for men and women, including among Chicanos, that requires women to keep their private lives and political lives separate in order to be respected. Irma avoided personal relationships. She also complained about women who were groupies. These groupies were there for the men and gave serious women a bad name.

In 1973, the RUP leadership asked Irma to coordinate a scholarship program for Chicanos studying medicine in Mexican universities. While in Mexico, she felt as if she was being followed most of the time. At first, she figured it was paranoia and just that she was unaccustomed to living in Mexico, but later she concluded that indeed she was being followed, since the same man was always watching her no matter where she went. The Becas Para Aztlán program ended up graduating some students and some are practicing medicine in the United States today.

Irma was elected in 1974 as Bexar County chair of the Raza Unida Party. As county chair Irma submitted paperwork to fund primaries based on the number of votes the candidate for governor had received the year before. She had to make sure there were election judges and clerks for the precincts in Bexar County. She had to recruit candidates, including other precinct chairs, especially in key contested precincts. According to Irma, precinct chairs were hard to find, but once found and put through training they were there "*hasta el fin!*" (until the end!).

By the mid-1970s, Irma was ready to become a candidate for public office. Even though she picked an office that was not a partisan election, she carried the banner of the Raza Unida Party. She made sure people knew she was an active member of the *partido*. Irma ran for the San Antonio River Authority (SARA) in 1976, which was a regulatory agency with jurisdiction over a large multicounty area. The politics of water figured centrally in the work of the SARA. The board of directors consisted of twelve people, six from Bexar County, and two each from Wilson, Karnes, and Goliad. It was a large board and service was not handsomely paid, only fifty dollars per meeting, plus expenses.

In order to qualify as a candidate she had either to pay a filing fee of $100 or gather signatures of nomination from voters in the district. She chose the petition route. She already had prior experience with gathering signatures. Ramón Vásquez y Sánchez, who worked in the courthouse, called her and told her that the clerk's office was checking each signature. She had collected closer to 200 signatures. The election took place in January so she campaigned during the Thanksgiving weekend and Christmas holiday season, which were difficult times to get people's attention. She raised only $76. "I remember that all I had enough money for was to buy the palm card or you know . . . I would go to cantinas . . . and a lot of parties . . . or any kind of functions."

During her campaign she took advantage of all the free radio airtime provided on Spanish radio stations, KCOR and KEDA, and the Spanish television station, KWEX, Channel 41, with Marta Tijerina, a RUP sympathizer. While on the Marta Tijerina show her opponent accepted a debate and arrived with a translator. Irma did not need a translator. The viewing public loved her. But she had her detractors, as well. "I remember going to the Villita and one of the other candidates was out there. And I was running against the incumbent, but he wasn't there. This man asked me how could I possibly be running for office. He wanted to know what kind of degree I had and all these, you know, education. And I said, 'I don't have any.' And he says, 'Well how, how dare you? How could you?' or something to that effect even consider running. And I told him, 'I have a certain degree of intelligence and common sense and that's all it takes.'"

On the day of the election, her home phone went dead at around 10:30 a.m. to 11:00 a.m. She thought it suspicious because it had never happened before. Instead of continuing to make phone calls to voters she went to the polls to solicit votes there. She figured that those arriving were going to vote so why not ask them at the last minute in case her name did not register in their minds among the large group of candidates. At one polling place she spoke with Bishop Patricio Flores, the first Chicano Catholic bishop, who was about a half block away at a church *fiesta*. He spotted her and called her over to wish her luck. The crowd that was at the *fiesta* saw the greeting and perceived it as an endorsement of her candidacy, so they walked over to the polling place to vote for her. At another polling location in South San Antonio, she started to approach two elderly women walking to the door of the election place. "And they told me that they didn't want anything handed to them because they knew who they were going to vote for and the person they were going to vote for was me."

When the polls closed at 7:00 p.m. Irma and Anna went back to her home to listen to the election returns. By now her home phone was working again. At about 7:30 p.m. it rang. The chairman of the SARA board, Mr. Heard, called to congratulate her. She had won. While only spending sixty-six dollars on her campaign and having ten dollars left in her campaign account, she had received 70,000 votes evincing the power of the growing Chicano vote in Bexar County, particularly San Antonio. "That was the first time both my parents voted. Registered and voted. And my brothers, the three who could vote at that time, voted. But I realize that there were so many people that I made such a big impact on and all this media."

With this victory Irma became the first Chicana as well as the first woman to serve on the San Antonio River Authority. More importantly, her election was also the first time a Chicana had been elected to office in an urban county nationwide. She was twenty-nine years of age. The swearing in ceremony was scheduled in downtown San Antonio. "And so it was a really neat ceremony having *toda nuestra gente allí* (having all of our people there). And after the swearing in, this woman came to me. She must have been . . . in her late fifties or maybe early sixties. And she had walked from San Fernando Cathedral to Gunther Street, which is far . . . but she got there because she said she wanted to be part of history, that she wanted to see a *Mexicana* in San Antonio getting elected in her lifetime. And so she was there."

"After the swearing in, well, I was invited to a reception at the Frost Towers. I had never been to the Frost Towers. And my two best friends went with me. It's the three of us. Three women who look so completely different. Rosie and Anna. And three colors of brown, too." Irma was tall and slender. Anna was short and vivacious. Rosie was heavier than either Irma or Anna, shorter than Irma but taller than Anna. "Oh, and are these your two sisters?" the board chairman asked her. And he followed up with, "Well, perhaps now for the party at Christmas this year, you can bring the tamales." I told him, "Sure, if you bring the sauerkraut." That was her initiation into the River Authority.

During her tenure, she thwarted misuse of political power on the SARA board and helped to open up the political process to Chicanos in San Antonio. She complained about several aspects of the board meetings she was now a part of. During the first meeting, she noticed, "some of the people, who were the board members, are coming out of an office. And I thought hmmm, how strange." The second meeting takes place and the third and, "Again, I see these people coming out of the office because I would get there earlier. So, this time I asked, 'Were you having a meeting before the meeting?'" It is illegal for public officials in Texas to have pre-meetings in private while not in session. Public meetings are to be held in public and the proceedings recorded in minutes. Subsequently, she noticed that reading the minutes her comments were never reported. "Nothing I said was ever on the minutes." She began to second motions and speak on the motions during discussion. "That was a very frustrating six years because it didn't matter what I said or did." All the others on the board were old white men who fell asleep during the meetings. She was considered and treated by the old men as an outsider.

She learned to accomplish significant things by using the Spanish-language media. San Antonio residents who frequented the area parks called the media to complain that they had no public rest rooms. KCOR, the Spanish radio station, began to air these complaints and Mateo Camargo, a supporter of Irma's bid to get on the SARA board, called her to respond. Together, they began a radio campaign to get bathrooms installed at Mission Espada Park, which was located on the banks of the San Antonio River in the southernmost part of Bexar County. The closest restroom facility was at a gas station across a busy highway from the Mission park. She raised the question at one of the SARA meetings and met with resistance by the River Authority executive director, who said there wasn't any money for that. Irma felt the reason for this was that this was a mostly Chicano-used park. KCOR again gave her extensive airtime. Irma went public urging people to call the San Antonio River Authority to complain. She gave the number of the executive director over the air. After a barrage of phone calls, the money magically appeared to pay for the bathrooms and construction began.

During her six-year tenure on the SARA board she became pregnant. "My dream, you know, I was going to have this child." She decided not to marry. "I talked to the manager and chairman of the board and I wanted to tell them that I was pregnant and I wasn't going to get married. And I was letting them know before they heard it anywhere else. And that I didn't want to hear about it again. And it was not to be a political issue of any type. That there was no way I was going away." They sent her flowers and a card at the time her son was born. No one on the board or any of her friends gave her any problems about not marrying even though she had a strong Catholic religious background.

After her term ended in 1983 the Raza Unida Party had lost ballot status and was no longer a viable political party. Irma became a member of the League of United Latin American Citizens (LULAC). Eventually she became president of her local chapter and later held positions at the state and national levels. She also participated in the campaign to elect Jose Garcia de Lara as LULAC national president.

In April 1990, she left Texas for Juneau, Alaska, whose population was about 28,000, of whom 1,000 were Hispanics. The economy in Texas was bad for her and her child. "The company I had worked for went bankrupt . . . after ten years, I had nothing to show for it. I was ready for change. I needed that change." A sister and her family were already in Alaska. In her first year there, she noticed there were no celebrations of *cinco de mayo* (May 5), *diez y seis de septiembre* (September 16) or even mention of *el doce de diciembre* (December 12), which honors the Virgin of Guadalupe.

By the end of that year she had started working for the city of Juneau and met the wife of Mayor Bruce Botello, Lupita Botello, who was of Mexican ancestry. They became friends. Mrs. Botello had sponsored a *ballet folklórico* (a group of women who dance to a particular kind of traditional Mexican music) in Mexico City. Along with others she formed a committee to begin promoting Hispanic Heritage Month in Juneau. Irma called on friends in San Antonio and elsewhere to obtain posters and cultural items. The committee also taught students at the schools about Hispanic culture. The Hispanic kids at the schools seemed very interested.

In Juneau, she interpreted for immigrants in court, at social services, and taught some citizenship classes. In 1993, she testified at the Civil Rights Commission hearings on behalf of Mexicans and Alaskan natives about the mistreatment they received. Subsequently she received a letter asking her to accept appointment on the next vacancy that occurred at the commission. She accepted and filled a vacancy that soon opened.

She became a member of the State Advisory Committee to the U.S. Commission on Civil Rights. She also helped to bring Univision (Spanish-language television) to Juneau by persuading the local cable owners, whom she met with at the invitation of then ex-mayor Bruce Botello.

The Health and Social Services Committee for the state of Alaska consisted of three Republicans and two Democrats. The committee began to hold hearings on the issue of English Only and opposing bilingual education. Irma signed on as a lobbyist and wanted to testify. Irma's position was that English Only would hurt tourism, plus the various Alaskan tribal groups would have trouble voting. During the hearings, things became heated as one of the Republicans on the committee became irked at her comments. He said that she was calling him a racist; she replied, "If the shoe fits, wear it!" After leaving the meeting, she was cornered by one of the opposing lobbyists, who was calling her a liar. She pushed him away from her, but he wouldn't leave her alone. They were yelling back and forth until he was escorted out. Her views eventually were persuasive enough to kill the English-Only bill in committee.

Irma then became a member of Network, a Catholic social justice lobbying group, with headquarters in Washington, D.C. She became a member of the board and served for six years in that capacity. She increased representation for Alaska on Network from five to twenty-five or thirty.

She missed her mother, still in San Antonio, and she was ill. Irma had worked for the city of Juneau for five years and the retirement programs in that state vested employees within that time. After seven years in Alaska, Irma returned to San Antonio. She took a job as the administrative secretary with the Mexican American Cultural Center (MACC), whose purpose is to be a national Catholic institute for the preparation of leaders to respond to the religious and social needs of Hispanic communities.

## Note

1. See Ernesto Vigil, *The Crusade for Justice: Chicano Militancy and the Government's War on Dissent* (Madison: University of Wisconsin Press, 1999) for an account of the crusade, its leadership, including Corky, and police relations. See also Juan Haro, *The Ultimate Betrayal*, 2nd ed. (Denver: J. Haro, Inc., 1998) for a very critical biographical narrative by the head of security for Corky and the Crusade for Justice.

# CHAPTER NINE

~

# Rosie Castro

Rosie Castro was born to Victoria and Victor Castro. Her father left the family early in Rosie's life. Her mother, Victoria, had been orphaned at age eight and was brought from Mexico along with her younger sister, to the United States. Rosie did not know her father until she was about thirty-four years old. She sought him out to meet him. He passed away shortly after that. Apparently, he was self-employed selling funeral caskets, perhaps making them as well. He was of Indian descent, and his ancestors had always lived in Texas.

Her mother and a guardian, Marcia García, raised Rosie. Victoria and Rosie lived with Ms. García in her house. Rosie lived in this household until she was twenty-three years of age. Ms. García and her father were devout Catholics and insisted that Victoria enroll Rosie in a Catholic school. Victoria herself had only attended school to the fourth grade. She did know how to read and write in Spanish and English. Therefore, Rosie attended Catholic schools into high school, which had a great impact on her. On a field trip during the elementary grades, she visited the Alamo Mission. The exhibits were shocking to her. The manner and description of Mexican people as "terrible" disturbed her greatly. She recalls not being too fond of the Alamo.

Rosie as a child became very interested in social injustice because she saw firsthand how this victimized her mother. Employment opportunities were very scarce for her mother with a fourth-grade education. The only type of work that Rosie's mother could find was that of a housekeeper, maid, and cleaner. Rosie stated her mother would sometimes "bring home eight dollars a day for [her] whole day's work . . . and she did a lot of work." Not being able to afford childcare, Rosie accompanied her mother to these houses, many located in Alamo Heights, a rich white neighborhood in northern San Antonio. Rosie would go with her and entertain herself by pulling ticks off the dogs living there or throwing rocks at cars passing by the house the mother was cleaning. Victoria worked on all holidays. Rosie had no opportunity to celebrate the holidays as other children did. Early in life Rosie realized boundaries existed along racial and economic lines; she could discern the difference between her west side *barrio* and the affluence of the Anglo north side. Rosie's household was in a predominantly black neighborhood with only seven or eight Chicano families nearby. She often was a "latchkey child" left alone under lock and key until her mother or guardian would return. Most often Rosie would fix her own meals and entertain herself by reading. Rosie also invented ways to invite children over to play. At times she would wander over to a favorite black family and get herself invited in. The family had a television set. Rosie's mom did not own a television set until many years later.

Rosie also still has vivid memories of the inevitable telephone calls from the owners of the houses her mother cleaned that would inquire whether Victoria had taken or stolen some of their household items. Being a suspect of theft was very difficult on her mother and particularly Rosie. "Those memories . . . colored the way [she] has thought about Anglo Americans."

For fun occasionally Rosie's mom would take her to view Mexican movies at the Teatro Internacional on West Houston Street downtown. And they would visit the main library. Rosie loved reading. A local priest always gave her books to read, and among Rosie's Christmas gifts were books.

In high school, Rosie's leadership qualities began to emerge. She sought and obtained numerous positions. She was the editor of the school paper and president of her class. Rosie was an overachiever and had a rebellious nature about her. Her extracurricular activities, besides reading, included membership in the Catholic Youth Association (CYO). The CYO was a citywide organization with competitions and gatherings of the youth. She met many other kids from across the city. It dawned on her how few blacks were involved. In her own school there were no blacks. Yet, she lived just down the street and the neighborhood was predominantly black. On television she began to take an interest in the news reports and the coverage of the black civil rights movement. She knew the downtown Internacional was the Mexican theatre and that the Majestic theatre a bit further down the street did not allow blacks or Mexicans except in the balcony. Downtown was segregated and neighborhoods were also segregated. "Everything from the houses to the actual streets . . . were so vastly different." The *barrio* had no sidewalks, no well-paved streets, no streetlights, no drainage system in place, and was in general disrepair. The Anglo side of town was meticulous and upscale with all amenities.

Rosie's rebellious nature prompted her to begin asking the Catholic nuns about segregation and why no blacks attend their school or their church. "It occurred to [me] that there weren't blacks among [us.]" She wanted to know why blacks were "invisible" in the institutions she frequented in her life. She also wanted to know if the Catholics valued ethnic and racial diversity. Her rebellious nature manifested itself often as open defiance and disagreement with convention. Rosie had a "tendency to not see things the way everybody seem[ed] to see them." She was also developing a greater interest in politics and learning organizing skills. Rosie had developed a strong sense of justice, which later led her to join and become a very strong activist in the Chicano movement.

In high school a nun she crossed because of that rebellious nature prevented Rosie from becoming the president of the Sodality, a Catholic youth group. Rosie languished in the shadows of others as a minor officer in the Sodality. She reached the rank of lieutenant in the drill team but sought to become captain. Her class consisted of twenty girls and only six boys. They did have a prom and a dance, but Rosie was not interested in those types of social activities. She did want to be valedictorian, but Mary Helen Askay had a higher grade point average. She and Mary had competed with each other since elementary grades. They grew up together. Rosie viewed Mary Helen as "more superior on all levels." But Rosie was motivated and a hard worker. She was frequently astonished at receiving a good grade or the highest in the class. The nuns actually told her she was not that smart, but added that she was a hard worker and motivated, which explained her academic success. Mary Helen did not graduate from high school, she got married her senior year. Rosie did graduate and by default became the class valedictorian for Little Flower High School.

For unexplained reasons, her mother and the guardian, both, informed Rosie she was not going to college. Perhaps it was financial constraints or gender bias or ignorance of the opportunities that higher education brings, but Rosie was going to go to work. Rosie was surprised to learn that many other authority figures in her young life also disapproved of her getting a higher education. But Rosie had her own ideas. She frankly "never agreed with that, because her whole sense of *Mexicanos* during that period of time was very much that they wanted their kids to go to college." Money was a problem, undoubtedly. The valedictorian title brought with it a scholarship. Rosie visited Our Lady of the Lake College (OLL) in the San Antonio *barrio* and with help from advisors there, obtained a mix of loans, grants, and her scholarship to package enough money to enroll and eventually complete her college degree. Rosie wanted to become a teacher. During her college days, Rosie also worked as a work-study student, plus other jobs. At one point in time she was juggling a full class load and three jobs.

Margaret Kramer, a psychology professor at OLL, took an interest in Rosie. Within months of being on the campus, Rosie had joined the Young Democrats (YDs) on Dr. Kramer's advice. Rosie was one of the few women involved with the YDs but soon made it an almost all-woman organization. OLL administrators advised her that for the Young Democrats to be permitted on campus, a Young Republican (YR) chapter also had to exist. Rosie recruited a Republican and assisted him in organizing a chapter of YRs.

She worked as a volunteer in the Lyndon Johnson presidential campaign of 1964. The Kramers, her professor and husband, were part of a liberal group in the city. "They were trying to be more progressive and [wanted] to open up the [Democratic] party." Liberal Democrats met for lunch regularly at a West Side restaurant, Karam's. The luncheon had a purpose. "The liberal faction wanted to be able to network, touch base with each other, tell each other what was coming up politically, and support one another." The Kramers would invite Rosie to accompany them to these weekly sessions. Rosie met many prominent individuals and politicians at these meeting, such as Bexar County Commissioner Albert Peña Jr., San Antonio City Council members Pete Torres and Ford Neilson, State Senator, State Representatives Johnny Alaniz and Rudy Esquivel, and Congressman Henry B. González. It was at these luncheons that she noticed other young people, mostly young men, present and participating. These were the young men from the Mexican American Youth Organization (MAYO). Rosie wanted to learn more about them and MAYO. She had heard that MAYO was encouraging young Chicanos across the state to boycott classes as a way to force reform in public education. Meanwhile, she too was beginning to participate in discussions of issues and began making recommendation to the adult crowd at the Karam's luncheons. She often disagreed with the many positions taken by the liberal group. "It was scary, but it was a good experience. . . . It gave you an opportunity to take these things on." This early partisan political involvement led to her interest in Democratic Party politics. She began attending precinct conventions and ultimately state conventions. The Kramers also were involved with precinct politics.

Rosie learned the basics of party politics, voter registration drives, lobbying, and getting-out-the-vote. When the initiative to lower the voting age became the public policy issue for her group, Rosie went to Austin to testify in favor of lowering the voting age to eighteen. "The rural type of senators were real bad ass. They were really hard on me." But the lobbying and testimonial experience for a young twenty-one-year-old Chicana was fantastic. "It added to my ability to stand up and articulate. The process was a sham, so much of it was." The voting age was lowered to eighteen.

During voter registration drives in the *barrio*, Rosie was appalled that too many women refused to register to vote until they would ask their husbands. Some women reported on a subsequent visit that the husband, "he doesn't want to." Reliance on male partners was not in Rosie's life experience. No father in the household, few boys in an almost all-girl Catholic school, and no brother, Rosie was developing into a clone of her mother—single, tough, smart, assertive, rebellious, and hard working. Rosie concluded that girls developed better leadership skills in all-girls school settings than in coed institutions, where the male leadership is imposed, not earned.

Rosie enrolled in a master's degree program and was offered an opportunity to work in Michigan for course credit. The program was sponsored by a regional educational agency, the Southwest Educational Development Laboratory, headed by two young and emerging educational Chicano leaders, Drs. José Angel Cárdenas and Blandina "Bambi" Cárdenas. Together they recruited many young aspiring Chicanos into the master teacher training program. "That was supposed to give a master's degree." Disagreements with the administrators over living arrangements and working conditions caused the program to fall apart, leaving many of them stranded in Michigan. Rosie returned to OLL and finished her master's degree.

During the late 1960s the MAYO members had organized many school boycotts across the state and several in San Antonio. While Rosie did not participate in those walkouts, she did join MAYO and even helped with some teaching in the Crystal City Walkout of 1969. She also got involved in an economic and community development program, the Mexican American Unity Council (MAUC), also organized by MAYO members. A major direct-action movement Rosie joined early was the boycott of the San Antonio Savings Association (SASA). This was a savings and loan operation owned by Walter MacAllister, the mayor of San Antonio and leader of the Good Government League (GGL), the controlling white group in the city. The boycott was aimed at SASA to get to MacAllister. "This guy was a racist . . . and a real dictator. We picketed the building." MacAllister had stated on public television that Mexicans were poor because they lacked ambition. In the course of these demonstrations and picketing, Rosie was arrested and jailed. She had earned her first Chicano movement merit badge. On another occasion an incident occurred in the lobby of the Frost Bank, a pregnant Chicana was pushed and beaten by the police. The police had been summoned to prevent the Chicanos from staging a demonstration in the bank lobby. A huge fight ensued between Chicanos and more police that arrived. Rosie believed that this official violence was designed to show that "Mexicans were not to get out of line." Rosie now had two Chicano movement merit badges.

On the OLL campus, Rosie as leader of the Young Democrats invited Congressman Henry González to speak on campus, and he declined. Rosie invited the MAYO representatives to speak on campus, and they accepted. Congressman González reported to the media that he declined the invitation to speak at OLL because the YDs and MAYO were "race mongers" given their anti-*gringo* rhetoric. Rosie took exception to his remarks and began a miniwar against the congressman through the media. Apparently, a fellow member of the YDs, Yolanda Galindo, who had become "very close to Albert Bustamante," an aide to Congressman Henry B. González, had poisoned the well. She was "a more conservative traditional Democrat" and opposed MAYO speakers being invited to the campus. Her unflattering remarks about MAYO to Albert Bustamante found their way into the congressman's press release, attacking both MAYO and the campus YDs. This media miniwar embarrassed and concerned the administration of Our Lady of the Lake College. The administrators were conservative Catholic nuns in charge of OLL. Rosie persevered and graduated to other activism.

She became involved with the initial campaigns of the latest MAYO project, that of incorporating a regional political party, La Raza Unida Party (RUP) in 1970. By 1972, the RUP was running statewide candidates for a multitude of positions from governor to local candidates. Rosie also got involved during these years with the Committee for Barrio Betterment (CBB). In a joint project between the RUP and the CBB, they were going to file candidates seeking seats on the San Antonio City Council. RUP/CBB versus the GGL, Chicanos versus *gringos*. She campaigned tirelessly for the slate of *barrio* candidates that were not successful. In 1971, she became a candidate together with another woman, Gloria Cabrera, for the CBB. Again they lost, but not before carrying every voting precinct in San Antonio's West Side. In other words, the CBB candidates won the Chicano vote, but it was not sufficient to counter the Anglo vote against them. Chicano voters were not enough of a critical mass of voters to win at-large elections in San Antonio in the 1970s. In the concession of defeat of 1971, Rosie ended her emotional speech with a clenched fist in the air and the words, "We will be back!"

The CBB then redirected their energies and worked to bring San Antonio and Texas under coverage of the Voting Rights Act of 1965. And in 1975, the U.S. Congress extended the Voting Rights Act and amended it to include protection for language minorities, including Texas. In separate litigation, San Antonio was ordered to elect its council members from single-member districts. The election losses by Rosie Castro and others running against the GGL under the banner of the RUP and the CBB were the evidence required to obtain the court order mandating single-member districts in the city. This structural opportunity opened the door to Chicano representation on the city council. The Raza Unida Party had won seats on the Edgewood Independent School District and the San Antonio River Authority.

Rosie Castro's personal life took a different turn and awesome responsibilities. Rosie became pregnant and chose to have the baby, except it was not one baby but twins: Joaquin and Julian. Family history was repeating itself somewhat. Rosie was a single mother and poor. She never earned as much money as she should, given that she opted to work at organizing causes and reforms. Often she took jobs dependent on soft money and not as career-enhancing as teaching, which contains employee benefits such as health insurance. But she raised the boys by herself. By 1996 her mother, guardian, and an aunt had died. Even the father she met only once was dead. She was alone with the boys. The biological father has helped somewhat but never enough. Rosie, the hardy party animal, heavy smoker and drinker, quit her vices for the twins. "Drinking was a real way to find relief for a lot of things . . . during the period. I could have done a lot better in many different areas or components had I not got as involved in drinking."

As the boys grew into manhood, she worked with them. She took them to political meetings. She took them to school and church functions. She helped with schoolwork and "kind of let them do it themselves." Rosie modeled for the twins the role of an assertive woman and an activist Chicana. The boys learned well. They excelled in public school and obtained full scholarships to Stanford University, graduating with honors. They proceeded to Harvard Law School and graduated with honors. They came back to San Antonio and promptly got involved in local politics with Rosie at their side, advising and organizing. Joaquin ran for the city council and beat several candidates without need for a runoff election. Julian ran for a state representative seat in 2002 and won without a runoff. At the time of the first electoral victory party for Joaquin, in an emotional speech to media and campaign workers, he made reference to his mother. He quoted her 1971 concession of defeat speech and added, "We are back!"

# CHAPTER TEN

# Severita Lara

Chicana warriors are those women who fought for their people during the Chicano movement and who continue to fight against oppression of any kind. They are the women who fought alongside men and sometimes in front of them during the *movimiento*, taking leadership roles, often speaking publicly when no one else would, and doing much of the groundwork needed to spread the message of liberation. They suffered under male chauvinism a lot of the time, but some of the time they had the support of their male peers to run for office and to make decisions that effected change.

One such woman was Severita Lara, who played a key leadership role in the historic student walkout of Crystal City High School in 1969, co-organized by then-MAYO (Mexican American Youth Organization) leaders José Angel Gutiérrez and Luz Bazán Gutiérrez. The walkout was the thirty-ninth in MAYO's history of orchestrating walkouts throughout Texas and California. They all shared common themes of resistance against assimilation and of protest against oppression and discrimination, such as being excluded from high school popularity contests and activities.

At an early age, Lara challenged the oppressive educational system that existed in *Cristal*. Her father, José María Lara, attempted to enroll her in the first grade, bypassing the school's practice of enrolling all Mexican students in what was called Zero Bell, because Severita already knew how to read and speak English. The school system insisted that she stay segregated with the Mexican students in Zero Bell. When she was in junior high school, *Mexicanos* were forbidden to speak Spanish in school. She spoke up, as she was prone to do, in Spanish, and was punished severely for it. In an interview years later, she recalled the scene vividly as the first time she noticed herself being discriminated against.

"I was caught speaking Spanish in the halls and I think it was in eighth grade. Mr. Harbin called me in and says, "You know the rules. You are not supposed to do this and you have been warned before." And, so I said, "Yes sir." And so he called me in and he lifted my skirt, because I had petticoats on, you know, and so he gave me a two paddles or paddled me twice and I ran all the way home crying and crying and so my dad came in, into the office."

Her father shoved the principal up against a wall, holding him by his shirt collar, and warned him never to touch his daughter again for speaking their language. This let Severita know that her dad would support her when it came to fighting for her culture, and more importantly, her dignity. From then on, she was punished for speaking Spanish by sending her to the library, which proved to be a godsend.

"I came back and after that I knew that I wasn't going to get hit, so I would challenge the teachers by speaking Spanish there in the halls. And everybody would say, 'Golly, how come you can get away with it?' you know. But they would send me to the library and that is where I would go. And that is where my love of books came from. I used to read a lot because I was punished a lot and sent to the library. And that was my first, my first incident, incidents with seeing what, what they did to us."

Severita said she had a very close relationship with her father. He taught her and her two brothers and three sisters to stand up for themselves and question authority, even their teachers and principals, if they thought something was wrong.

"My dad always talked about not being afraid to stand up for what you believed in and now those were things that every, *a las cinco que cenábamos* (at five when we ate dinner), those were the things that my dad would always tell us and I always felt that I could do anything. *Tenía cuatro mujeres mi dad y siempre nos decía que la mujer podía hacer igual que el hombre.* (He had four daughters, my dad did, and he would say that the woman could do the same as a man.) And *que no tuviera miedo y si una maestra o principal me decía algo* (not to be afraid and if a teacher or principal said something) for me to stand up. And so I wasn't afraid. I always knew that my dad will be, would be there and he would always come to the office and speak up for me."

Severita remembers her dad also teaching her to make responsible choices, and to learn to live with the consequences of her choices. When she was sixteen, she and her sister, Linda, thought it would be "glamorous" to be migrant workers, and go with other migrants from *Cristal* to the north. She begged her dad to let her go, and he finally gave in, on one condition:

"You can go, but there is only one thing I am going to ask of you. You go, but you stay the whole time. You cannot come back. I will not send you money to come back if you want to come back. *Se tienen que aguantar.*" (You will have to tolerate it.)

So she went to Shelly, Minnesota, to pick sugar beets with a long hoe, and she lived in a horrible house with rats and no running water.

I remember the first three days I couldn't even raise my hands up to comb my hair. It was so painful and it hurt so much that I couldn't. I couldn't even see the end that we were walking and walking and we couldn't see the end, and they would try to show us how to do the cleaning and they told us to make sure to do the job right because they marked *a los surcos, a cuáles eran de quién* (the rows, which belong to whom).

And we called my dad, I think it was in about a week's time, that we were sorry that we wanted to come back and that it was really bad and the rats and all these stories about the weather being so ugly. And my dad said, *"NO, mi'ja yo les dije que las iba a dejar ir, que cuando se fueran con Mague, se regresaban con Mague."* (No, daughter, I told you when I let you go with Mague that you would have to return with Mague.) But we told him, "No, Dad, no. We have money for the *pasaje*" (return fare). And my dad said, "No. You cannot come back. You have to stay. You are going to learn a lesson and you are going to find out what it is like to be a migrant."

We stayed. Linda, my sister, turned sixteen in the field on her birthday and she was crying in the middle of the field, saying, "It is my birthday. I am sixteen. I should be having a big party." And all of this. And the people there were all laughing because, you know, I was hugging her and we were both crying because she had turned sixteen in *la labor* (the fields).

So, we came back in the truck and we were pretty excited and we went and hugged Mom and Dad. And every year, it was a joke when the summer came up and my dad would say, *"¡Mijas, están listas? ¡Hagan sus telichis! Ya mero es tiempo de ir al norte."* (Daughters, are you ready? Pack your bags! It is almost time to go up North.)

After that summer, Severita returned to high school a junior. She and her friends were upset that the year before, the school board had asked teachers to select the baseball tournament queen, instead of leaving it up to a vote among the overwhelmingly predominant Chicano student body. And of course, the Anglo faculty selected an Anglo queen. Similarly, a group of Anglo alumni requested that the school board adopt a policy saying the homecoming queen had to be chosen from among the daughters of parents who had graduated from Crystal City High School. This left only 6 out of 280 Chicana students eligible, since most of their parents had been pushed out.

These were not their only grievances. The school had a history and pattern of discrimination against Mexican students, starting by segregating them when they were in primary grades. Severita and others remembered these practices well and agreed it was time to change them. They had grown tired of the school's practice of choosing white students to dominate the cheerleading squad, even though Mexican girls outnumbered them ten to one. Severita and other students had heard about the student walkouts in Los Angeles and San Antonio. They had wanted to stage a similar walkout in the spring of her sophomore year to voice their concerns. But MAYO leaders had persuaded them to wait until the fall, to keep from falling into the administration's trap of failing all the protesters at the end of the school year. In the fall it was time to make a stand, and Severita didn't shy away. She stood front and center, face-to-face with the school board and with the principal. She had been involved since the initial planning and carried the walkout through to its successful end.

"We got together and we said, who is going to do this and who is going to do that? And I remember some of the other people were scared to go distribute the leaflets and I remember saying, 'I will do it.' You know, I was a little bit *más atrevida que los demás y no tenía mucho miedo*." (I was bolder than the others and I wasn't as afraid.)

The walkout provided another opportunity for her father to stand beside her because she soon found herself being disciplined by administrators.

> I guess I wasn't very good at hiding. I got caught distributing the leaflet at that time, and they brought me to the office and Mr. Lear told me that I was a rebel rouser and why was I doing this and that I shouldn't be doing this. That I was treated very nice and a whole bunch of other stuff and he suspended me for, I believe it was three days, and my dad came to pick me up and I thought my dad was going to be mad. Because to him, education was very important. We could never stay home unless we were running a hundred-and-something fever. If we weren't, we couldn't stay home. And so, he said, no, you are right. If you think you are right, I stand a hundred percent behind you, and he said it was OK, not to worry, because I was real worried about school, and he said don't worry about it. And you are right, you are right, then let's, let's wait and see what happens.

More than 1,700 students walked out of schools, from elementary to high school, for nearly a month. In that time, Severita had become a leader in her community, had represented Chicano students in Washington, D.C., had become a newspaper writer and subject of stories and had mastered the art of public speaking. She had a natural knack for knowing exactly what to say and how to say it to win her listeners' support. Her and all the other students' efforts paid off. The school board gave in to most of their demands, and granted them amnesty to return to school.

"All of that was a very exciting and a very important time in my life."

She was one of the most visible female leaders of the Chicano *movimiento* in Tejas. She felt that women had an equal say and that men were supportive of women running for offices. "I didn't grow up in that era where women were not supposed to go to school and you were supposed to get married. My mom had that idea. You know, you are supposed to not go to school. Find a good man to support you, but my dad didn't believe in that. Thank God. My dad was the opposite. He said, *'El día que las deje el viejo, ustedes pueden trabajar. Edúquense.'* (The day that your old man [husband] leaves you, you can work. Educate yourselves.) So, I have always believed that women could do anything, you know, that they wanted to."

In La Raza Unida, she felt like she was an equal. "The trend in *Cristal* has been *la mujer es la que es más fuerte, que sale en frente* (the woman is the stronger, the one that is out in front). I guess *se habre la puerta porque es más fácil, que el hombre dejen entrar* (she opens the door because it is easier for her than for the man to let her in). We have so many teachers, *mujeres* (women) now, because of La Raza Unida. They saw that there was a possibility that they could go to school and get educated."

After the walkout, Severita quit school and got married, mostly because her parents were so strict that she wasn't allowed to stay out late. She was afraid she would get a beating from her mother, Irene Cepeda Lara, when she came home late. So she opted to move out altogether with Ezequiel, her husband. She quit high school and went to college a year early. She had her first son, Ezequiel, when she was a freshman in college at St. Mary's University. After she graduated with a bachelor's degree in biology with a major in chemistry, she won a scholarship to medical school through Becas de Aztlán, a scholarship program between the Raza Unida Party and the government of Mexico. She studied medicine in Mexico City at the Universidad Autonoma Metropolitana for two years. She became pregnant with her second child and had to leave Mexico City because she got ill and her son was born prematurely. She wanted to prove to her mentors, José Angel and Luz, that she could finish school even though she had quit high school, gotten married, and had children while she was very young.

"Even though people think that, you know, I wasted that time out there, I didn't. I learned a lot from the, from the people there. I lived with another couple that were *becarios* (scholarship recipients) too. And we lived in one of the poorest sections in Mexico City. It was an *ejido* (communal land grant). And there were all kinds of rich homes around that *ejido* and our water and electricity got cut so that the other neighborhoods could have enough water pressure. And I learned to appreciate my kids first. I used to be very me-first. I have to do all of these things first and different attitude. And all the, the *Mexicanos* and the contact, the teachers, the, the *familias* around there changed my perspective on, on life and my kids."

Severita learned more about her own family history as well, including that her grandfather, Don Modesto, was a Zapotec Indian from Oaxaca, and her grandmother, after whom she is named, was of Spanish decent.

She returned to Crystal City for good in 1984, after her father had a stroke. Her plan was to run his store for him and stay out of local politics, since it had only brought her trouble before. "When I came back I promised Ezequiel I was not getting involved in politics. That we wanted a job and that we wanted to survive because every time that we got involved, he would get axed. If they couldn't get to me, he would be the one that would get axed and not have a job. So I promised him that I would not get involved and that I would stay quiet and I would work and he would work too."

But her lack of involvement didn't last long, because she saw so many things that needed to be done in her community. She began by working in the elementary school, but the school board didn't make it easy. Her reputation preceded her and posed a threat to the status quo.

"It was very hard that first year, and they made life miserable for me, tried to run me out and do all kinds of things and school board members were constantly in my, in my room, observing me. They said that I was going to teach them to be rebel rousers and I only had them singing 'Yo Soy Chicano'" ("I am Chicano").

After getting a job as a teacher at Crystal City High School teaching biology, chemistry, and physiology, she became interested in running for the position of county judge. It was 1986. It was a very painful experience by the time it ended.

"I decided to run because I felt that not enough was being done for *la raza*; that we had kind of regressed and there were not enough programs, grants being applied for; and that the people that needed the help were not getting help. When I declared that I was going to run, I didn't have any money, just the, the desire." She garnered the help of many volunteers, and they began campaigning door-to-door. With money they got from fundraisers and donations, they bought radio spots. She ended up borrowing $7,000 for the campaign. "Mr. José O. Mata, who signed that loan for me. Poor guy, I think he

was really scared there." Another obstacle she had to overcome was the belief among some men that because she was a woman, and a strong one at that,
she would hang them by the *huevos* for things like drunk driving, domestic
violence, and failing to pay child support.

She won a runoff to decide on the Democratic primary election, by one
vote. But a recount gave her opponent, Ron Carr, the victory. She tried challenging the election, but the judge didn't even want to hear it. "He said that
it was too late and that, that if I didn't like his decision, for me to appeal it.
He wouldn't even hear it. We didn't have, we didn't even, even have a trial
or have a hearing or anything. He just said that he was not going to hear it,
that if I didn't like it, I could appeal. And at that time, Jansen said it would
take like five thousand dollars to appeal and that is when I, Ezequiel and I
met, and some of my supporters and I, I didn't have the money. I mean, because I was already in debt too much and I just couldn't afford to, to go at it."

Severita tried the put the ordeal behind her—forget that she had been offered a bribe, that others had been bribed, and that she couldn't afford to win
legally. She also felt bad about letting down all her supporters.

> I started getting angry. It took me a week to realize that I had lost. I mean, it
> is very powerful when I won and I felt that I had won. The celebration, the
> people, *la pitadera* (the car honking), you remember *todo el borlote que se hace
> después de las elecciones* (all the commotion that goes on after an election) and
> then a week later, you know, to be completely stripped of that and not to, and
> then to work. We had put so much work. I never paid anybody; none of the
> workers were ever paid. All their work was free. The campaign office was
> packed with people wanting to do free work. They believed in somebody. And
> it hurts me for them because they had hope and it was gone. *Yo todavía tenía mi
> trabajo.* (I still had my job.) I was still a teacher and I had money coming in,
> but these people that had spent so much time and their money, their *diez*
> (tens), their *viente* (twenty) dollars, it was a lot to them. And after that, I cried.
> I cried for about a week or two. Every time I would remember and every time
> I would see him, you know, I would say, you know, *porque era gringo él lo podía
> pelear* (because he was white he could fight it.) And to me, it was the money
> issue. That if I had had money, I could have probably, possibly won it on, on
> an appeal because *había chuecura* (there had been crookedness). And there was
> a lot of things that were wrong. *Chuecura que se había hecho.*

Severita was determined to try again. She wasn't about to let these politicians get the best of her. But her health faltered in 1990, and she didn't feel
strong enough to campaign door-to-door like she had done before. She waited
a couple of years and ran successfully for the Crystal City City Council instead,

with the intention of accomplishing those things she felt were still not being done. One of her top priorities was to put a recreation center in the *barrio* called Mexico Chico. While on the city council, she was appointed mayor for a year. During that time, she succeeded in getting eleven houses approved for the housing department. And a mural was refurbished, although it was changed somewhat to deny that part of *Cristal's* history that was marked by the walkouts. Some people would like to forget that period of time, or to blame it for *Cristal's* current high unemployment rate and other problems.

There is a lot of negativism in here, in *Cristal* and the Raza Unida. I encountered it with my students. *Sus padres les han dicho, Verdad, que Raza Unida fue lo peor pa' Cristal, que José Angel Gutiérrez . . .* (Their parents have told them, right, the Raza Unida was the worst thing for Crystal and that José Angel Gutiérrez . . .) *Vino e hizo cambio todo. Hizo la revolución y luego se fue y nos dejó. . . .* (He came and changed everything. He made a revolution and then left, leaving us. . . .) And they feel that all the businesses left. *Se fueron los Americanos. Se fueron los negocios. Ahora no tenemos negocio. No tenemos nada. Y que Cristal está aruinado por Raza Unida. Que sino hubiera habido Raza Unida entonces los gabachos estarían todavía. Tuvieramos negocios. Y yo les pregunté a ellos, y una es amiga mía, y le respeto su opinión, dice que por la Raza . . . y me dice a mi cara . . . "por ti, por José Angel, tenemos este mugrero aquí Severita, y que ésto y lo otro. No entra la gente. Necesitamos a los gabachos que manden y compongan aquí." Le digo, "¿por qué tienes la 'P' en la frente? ¿Por qué estás trabajando? ¿Estás de teacher aide? ¿Por quién te están educando? ¿Quién te paga el cheque? Lo que el hizo [José Angel Gutiérrez] fue que nos abrió los ojos y abrió la puerta. Nos dijo 'de aquel lado de la puerta hay mucha feria y educación para ustedes' y nosotros le dimos, pero sabes que, una patada a la puerta. Y muchos de ustedes nomás se topan y topan con la puerta. ¿Por qué hay tantos mexicanos . . . ?" Y le comienzo a dar listas de todos los que se han graduado—el superintendente . . .* (The Anglos left. The businesses left. Now, we have no business. We have nothing. And Crystal was ruined by Raza Unida Party. If there hadn't been Raza Unida Party we still would have business . . . and she is a friend of mine and I respect her right to an opinion. She says that because of the Raza [Unida] . . . and she tells me to my face . . . "because of you, because of José Angel [Gutiérrez] we have this mess here. People don't come. We need the white people to control here and fix everything here." I tell her, "Why do you have 'P' stamped on your forehead? [P stands for *pendeja*, meaning "stupid."] Why are you working? You are a teacher's aide. Because of whom are you being educated? Who pays you your check? What he [José Angel Gutiérrez] did was to open our eyes and open the door. He told us, 'Behind that door is money and education for you.' And we hit and hit, but you know what . . . we kicked that door open. And a lot of you just butt and butt that door. Why are there so many Mexicans . . ." and I start making a list of those who have graduated—the superintendents . . .) from that, that Carnegie program, that even though I wasn't here at that time, I know that there was a PhD program or program for superintendents; that COPS programs for all the teachers, *todas esas mujeres platican y platican como se educaron* (all those women talk and talk about how they educated themselves). And let me just go back. I had, I just went through the New Jersey writing project. It was a three-week workshop with other teachers, *unas de las antiguas que se educaron con el* (some of the old ones that were educated by the) COPS program. And they did essays about *su vida de migrantes y lo que batallaron y se educaron poco a poco, afuerzas. Pero ni una menciona quién les ayudó. ¿Quién fue el que abrió la puerta? ¿Quién les ayudó? Nomás las oigo porque no debiamos comentar. Y yo pense, esta gente no aprende. ¿Quién nos empujó? ¿Quién les enseñó y todo?* (their lives as migrants and how they struggled and educated themselves slowly, struggling. But not one mentioned who helped them. Who it was that opened the door. Who helped them. I just listened to them because we are not supposed to comment. And I think, these people don't learn. Who pushed us? Who taught us how?) I mean, you can't be here always. I used to be angry at you when you left *Cristal*. Yeah, you know, I was angry. People ask me that in interviews, "Aren't you. . . . How did you feel . . . ?" You know. "He left." And I . . . sure, I was angry. But I mean, we are not his kids. He came and taught us something. It is like a teacher. He teaches us something and then we have to learn ourselves and we have to move on and you can't expect him to be here. Then if he would have stayed, you all said he would, you would all say he was a dictator. *No se queden aquí le hechan de todo* (Not staying her they still heap everything on you) and everybody *tantos años que han pasado y todavía mucha gente* (so many years have gone by an still a lot of people) still blames you for a lot of things. *Pero,* (But) the hard core . . . we don't feel that way. It is . . . . *Y tampoco no les enseñamos la historia esa en la escuela y . . . los que deberas andábamos, sufrimos, comprendemos . . . lo que era. . . .* (And we haven't taught this history in the schools and . . . those of us that were involved, suffered, understand, what it was. . . .)

She retired from politics and returned to college to get her master's degree. "I have enjoyed being out of politics. Peace and quiet. My phone doesn't ring past midnight. You know, with people needing this or that and I don't mind what I was doing there and I don't mind helping them, but I no longer feel that the world is on my shoulders or Crystal City is on my shoulders and I have to solve every problem."

Although she is retired, Lara has started working for the community in other ways. She and other women are beginning to write grants to bring in money for arts and recreation for the children. "We are seeing a need that is not being filled by the politicians and the people in office. I thought, maybe, going another route, I can accomplish more. I believe maybe, some of us need to put our necks on the line. But I keep asking myself, if those things didn't work when José Angel was here, what makes me think trying to bring in something is going to work, you know? I don't know. I still have dreams."

As a teacher, Lara has started teaching her students about Crystal City's role in the Chicano movement. A lot of the students had been taught by their parents that José Angel Gutiérrez had hurt Crystal, and Lara would tell them, *"Pregúntenles ¿con qué dinero se educaron? ¿Quién les abrió la puerta?"* (Ask them where they got money to get educated. Ask them who opened the door for them?) And, and I never got any feedback." She tries to give the students a different perspective of what happened by bringing in books where *Cristal* is mentioned for its *Raza* activism.

"They admire us because we stood tall and we fought for all those things. I tell them about *el gas* (the gas [controversy with Lo-Vaca Gas Gathering Company]) and what happened. And they are like, 'Wow.' They have never heard this story."

Even her own son didn't know the extent of his mother's involvement in the *movimiento*. When he went away to college at the University of Wisconsin in Madison, he got involved with a MEChA chapter because he was so lonely among all the white kids. He helped with their Dieciseis de Septiembre celebration and learned more about the Chicano movement and Cinco de Mayo and other things he hadn't appreciated before.

"They are going to know their history of *Cristal* and they are going to be political and when something happened, I would tell them this and this about a political thing. They would come to me and say . . . 'Miss, what do we need to do? We are having trouble with this rule. . . .' And I would sit down with them. 'This is what you need to do. I can't go speak for you.'"

## Note

See José Angel Gutiérrez, *We Won't Back Down! Severita Lara's Rise from Student Leader to Mayor* (Houston, TX: Arte Publico Press, 2005).

# CHAPTER ELEVEN

~

# María Jiménez

María is the oldest child of five born to Raúl Jiménez and Elva Flores. She was born in Castanos, Coahuila, Mexico, on August 2, 1950. Her siblings are Alva and Olivia, sisters, and Víctor and Raúl, brothers. "Everyone lives in Houston except my sister Olivia who went to study medicine in Notre Dame, met a doctor there and she married. And had her children there, and she's now working in a hospital in Torreón, Coahuila." María's mother was the daughter of a school teacher, Ramón Flores Ortega, and in Monclova, Coahuila, there is a school named after him. He is revered because he was "one of the first to institute adult education among the workers there in that area." The maternal grandmother, Manuela Guerra de Flores, "was a very strong woman figure." María said, "It was up to my grandmother to develop businesses on the side to sustain the family." The reason being that the grandfather's dedication to teaching and education generally meant "he would put his own salary to keep these adult education classes going."

Grandfather Jaime Jiménez and her father, Raúl, were active in union politics in Mexico. "From a very young age I understood that, that politics was a way of life. When we came to the United States, one of my earliest memories was of being in San Antonio. And seeing the segregated buses and not understanding that." The Jiménez family, the grandfather, had emigrated to Texas in the 1920s. "He didn't want to fight in the revolution. My great-grandfather was one of the closest collaborators of Venustiano Carranza and had all his sons in the revolution. But I think my grandfather didn't want to be in the revolution." The grandfather kept the family in Mexico while he worked in the United States. "During his last time he actually worked in nineteen different states of the United States. He was into railroad. My father—from Zaragosa they moved to Monclova and was—worked in the largest steel plant in Latin America as a machinist. And so, when he migrated, first migrated to Chicago, because most industrial workers of México migrated to Chicago, but he didn't like it. And so, he returned and someone told him about Houston." So a group of people from Monclova started migrating to Houston.

Her father "migrated in 1956 and he brought us over, legally at the time. A skilled worker like him, it was very easy to get our paperwork done. And we migrated in 1957 here to Houston." Her father, although a skilled machinist, only went to the sixth grade in Mexico. "He made it a practice that we would watch the news together as a family and, and discuss the news when we have dinner. . . . By the time I was thirteen years old, I remember I had already decided to study political science."

María "became a naturalized citizen in September of 1968." She was eighteen years of age. Her childhood was unlike many of her Chicano peers in Houston. First, her family was very politically oriented. Second, her upbringing was very traditional. No dating, no dancing, and no extracurricular school activities. "That was forbidden in a Mexican household." And the Jiménez family spoke no English at home. It was *Español*. "They wanted us to learn how to speak in English, but they forbade us to speak in English at home because they felt like that the institutions around us would teach us English. And they were the only ones to teach us Spanish. So we have always spoken Spanish at home."

María managed to get on the debating team while in high school. "And I do remember losing tournaments because I was Mexican. We won the state championship because I had an Anglo partner in the women's division. And we debated the boys to go to national. And there were three judges." A judge said, "I have to break the rules. You clearly won it. I think the other judges told me they voted for the boys because they felt that they would do better nationally rather than the girls." The gender discrimination was there.

María attended Milby High School in Houston. She was keenly aware of the discrimination leveled against Mexican Americans in school, in Houston, and in American society. "And my speech in, in the oratory contest, was . . . about the situation of Mexican Americans in the United States. And the reaction of the judges, either they liked it or they hated it. I either got first place or I got last place."

During her high school senior year, the Chicano students were only "maybe 15 percent of the, of the student population. The rest was Anglo." A student, Mario Gallegos, now a state senator from Houston, ran for student body president. "It was interesting to see how everyone was horrified at the idea that they would have a Latino class president. And so, the Anglos that normally didn't organize got going and organized and to assure that Mario didn't get it. And he didn't get it."

Because she was a Mexican citizen while in high school, she also lost out on scholarships. "That influenced me in becoming a citizen." She enrolled at the University of Houston. "I was looking for political activity." She chose to join the Young Democrats over LOMAS, League of Mexican American Students, because the group was "known to be sort of a social organization where people just, you know, went to dance and have fun and all the stuff that, that students are supposed to do. I just wanted to concentrate on political activity."

The Young Democrats (YDs) provided some political activity for nineteen-year-old María. The YDs were involved in supporting César Chávez and the incipient United Farm Workers in their call for consumers to boycott the purchase of nonunion grapes and lettuce. The union boycott was part of the growing national Chicano movement. This prompted LOMAS to change not only their orientation away from social activity but also their name. LO-MAS became MAYO, the Mexican American Youth Organization. She joined MAYO. "My first picket line was in support of the people who had taken over from the Presbyterian church." Houston MAYO had taken over a building and demanded that it become a Chicano school. "There was Ramón Villagómez . . . Cynthia Pérez, Vangie Vigil, Lorenzo Cano, Ray, Willie Rodríguez, Ed Castillo, Poncho Ruiz was in the community, Gregory Salazar, Yolanda Birdwell. All of these people were part of that experience."

MAYO's political program across the state was very critical of the noneducation of Chicanos in the Anglo-run public schools. MAYO encouraged school walkouts by Chicano students and led many such student boycotts of classes.[1] The MAYO group also initiated a food cooperative in the north side of Houston. "Ed Castillo was in charge of that, I remember . . . there were two hundred families participating."

María and many other Chicanos at the University of Houston also began to promote political activity on campus. They demanded a more flexible and open admission policy to increase Chicano student enrollment. They were instrumental in getting a student recruitment program started. And they also demanded Mexican American Studies be added to the curriculum. "We actually went down to the state legislature with a proposal that we wrote. And, and a line item was, was placed for funding of the Mexican American Studies." María was also involved in the Chicano mural project on campus. The students decided to paint a mural depicting the history of Chicano people. As the painting began María protested, "Wait a minute. I always tell people I am responsible for Sor Juana Inez because they were just painting males."

María was always a feminist. "It came with a position of inequality, having you know, sensed inequality and injustice from a very early age. And I just always any, any statement or anything which, which created unequal conditions of expression or as a person or as groups, I opposed. And I remember the comments of my father's friends about educating us, and the equality. My father's concept was that our role was to study. And that's what we did."

Her mother did all the housework. María did not cook, wash dishes, or iron clothes. "Oh, I never did any of that. My mother had to do it all. She never had a job outside the home and very much does what my father says. And, and my grandmother Manuela, who was such a strong woman figure. I think that helped in, in understanding that a woman could be very strong figures in that context."

María was studious and smart and talented. She also researched the history of the Mexican people, not just their historical experience in the United States. "I wrote my first article defending the right of women to participate for the *Papel Chicano* [newspaper] which Alfredo Vasquez had in, in Houston. And I remember the reaction amongst some of the fellow Chicano activists was, 'Well, you're OK. That's good *gringo* way viewing the role in the family, the culture.' There was a lot of opposition. . . . That's why Sor Juana Inez, about the feminist movements in the Yucatán, the participation of women who, for one thing or the other *como Doña Pepa, Josefa Domínguez* (like Mrs. Pepa, Josefa Domínguez), and the revolution, and you know. The many women who led battalions and fought in the revolution and you know, to fight for the right of education, of women in México. They fight for the right to vote in the fifties for the women of México. That's my history. I don't know where your history comes from, the history of the Mexican people. It includes the history of struggle for the equality of women."[2]

The campus MAYO group also obtained funding to bring César Chávez to speak at the campus, and of course, help the boycott across the city with his presence. But María was restless. She wanted more campus political activity, as if their accomplishments were not enough. María schemed to take over student government. She cut a deal with the liberal Anglo students to support her candidacy for student body vice president. "It was a deal we made before I ran with, with that group of people, which they represented more of the white liberal. That he would resign in six months and I would be president six months because the Chicanos didn't want us to run with an Anglo, but, nor the blacks. And then, the women didn't want me to run with a man. So we, we negotiated and, and that was the agreement. Neat deal. And it worked out. "I was elected to the student body president. No, I was elected to the vice-presidency and then the president resigned, but that was an agreement we made." María became the first Chicana to become student body president at a major Texas university.[3]

Statewide MAYO began in 1970 to promote the organizing of a political party, La Raza Unida. María joined that effort also. She gathered signatures to qualify the *partido* on the ballot. By 1972 the Raza Unida Party was running statewide candidates, including various persons for state representatives and senators. María had graduated from the university and had a job. Reluctantly she became a candidate for state representative under the Raza Unida Party ticket in 1972. "I didn't like the idea of running. I, I don't like electoral politics. And I didn't like the decision, but, but I felt that it was necessary at, you know, at the time we didn't think we could win. We didn't have a majority of, of, of Chicanos in the district. And, but it was necessary to run for something because we, we were talking about community control. Of, of our own political destiny. And this was a way that we could attempt or to organize the, the 45 percent Latinos who were in the district. And so, as a party goal, I accepted, but not, not as a personal."

"I quit my job." And for the next three months, rain or shine, María walked the streets in the precincts of her district, knocking on doors asking for votes. "Three months I walked streets, you know, every day. Raining, I had an umbrella in this thing and I walked streets. And then, the, the whole Raza Unida county organization also walked. And I think we walked about a hundred thousand, knocked on a hundred thousand homes here in Houston. I think we were idealists. I only got 19 percent of the vote."

They were also really naïve about hardball politics and corruption. Many of her voters were instructed to vote for her opponent, Ben Reyes, by the Democratic Party election judges staffing the polls. María got word of the stealing of votes from her race and set up a scenario to prove the machinations of the Democrats. She recruited an African American voter, Omawali Luthili, to attempt to vote for her without his registration card and pretend that he was illiterate. The precinct judge approved his eligibility and instructed him to "Go ahead and vote." Mr. Luthili said, "I can't read. I want to vote for María Jiménez." And they instructed him how to vote, but the instructions actually were to vote for Ben. "And so, we took the complaint to, to whoever you had to have a complaint, the officials says, 'Yeah. We are all part of the Democratic Party. We are not going to take your complaint seriously.'"

María never returned to electoral politics as a candidate. She instead developed great skills at policy impact organizing. She defines policy impact organizing this way: "I believe that it doesn't matter who is in office; if we don't have active groups of citizens, then we don't have what we want. If we don't seek power, power in the sense of running the government. What we do is, is we want changes. So how do we achieve those changes? So, it doesn't matter what government is in power. It's, it's how you develop the political forces that can impact those who, who, who govern to achieve the changes for the well-being of the collective entity. It's more impacting policies and practices and not through being the direct governmental actor." María had also become a socialist in thought. That is how she met her husband.

At age nineteen, after her first year in college, María accompanied her aunt, a teacher, on a summer trip to Oaxaca, Mexico. At the hotel in Oaxaca were a group of teachers from Monterrey working at certifying local rural teachers, her husband to be among them. The group organized a dance. Her aunt insisted they attend, "You have to. It's not polite. The Mexican . . . it's not polite to not be there." María grudgingly accepted. It was not that she didn't know or like to dance, she loved to. She just hated going to dances.

María promised the *tía* (aunt) she would go. María positioned herself in a chair by the stairs. Her plan was to be there for a little bit. "So when my hour was up I could disappear and not causing any ruckus. Her husband to be, Francisco Villarreal, was being pressured to dance with someone. He eyed young María sitting by the stairs. "When somebody asks you to dance, you have to dance seven dances together and, and then, the, the man, the young man, or the, the man would sit you down. So it was an insult if you didn't dance, you know, if you didn't dance the seven dances. So I figured well, I am going to talk to him about politics and history, bore him to death. And he'll set me down before the seven dances and I can go up to my room. And so, that is what I did. I started talking to him about politics and history. It turns out he loved politics and history. And then, he knew about Chicanos, which is kind of rare. He was six years older than I. He wanted to marry me immediately, but I didn't. I wanted to finish my school. And I, I just didn't want to leave the states. I married the first man I dated."

Five years went by, however. The couple wrote letters to each other; he would come to visit her in Houston. She finally accepted Francisco's marriage proposal. They married on April 23, 1974. His family lived in Los Angeles, but he didn't like the United States. He had a teaching job in Sinaloa. "We went to Sinaloa." Her husband began teaching at the local university. She and her husband and others became involved with student protests over a hike in bus fares. "The governmental agency I worked for basically said, 'We either fire you or you go to Yucatán.' So, they sent me over to Yucatán."

It did not take long for María to get politically involved in Merida, Yucatán, or have babies, twins in fact, in 1978: Carlos Francisco and Stalina Emanuel Villarreal. "The struggle with family was that when I married in México, you know, women had babies right after they are married. And we decided not to have children immediately . . . and when we finally decided, we had two of them. I remember it tickled my father to death. He told me that. He said, 'You waited three years to have two just like if you had one right after the other.'" Twins run in her side of the family at two levels. Her uncle, father's brother, has twins, as does the other uncle, the oldest brother. Her *primas hermanas* (first cousins) on her mother's side also had twins.

María did not take on his Villarreal name. He did not object to her activism. María did not know how to cook. Francisco, her husband taught her how; he remained the better cook. The twins loved his pancakes, not hers. He washed clothes, even the diapers when the babies came. He hung them out to dry. He changed the babies, fed them, and bathed them. "All the neighbors would be shocked to see what was going. . . . So people were a little shocked about his participation."

Her activism in Mérida may have caused her divorce in October 1985. "He was looking for a woman who was politically active, but as time went on, he changed his mind. I didn't change. And so, I did union organizing, independent union organizing in México. And I remember there was a, the only steel plant in Yucatán at the time in the area we had helped organize. And it went into lockout and the riot police . . . and it was finally was broken violently. And it was the only time I have had to hide and which for about a week. But I think that did in the marriage because I put myself in danger, put the children in danger, put him in danger, put the household in danger. It's just that I think as time went on I got more and more committed to organizing the political movements in, in México. And he got more and more interested in just leading a private middle-class life. And we were, became two different people, just like we sat down and, and decided to get married, we sat down and decided to get unmarried. It's kind of accepted that men, like executives, you know, are out of their house all the time and doing things. But it's not acceptable for a woman to, to have that type of schedule."

María and the seven-year-old twins returned to the United States, Houston. "A lot of people that I was active with I had found out that they were not active anymore." Eddie Canales with the Service Employees International Union (SEIU) was organizing janitors in downtown buildings in Houston. She joined the effort, and toward the end of December 1985, her first building voted to unionize. "About a month later, the INS [Immigration Naturalization Service] conducted a raid in the old, in the only buildings where the union had won. Clearly a union-busting tactic. In México the reaction was to, you know, beat you up and put you in jail. Here it was to deport you." This unionization effort of undocumented workers and those from Central America now residing in large numbers in Houston, together with U.S. immigration policy, became María's new focus for policy impact organizing.

The Quakers, American Friends Service Committee (AFSC), advertised for a job opportunity working on immigration policy and immigrant groups. María applied and was flown to Philadelphia to interview. The problem was that the position was in Philadelphia, at AFSC headquarters. But she told them during the interview, "I cannot go to Philadelphia. I have two young children and the network support that will take care of them while I am traveling would be my parents, and they are in Houston. And if you want to hire me, you have to open up an office in Houston." A few days later AFSC headquarters called and said, "You are hired. You have your office in Houston." For the next sixteen years, María traveled the United States, particularly the U.S.-Mexico border area, meeting with immigrant groups, INS authorities including the Border Patrol, other police agencies, immigrant service groups, political figures, and Central American refugee organizations. She monitored the violence of the Border Patrol, white terrorist groups, and smugglers that preyed on the undocumented persons crossing into the United States from Mexico and Central American countries.

To María, immigration policy is "a method of insuring inequalities at the international level. Because the very wealthy and the political elite have no problems in obtaining legal methods of entry into all of the countries of the world. The Border Patrols on the militarized borders are for people who are the international working poor who are internationally displaced poor. It's reflective of our inequality at a global level."

As the field representative and organizer, María contributed centrally to the building of the Border Network for Human Rights (New Mexico and Texas) and supporting Proyecto Libertad in Harlingen, Texas, to continue service operations. She also was most instrumental in building the Association of Residency and Citizenship of America, Mexicanos en Accion, the International Coalition for Mexicans Abroad Houston Chapter, Houston Coalition for Dignity and Amnesty, and the Committee for Justice for Servin Olvera. In this latter case, Ms. Jiménez was instrumental in bringing to light the fact that Mr. Olvera died from a broken neck while in the custody of an agent of the Immigration and Naturalization Service (INS) during a raid. Mr. Olvera was denied medical assistance for six hours even though it was evident he had been paralyzed by the Border Patrol agent.

María's work has not gone unnoticed. Janet Reno, as U.S. attorney general adopted María's recommendations for civilian oversight of INS. Section 503 of the Immigration Act of 1990 was largely the effort of María's work on reporting the physical abuse of detainees by the INS. This section provides for certification and training of INS officers and required a review of the use-of-force policy. Her work with the Association for Residency and Citizenship in America resulted in regaining residency status for 400,000 or more immigrants across the United States, 20,000 of them in Houston, with the passing of the LIFE Act of 2000. INS had "lost" the applications and processing payment fees of these immigrants and had failed to solve that dilemma for the applicants. Houston Mayor Lee Brown issued a proclamation in recognition of her work and that of AFSC-Houston on September 29, 2002.

Meanwhile, as a private citizen María rethought and reevaluated her own citizenship status and sought to recoup her Mexican nationality. She became a Mexican national once again in 1997. She was one of three U.S. citizens of Mexican ancestry asked to speak at the ceremony at the Mexican National Palace for those recuperating their Mexican nationality. Perhaps, one day when U.S. persons of Mexican citizenship are elected to sit in the Mexican Congress, María will be among those.

María worked for the AFSC until they decided to close the Houston office and end the monitoring project at the beginning of 2003. She protested the decision and was terminated for insubordination on January 28, 2003. But María continued. "I am going to die doing this work whether I am paid for it or not."

María is still protesting and causing change. She and others delivered 2,000 letters in support of the CLEAR Act pending in the U.S. Congress to the local Harris County Republican Party office. The officials had on past occasions accepted letters from María and others with respect and cordiality. Not this time. As the group attempted to leave the letters on a table, two staff members rebuffed them by refusing to accept the box; instead they asked, "Why didn't you mail them?" Obviously, 2,000 letters are an expensive mailing. Regardless, María and the group left the box on a table and walked out of the office. As they turned into a corner hallway and out the door, they noticed the box of letters being placed outside on the street at 3311 Richmond. They retrieved the letters, called the media to complain about this treatment, and proceeded to hold an impromptu press conference on the sidewalk. Police came and entered the building. As they emerged, an officer singled out María Jiménez for citation with "assault by contact." Koenning and Ryan Patrick, staff members of the local Republican Party, complained that María had pushed them violently while placing the box of letters on the table in their office. The charges were eventually dismissed when the Republicans failed to appear in court.

This type of harassment has not deterred María. She has written numerous articles and reports. She has won dozens of awards and honors, including the Liberty Bell Award from the Mexican American Bar Association in Houston; the Carol King Award from the National Immigration Project of the National Lawyers Guild in Chicago; the Hall of Fame Award for Hispanic Women in Leadership in Houston; the Community Leadership Award from the National Hispanic Institute in Austin; the Matt Garcia Public Service Award from MALDEF in San Antonio; the Willie Velasquez Hispanic Excellence Award; the Dedicated Service Award from the Association for Residency and Citizenship of America in San Jose, California; two proclamations of "María Jiménez Day" by the City of Houston mayors in 2003 and 2005; nomination to the Wall of Tolerance by Morris Dee and Rosa Parks, at the Southern Poverty Law Center in Montgomery, Alabama; and more. She organized the Houston contingent of the Immigrant Worker Freedom Ride of 2003 to Selma, Alabama. She moderated historic roundtable discussions among Mexican and Texas legislators about immigration reform. She became a visiting scholar in the UH Center for Mexican American Studies, teaching students about Chicano activism and organizing. She currently serves on the board of the National Network for Immigrant and Refugee Rights and was at the epicenter of organizing the massive immigration marches and rallies of April 10, 2006, and May 1, 2006.

As to her future, María envisions herself as some old lady passing out leaflets on some issue or cause. "I don't think that *no tengo remedio* (I am without remedy). That's, you know, I guess that's why I am not married. *No tengo remedio* a hopeless cause in that sense. I've never remarried since my divorce because I feel *nadie me aguanta*" (nobody will tolerate me).

## Notes

1. See Armando Navarro, *The Mexican American Youth Organization: Avante Garde of the Chicano Movement in Texas* (Austin: University of Texas Press, 1999) for an account of this organization.

2. See Vicki Ruiz, *Soldaderas in the Mexican Revolution* (1999) for an account of the role of women in the Mexican Revolution of 1910.

3. State Representative Roberto Alonzo (D-Dallas) also ran for student body president at the University of Texas in Austin in 1976. In his case, when it became apparent that he would be elected student body president the various Greek organizations on campus began an initiative to abolish student government. On election day, the students did in fact elect Roberto Alonzo student body president, the first Chicano ever to gain this position, but the students also voted to abolish student government. Roberto became a president without a government. See his interview at Special Collections Department, General Library, University of Texas, Arlington, Texas, May 20, 1998.

# PUENTES Y LAZOS:
# THE HISPANIC CONNECTORS

The women in part III are beneficiaries of the early *Adelitas* and also of those that labored and suffered loss of opportunity for their activism during the Chicano Movement. By the 1980s the *Adelitas* were out of the public arena and partially forgotten. Most of them were beginning to experience health problems associated with aging. Even Rosa Tijerina, the youngest of the group, was in and out of hospitals and unable to find stable employment at a wage that afforded minimum standards of living.

The young women of part II involved in the Chicano movement were married with children, divorced with children, or left behind as single heads of households in the historical trash basket and still taking care of family members economically and as caregivers. They still hold important jobs: judge, librarian, consultant, journalist; and they continue to advocate for social justice, some more than others. They too are experiencing the ills and malaise associated with the middle-age life of women. Few among us remember their names, much less contributions; they became the bridges between prior generations and the 1980s.

None of the members of part III were early pioneers breaking down barriers, and none were directly and personally involved in MAYO or the Raza Unida Party. U.S. District Judge Hilda Tagle best personifies the beneficiary status of those that came after the doors of opportunity were opened and discrimination against women generally had ended. Judge Tagle suffered early indignities based on her Chicanismo and gender, but once on track for judicial posts, she climbed the ladder to become the first Chicana federal judge in Texas. The nomination and appointment process were brutal, but she endured and has made history. Elvira Reyna, Leticia Van de Putte, and Socorro "Coco" Medina all entered the public arena after marriage and were either raising a family or had raised a family.

Coco Medina was in business and a mature middle-aged woman in the Texas panhandle. Like most middle-class persons, she volunteered for civic projects and sought to establish a business, a radio station. She was very much a part of her community and that is what prompted her to seek public office, no one else would. She believed it was time for Hispanic representation and took the lead.

Leticia Van de Putte began working on someone else's campaigns until it was obvious she could do a better job as candidate than those she supported. Despite the fact she was operating her own pharmacy, raising children, and had minimal political party involvement, she parlayed her precinct position to the nomination and subsequent election as state representative. She is now one of two Chicanas in the Texas State Senate.

María Berriozabal has almost the opposite trajectory to Leticia, Coco, or Elvira Reyna. María married late, had no children, but worked for well over a decade as the secretary or assistant to the Democratic Party county chair. She learned politics by observation and by listening to the men talk politics. She witnessed the deals brokered by powerful Anglo men in her midst. She tiptoed into a city council seat vacated by Henry Cisneros because the focus was on him and not her. She walked her district, meeting voters face-to-face, house by house, garnering overwhelming support. While on the city council she became a strong advocate for the poor and often opposed Mayor Henry Cisneros on the high-dollar development projects. She ran for mayor of San Antonio, hoping to become the first Chicana elected in a major city; the good old boys, including many Chicanos, denied her that bid, opting instead for an Anglo male. Later she ran for the U.S. House of Representatives, only to have the scenario replayed, this time in favor of the son of Henry B. González.

Elvira Reyna is the only Republican included in this book. There are not many Hispanic women Republicans in Texas, plenty of Anglos though, and a few African Americans. A former beauty queen, Elvira was a housewife and mother for years. She managed to graduate from college together with her daughter. Eventually she joined the district staff of a state representative. She became his voice, face, and doorkeeper for constituent access. When he died, the widow insisted Elvira be appointed to serve out the term. She did and worked astutely to stay in office. Her district is a heavily Republican constituency with few Latino voters; nonetheless, she continued to get reelected by strong majorities. Elvira has learned to forge coalitions and alliances with different groups to get things done. She knows how to be a *lazo* and bring people into her circle. In the 2006 Republican primary she lost her seat.

These Chicanas were pushed into leaving their ethnic label behind for a new one: Hispanic. The terms *Chicano/Chicana* not only had been politically charged but also were generational. Since 1970 the U.S. Bureau of the Census has imposed the Hispanic label for all Spanish-speaking persons in the country, the beginning of the era of the Hispanic generation. These Hispanic women remain very involved in the political system, some directly as elected officials and others as important connectors and vocal advocates for what remains to be done.

# CHAPTER TWELVE

~

# Hilda Tagle

Hilda Tagle was born in Corpus Christi, although she spent most of her formative years in Robstown. Her mother had seven pregnancies, but two children died during childbirth. Of the five surviving children, Hilda was the only daughter and the eldest. Her four brothers were named Manuel Jr., Jerry, Joe, and Santiago. Manuel is currently a foreman for the county public works department. Jerry is a contract welder with the army depot. Joe is a plant operator with Reynolds, and Santiago works at a body shop, repairing automobile damage. All four of her brothers live in the Corpus Christi area.

Her parents, Manuel and Dolores, were both born in 1921. Dolores was originally from Candela, a small town in Mexico between Nuevo Laredo and Monterrey. Hilda's maternal grandfather worked there in a local flour mill before immigrating to the United States. Her paternal grandfather was born in the Austin area, but he died before Hilda was born. Estefana Tagle, her paternal grandmother was born in the Valley in a small town named Santa Rosa.

Both of her parents were migrant workers, working in agriculture throughout the state. They worked with a variety of different crops, not specializing in one area. During the Second World War, her father served in the army. In the meantime, her mother worked as a beautician and other jobs to keep the family stable.

Tagle is a Spanish surname with Arabic origins, meaning frontier. Her last name was a mystery for years until she looked up its origins as a college student. Hilda never encountered anyone with her last name, and the only people with similar names seemed to be of German background. In Spain, there is a small town named Tagle in the Santader province. The last Spanish governor of Perú was named Torres Tagle, so it possible the name was more common in Spain in the past. Otherwise, little is known about Hilda's family history on her father's side.

Hilda attended a Catholic school in Robstown, where she excelled. She skipped the second grade because of her advanced reading skills. She is unsure what the racial makeup of her school was, but in elementary school she experienced overt discrimination for the first time. The principal, Hattie Martin, was adamant that she did not want Hilda to attend that school. Hilda later assumed that it had something to do with her ethnic background, but she was too young at the time to draw the connection. While the principal eventually relented, Hilda was warned that she would be watched especially.

Ms. Tagle was always been a voracious reader, and that played a significant role in her academic success. She spent most of her summers in the libraries, partly because it was one of the few places that was air-conditioned. When she was ten years old, her mother allowed her to take the bus to the Corpus Christi library. This was her mother's way of encouraging her to become independent. Hilda was able to spend her days at the library and the movies and return in the evening. This atypical experience was instrumental in her educational achievement, because it gave her a steady stream of new challenges.

Before beginning middle school, Hilda started attending the local Disciples of Christ church. While she had been raised Catholic, she found the new environment very comfortable and rewarding. Her mother went to church with her, and they were baptized together. This church brought her and mother closer together and served as a very powerful experience. Hilda's willingness to explore a new religion is illustrative of her independence and her open mind. Her willingness to try new things was evident at a young age and has played a role in her success.

Dolores Tagle desperately wanted her daughter to be financially independent. She feared that her daughter might be left some day without other support, and she encouraged Hilda to train for a vocation in case the worst came. Her mother pushed her to become a beautician, and Hilda was certified at sixteen. Although, she never used it, this certification was a perennial fallback option. This experience encouraged her further for college, "I wanted college so bad that I could taste it."

Her desire for collegiate success did not come from her parents because that was outside of their frame of reference. That is not to say that her parents discouraged her from academic achievement, but it was not something that they expected. Hilda did not know what applying to college entailed, but she was helped by knowing several other college-bound children. One of her friends was physically handicapped, and she helped this girl with her books. Hilda got into her first integrated class because she altered her schedule to be in the same class as this friend.

Hilda never received any college counseling, but enrolled at Del Mar College after graduation. After going undeclared for two years, commuting from Robstown, she transferred to East Texas State. While there, she decided that she was interested in becoming a librarian. With her incredible love of reading, that seemed to be a logical choice. After graduation she moved to North Texas to begin her graduate study.

Hilda finished her degree at North Texas in two years, and for the first time in her life she did not have to work full-time. Having this additional time to herself she could explore new things, but she was very lonely because most of her closest friends had moved on to other schools. She graduated with her masters in 1971, and she got a job teaching at a Jesuit school in Houston. After teaching there for four years, she decided while the job was rewarding, it was not what she wanted to do for the rest of her life.

After a frustrating period of introspection, she decided to go to law school. Hilda was accepted to the University of Houston, the University of Texas, and the South Texas School of Law. From these choices she chose the University of Texas. She was accepted as part of an affirmative action program that has since been found to be unconstitutional. After beginning in the summer of 1975, she finished in merely twenty-seven months going straight through, including three summers.

While she finished her law school career very successfully, there was a significant period of doubt in Ms. Tagle's mind. The adjustment to law school was very difficult, coming from being one of the best students to closer to the middle. Several encouraging classmates pushed her to be her best. The weight of being an affirmative action student added additional pressure to succeed, but in the end she completed the course effectively. Hilda knew that she was viewed differently than her Anglo classmates, and if she did not completed her degree, it might reinforce some people's racist ideas. This idea coupled with her natural desire to achieve, made her push harder and complete her course of study.

After graduation Ms. Tagle was not prepared for the cutthroat competition that surrounded law employment. Unlike some of her classmates who came from legal families or had valuable experience as clerks, Hilda did not have that background, partly because of her aggressive law school schedule.

A fortuitous phone call from the city attorney's office garnered an informal interview and later her first law job. Even with this great job and academic success, shyness has been a problem for Hilda throughout her career. In fact, "I never had the courage to go into private practice." Despite this difficulty, she pushed herself and has managed to control this potential problem.

Her time at the city attorney's office was very intense, and she was forced to push herself to stay afloat in the competitive atmosphere. One day she received a call from the county attorney, Mike Westergren, asking if she would be willing to apply for a recent vacancy. After less than two years, Hilda was recruited out of the county attorney's office and hired by the district attorney. In all three of her early law jobs Hilda excelled, despite being one of the few non-Anglos. Her reputation was growing, and rather than actively pursuing employment, potential bosses were seeking her out.

While interning with new congressman Solomón Ortiz, Hilda learned that a new county court had been created in Nueces County. After deciding that she was in need of a base, she sought out the support of the Mexican American Democrats. This group exposed her for the first time to a passionate political group. Outside of her aunt, who was a strong and vocal supporter of Congressman Ortiz, this was Hilda's first exposure to strong electoral politics. In order to get on the court she needed the support of the five-member county commissioner's court. While she had one vocal supporter on the court, she also a vocal opponent, a sexist named William McKenzie, who did not think that women belonged as judges. In the end she was not appointed, losing out to a better-prepared candidate.

Less than a month later, another opening appeared at court at law number three. Hilda won the endorsement of the county commissioner's court over the objections of McKenzie. In her first election, she went unopposed and did not have to face an opponent until 1990. The stress of the campaign weighed on her very heavily. With the encouragement of her ex-husband, she began to campaign and use the power of incumbency. She was married very briefly in 1979. Trying all of the various media types, she relied largely on radio and volunteers knocking on doors. After a hard-fought campaign, she was able to fend off her challenger by a safe margin.

By 1994, Hilda began to grow restless with her position and started her committee to run for the 148th District court. There was a vulnerable incumbent in that position, a well-known judge, Margarito Chapa Garza, but one that had suffered from a public censure. Knowing that the race would be difficult, she was able to rely on her faith, and that allowed her to keep a positive attitude. Aggressive fundraising allowed her to raise more money than the incumbent. She spent it wisely and came out with the most votes in the primary election with 14,182 or 45.94 percent to Judge Garza's 39.99 percent. A third candidate, Anne Marshall, received only 14.06 percent of the vote. She eventually beat the incumbent in the runoff election obtaining 17,829 votes or 57.97 percent of the votes. Although she started out at a disadvantage, hard work allowed her to narrow the gap and be successful. While her race saw several setbacks in relations with the elite of Corpus Christi, the race left her stronger both politically and personally. In the general election she was unopposed and won handily. Republican candidates did not contest many elections in the border area or Nueces County in 1994.

Even before her dramatic win over the incumbent, Tagle had been getting encouragement from various sources to submit her name for a federal judgeship. Several groups and individuals sought her out to offer support for this competitive appointment. After getting a late start, she announced her attention for the federal bench in 1995. While she did not get that position, it taught her a lesson about the importance of being aggressive when going after something as competitive as a federal judgeship. Even though she was getting support for her appointment, Hilda knew that she would need to work harder if she was going to reach her goal.

In order to position herself better for future consideration, she began to meet the decision makers that could help in her quest. Most of the gossip pointed to Congressman González being a point man on the federal judge nominations. Unable to get a meeting with the congressman, Hilda arranged to meet with one of the congressman's biggest backers. Although this did not allow her to meet the congressman, it did get her name in the door with the staff at his office.

After that politicking, it turned out the word on the street had not been entirely correct. All of the congressmen from South Texas were going to be part of the committee. Hilda went and visited Congressmen Solomón Ortiz and Eulogio "Kika" de la Garza and discussed her intentions. She spent several months dealing with the paperwork need by Congress, the FBI (Federal Bureau of Investigation), and the ABA (American Bar Association). Despite all of this work, her nomination was not voted on before the fall recess in 1996.

The next session, the pertinent congressmen had changed and it was necessary for her to meet with several new members. After a long, drawn-out process, her candidacy ended up being a compromise between the Valley congressmen and the Houston congressmen. Being in the middle, Hilda's candidacy was acceptable to both groups. She was officially renominated in spring of 1997. The Republicans in the Senate had been sitting on a number of nominations, hoping to delay the process indefinitely. After meeting the

two Republican senators from Texas, Hilda was able to gain their support, and she was finally approved and sworn in, March 1998.[1]

Since her appointment, Ms. Tagle has served on the court with distinction. Her tenure has included several difficult cases, such as an INS corruption case and the Republic of Texas case. She remains on the federal bench as the federal judge for southern Texas.

Throughout her life, Hilda Tagle has shown herself to be very capable of dealing with adversity and difficult changes. Several career changes did not dilute her passion, rather the opposite, they strengthened her character. Her setbacks, such as the two times she was passed over for appointments, solidified her desire to reach her goals. Hilda credits her mother with being a great example of strength through adversity. If her career is any indication, she has learned the lesson well.

## Note

1. State District Judge Tagle resigned her position for the 148th Judicial District and Governor George Bush appointed a Republican to the post. He was defeated by Rose Vela, who was nominated to fill in as the Democratic candidate. Judge Vela won the general election with 50.85 percent or 31,696 votes.

~

# CHAPTER THIRTEEN

# Elvira Reyna

Texas State Representative Elvira Reyna of Mesquite is the first Hispanic Republican ever elected to serve in the Texas State Legislature. She was first elected in 1993 under the Democratic governor Ann Richards. Elvira was born in Harlingen, Texas, on October 28, 1950, the daughter of a single-parent family headed by a Mexican-born, Catholic mother who worked in canneries, cleaned houses, and realized her goal of becoming a United States citizen in 1998. Reyna never knew her father. "My mother was a single parent in a strange country. She didn't know any English. My mother and father divorced when I was an infant. I am the middle child (of three children). My brother is the oldest and we are all a year apart." Reyna says her mother was a feminist.

Her childhood was largely apolitical. The family moved to Dallas when she was thirteen. She embarked on an unlikely path to a college degree, the Republican Party, and a seat representing a suburban Texas House District that is only 8 percent Hispanic.[1]

Reyna remembers moving to Dallas because one of her cousins had moved to Dallas and said the education and job opportunities were better there. "We lived in the Little Mexico Housing Projects and we were getting subsidized even then, but my mother said no more." She remembers her mother saying that she was going to raise her children on her own. As a result, Elvira worked as soon as she was old enough. She picked cotton in Harlingen in order to help her mother pay the bills. "When we moved to Dallas, I started ironing for the next-door neighbors and babysitting. I worked all through high school and I just handed the check over to my mother and she would say, this will help with the phone bill and electric bill and whatever."

When asked about school or a career, Reyna said she didn't think it was possible to go to college because she didn't have any money and was tired of working. She had to work through high school and so thought she couldn't go to college. "I didn't know that you could get scholarships or/and work part time and work around your schedule. I assumed that I couldn't have it all— that I couldn't work and go to school or even be married and go to college."

Reyna struggled because after graduating from high school, she married right away, started having a family and went to work as a secretary. She married Angel Reyna and had two children. She realized the hardships. The reality really hit her when her kids were in elementary school and she was involved in their school activities and everyone around her had a college degree and she didn't. She felt she was less of a person because she was less educated.

Reyna started attending Eastfield College and made excellent grades, graduating with a 3.0 GPA. She went to the University of Texas at Arlington and received her B.A. in Organizational Communications in 1989, the same year that her daughter graduated from high school.[2]

Politically, she felt like a Democrat. "I felt like I was a Democrat because I was not rich. I always aligned Republicans with the rich."[3]

"When my husband and I first started out, we lived in Oakcliff and then later we bought a house in Pleasant Grove. I was working for the Dallas Independent School District and heard that Mesquite had good schools, so we bought a house in Mesquite. We attended First Baptist Dallas and were very involved with the church. My husband was the Baptist in the family, so my children have been Baptist ever since."

Reyna recounted that after working for the DISD, she worked part-time for a while at Service Master Industries. Then she went to apply for a job as a teacher's aide and substitute secretary. While working at one of the schools, she met the wife of Bill Blackwood, who had just been elected to the Texas House of Representatives in her district. He was looking for someone to work with him part-time. His wife recommended Reyna.

She started working with the representative soon afterward. She answered the phones, addressed constituent's concerns, and kept the representative's schedule. She worked for Blackwood for seven years, until he died. During that time, she found that Republican ideals agreed with her own. "Less government, more individual responsibility," she said. "It was family values, and thinking back to growing up when my mother was bringing us up and somebody suggested that government could help us with welfare or food. I'd rather raise my children on my own," Reyna recalled. Like other Hispanic Republicans, Reyna sees it as a natural tie. But she sees the obstacle. "It's a tradition," she says of being Hispanic and Democratic. "Just like being Catholic is a tradition. Hispanics are very loyal, I find. It's difficult."[4]

Reyna recalls that her husband was the first to encourage her to seek public office. "I really didn't think I could do it. I liked the aspect of being a legislator, of being a representative of the people, but I didn't think I could do it. I didn't have any money; I didn't have the name identification; I knew who the other opponents were, especially the former mayor, so I didn't think I had a chance. But I did have the basics. I did have the understanding of the process, but most importantly, I had the dedication to serve the people and I knew how to serve the constituents because I had been doing it."

When she first ran in 1993, Reyna thought the district was between 5 and 8 percent Hispanic.

"But, I felt it was important enough for me to run because I had that same dedication that my predecessor had in representing and serving the constituents, so I thought I'd give it a shot. And it was a lot of hard work, but I did it."

"What helped a lot was the name of my predecessor, Blackwood; it was a very important name, had a lot of integrity. People respected the family and they supported me. I think that really gave me credibility."

"When I came to the first session, Speaker Laney gave me the Higher Education Committee, and Environmental Regulation. In fact the speaker gave me the assignments that I wanted and I got to keep Mr. Blackwood's seat on the House floor."

As far as the Hopwood decision and affirmative action, Reyna believes that it is a tough issue, because especially in her case, she doesn't represent very many Hispanics and she would like to stay race neutral. "I want to, but at the same time, I know that there needs to be the opportunities, the accessibility to higher education for all students. I think a root cause of the problem, though, goes back to elementary and high school."

"I am a Republican because I feel that my personal conservative beliefs are more aligned with the Republican Party. I think conservative in that I want less government. I don't like this big central government. I believe in more local control, less government intrusion in our lives, more free enterprise. I think the bottom line is that our government has built this too big. The scope of government, I think it should be educating our children, public safety, and transportation modes. Those are the three main areas that I think government should be involved. I am going to vote for the issues that represent the Republican conservative philosophy of the majority of my constituents, but I represent everyone."

Along the line of education, the subject of school vouchers was discussed. Reyna feels that schools need more competition and there is a lot of waste in schools today. "I think that parents need to have a choice of where they want their children to be educated."

Representative Reyna defines leadership as really taking the responsibility of whatever it is you are responsible for whether at home, in the office, or in politics and to be in the forefront and to set a good example, to be a positive role model, to follow through, and to be accountable for what you are doing, to be a responsible person.

When it comes to building trust, Reyna believes that you try to treat everyone like you would like to be treated: with dignity, courtesy, and kindness. "I try to overlook the political philosophy and look at the person, and look at the good of the person. Plus, it's a Christian attitude."

"I believe the most pressing issue facing Mexican Americans today is education. The high school dropout rate is very high. Education is the key and everywhere I go I love to talk to the children. My job is not just going to Austin and voting for or against a bill. It's more than that. I take it real seriously

because I feel that I am a role model and I want to be a mentor to the school children. I like to go to the schools, at any level and talk about education and how important it is."

Representative Reyna was first elected to represent District 101 in 1993. The district includes the cities of Sunnyvale, Mesquite, Garland, Seagoville, Balch Springs, and part of Dallas. Outside of Dallas, Mesquite is the largest city in the Fifth Congressional District.[5]

She currently serves on the Juvenile Justice and Family Issues Committee as well as the Human Services Committee and is the chairman of the Local and Consent Calendar Committee. Her past legislative appointments include: chairman of the Subcommittee on Tuition and Fee Exemptions; the Public Safety Committee; the State, Federal and International Relations Committee; and the Environmental Regulation Committee.

Representative Reyna is extremely active in Republican Party and legislative activities and remains involved in civic and volunteer projects within the district. Recently, she was awarded the "2003 Legislative Honor Roll" by the Texas Association of Realtors. And during the last legislative session, she received the "Fighter for Free Enterprise" award given by the Texas Association of Business.

During the Seventy-eighth Legislature, Representative Reyna authored or coauthored thirteen bills, of which six have passed and are now in effect.

Reyna's legislative priorities include fiscally responsible government, creating more opportunities for higher education, ensuring the public's safety, putting a stop to unfunded mandates, and keeping the foundation of the traditional family intact (Journal 2003).

## Notes

1. "Hispanic Republicans are Political Pioneers," *Austin American-Statesman*, February 1, 1998, p. A14.

2. "The Honorable Elvira Reyna," *Hispanic Journal*, 2001, available online at http://www.hispanicjournal.com/legislature/Elvira_Reyna.html.

3. "Hispanic Republicans are Political Pioneers," p. A14.

4. "Hispanic Republicans are Political Pioneers," p. A14.

5. "State representatives Elvira Reyna, Joe Driver endorse Jeb Hensarling for congress," 2001 available online at http://www.jebforcongress.org/press/press_15.html.

# CHAPTER FOURTEEN

~

# Leticia San Miguel Van de Putte

Baby girl Leticia started life breaking tradition. Shortly after birth on December 6, 1954, her parents, Daniel San Miguel and Isabel Aguilar, now Ortiz, debated what to name their firstborn. Tradition among Catholic families called for her to be named *María* plus another name after a grandmother or great-grandmother. On one side was a great-grandmother with a name of *María Tomasa*, and on the other side was another named *María Josefina*. Her dad wanted to name her *Tomasa Josefina*, and joked that "She can just be Tommy Joe." Her mom was adamantly opposed, "Absolutely not! If we're not going to have the *María*, she still needs a *Mexicana* name. And so that's why they decided on Leticia." She muses now, "If I would be Tommy Joe Van de Putte, chair of the Mexican American Caucus; chair of the Senate Hispanic Caucus, they would have gone, 'Huh?'"

She certainly has the Van de Putte surname, from twenty-five years of marriage to Pete Van de Putte. The maiden surname of San Miguel has a long history, several generations back before Texas was even an independent Republic. "The San Miguel family is ninth-generation *Tejano*, from Maverick County, from Eagle Pass. A very strong ranching family. I had a great-grandpa who was a Texas Ranger who died in an ambush in 1906. So, it's a very proud San Miguel family, San Miguel ranch. My family has been there through Spain, Mexico, France . . . the Confederacy." Her mother's family was from Guadalajara. "Left in 1910, like many families did in Mexico, went to Colorado, were on their way back, stayed in San Antonio for what they thought would be three weeks to make enough money *pa regresar*, to go back

149

to Guadalajara, and never went back." Both maternal and paternal grand-mothers were born in Mexico and had a strong education ethic.

Grandfather Daniel San Miguel was a pharmacist, one of the first *Mexi-canos* to own such a business, *una botica*, in San Antonio. It was called *La Botica Guadalupana* and located "in the area of San Antonio that's now known as *El Mercado* [Market Square]. But back then it was Produce Row. It was where the trucks came. It was the center of the *Mexicano* business com-munity." Grandfather Roy Aguilar owned a *hielería*, an icehouse, called Roy's Ice Station. It was located "almost at the corner of Commerce, as you come down the bridge on Colorado. And, and so on Friday and Saturday nights they had little *conjunto* (traditional Chicano three-piece band) there outside, little barbeque."

Leticia's fondest memories, however, were of the *botica* and her pharmacist grandfather. He never went to pharmacy school. "If you trained and you ap-prenticed in the early 1900s with a pharmacist, you could take the state boards. And if you passed the boards, then you could be a pharmacist. But he never called himself a pharmacist. He was a druggist or *un boticario*. My grandpa was one of these men that worked seven days a week, never took a vacation. And when I asked him, you know, '*Huelo*, why don't you go on va-cation? Why don't you take Grandma somewhere?' And he said, 'Why? My whole life is a vacation. My whole life is a vacation. Why would I, why would I want to leave this?'"

Leticia remembers the smells of *la botica*: the wrapping paper, tissue; the sawdust on the floor. "All the *acietes y pomadas* (oils and ointments), and the things that they would make up. I loved that smell." More importantly, "the reason that I really wanted to become a pharmacist was because I wanted to be looked at in the same way *los pacientes* (the patients) would go to get coun-sel from my grandfather. It was that sense of he was treated with such respect that I wanted that too."

Her parents were also her role models, "both born in San Antonio, both college educated, both teachers." They were the firsts in their families to go to college, "so there was never a question when I was growing up if I would go or not. It would be, it was more, '*Mi'jita*, where do you want to go to col-lege? What do you want to be?'" But her parents as newlyweds had a tough time in San Antonio.

Leticia was born at Madigan Hospital at Fort Lewis, Washington State. Her dad was stationed there upon his return from duty in Korea. When he was discharged and returned to San Antonio, the couple attempted to buy a home in "the University Park area, right by St. Mary's University, so that my dad could come back and finish school. They couldn't. Not that they couldn't qualify, but because of the deed restrictions that at the time said, "No Mexicans. No N-I-G-G-E-R-S. No dogs." They bought a home "closer to the *barrio* on the West Side in South Zarzamora" [street name].

Her mother, a graduate from Our Lady of the Lake University in San Antonio, was a talented musician and choir director. She started the *ballet folklórico* and *mariachi* movements in the San Antonio Independent School District when such activity was prohibited. "It was against the law." Her mother was charged with violation of school policy and state law. She fought the battle all the way to the school board. "She brought all the little choir members, little third graders, and elementary school students to the board room to this allegations thing that she was teaching Spanish, and she said, 'Absolutely! We're singing in Spanish. We are singing in German. We are singing in French. We're singing in all languages.'" Later, when Leticia was in the elementary grades, she was suspended from school for speaking Spanish on the playground. "I mean, everybody knew the rules: You don't speak Spanish in the classroom. But I was on the playground and a teacher caught me and so they sent me home." She reflects on the impact of that English-only rule, "We were sent home. And so my parents quit speaking Spanish to each other at home because they didn't want the kids to be in danger at their school."

Leticia Van de Putte also had her share of tough times in San Antonio and through her college days. She attended Horace Mann Junior High School. The family lived two blocks away from the school and just a block away from her elementary school. She was involved in a lot of activities such as the pep squad and student council. And she was a real tomboy, playing football, running, climbing, and wrestling with the boys. "I played baseball. I ran track. I played football until I was thirteen and my dad made me stop playing football. And I was really angry, but he said, 'No. The boys might tackle you even when you don't have the ball.' I was really upset about that, but . . . I couldn't quite understand what was the concept there."

During junior high election for the next year's president of the student council, a classmate nominated her to run for president. The boy president at that time, Jaime Garza said, "Well she can't. She's a girl." Leticia was dumbfounded. She could "beat him any time in a hundred yard dash. Why? What was the fact that I was a girl that I couldn't be student council president?" She ran because Jaime told her that she couldn't. She won the race and proved him wrong.

At Jefferson High School she got involved with the pep squad that had a dance team and a roping team, The Lassos. It was a very prestigious membership among the high school students. The school mascot was a Mustang. The students in organizations like these had to meet high scholastic requirements.

The Lasso president had to maintain a 4.0 grade average. Leticia always had excellent grades. She explains, "I was really lucky that, you know, how sometimes when you have deficiencies and you compensate, you never know that they end up being a plus. I had pretty terrible vision when I was a child. Couldn't see far away. And I always knew I had to be close up to the teacher so I could see the chalkboard. And I wore glasses. And so, I knew I had to be up there. But, because I couldn't see very well, I didn't watch TV very much because you'd have to be real close to see it. But I could read without any problem at all. So, one of the things, I think, that really helped is that I was an avid reader."

She also credits her father for her early academic success. "My dad would say, 'This is my daughter Leticia.' And the first thing out of anybody's mouth, '*Ay que bonita la muchachita, que bonita* or what a pretty little girl.' And the next thing out of my dad's mouth would be, 'And she's the smartest girl in the class.' Well, I thought I was. I mean, because my dad said it, it must be true. Correct? Well, I wasn't. But I worked harder at spelling and I worked hard at that because my dad kept saying . . . 'She is the smartest girl in her class.'"

She took advanced classes in high school and was very well read. Her dad pushed her to join and become president of the Lassos. "*Mi'jita* you have to. You have to. They're just not many. *Mi'jita* you would be the first Mexican American to ever be out there marching in front. You've got to do it." And she did and got elected. "And right before that first game, I just didn't realize the amount of animosity. Even from people who I knew that were in the band or who I was the leader of in the dance team in that. . . . Before the first game the band members, some of them, and some of the dance team, refused to march because a Mexican was going to be leading them out in front." The band director stood his ground and faced the racism. He said, "If you don't march the first day, you're not marching the rest of them." The local newspapers, including the student paper, and television media crews had a field day with that protest and confrontation. She remembers that being the first time she was interviewed by a TV camera crew.

There were a lot of good universities in the San Antonio area, but Leticia wanted to get away. She wanted to go to the University of Texas at Austin, but she knew that she would not get admitted because she was Mexican. It was very difficult for Mexicans to get in at the time, she believed. She did very well on her Scholastic Aptitude Test (SAT) and had a really good grade point average, but she did not get in. She applied to Baylor and was readily accepted, plus was offered a scholarship. But before she could go, the family had to make the decision for her. She was not able to make that decision. Her grandparents were the biggest problem with their gendered and provincial viewpoints. It never occurred to them or her immediate family that she should be able to decide for herself. The grandparents objected to Baylor because it was Baptist and they "don't even have a statue of *La Virgen* (Virgin of Guadalupe)." Her cousin, "male, graduated the same year, can make that decision, but *La Niña* (womanchild) can't. But *La Niña* could go to St. Mary's University. Because she could live at home. . . ." It mattered not to the family that St. Mary's did not have a pre-pharmacy program and Baylor did.

She attended St. Mary's for a year and had a lot of fun there. There were lots of anti–Vietnam War protests on the campus at the time. The school also did not have much of a female population because it had been an all-boys school before.

After her first year at St. Mary's University, the family relented and Leticia transferred to the University of Houston. She was one of eight women and four Chicano students in her pharmacy class of 1965. She also was very poor. Her parents had divorced and she gave her mother her car. Leticia then zoomed around Houston and on campus on a Honda 400 motorcycle. Leticia scouted around for a job and landed one on Sundays as a vendor at the Houston Oilers' home games. She sold programs. In addition, she had to work at the Foley's pharmacy as part of an unpaid school requirement.

She looked for financial aid and found a scholarship for band members. But she didn't play any musical instrument. She had been in the Lassos and could march and do tricks with rope. The Cougar band had letter holders as members of the band. The letter holders simply raised big letters: H-O-U-S-T-O-N when they marched on the football field. She begged the band director for an opportunity to try out letter carrying. The band director was most impressed with her marching ability and suggested she try out for the Cougar Dolls. It was a dance team. She didn't think she could make it because she did not meet the height requirement of five feet six inches. She was five feet four, a short and hefty girl. Most of the girls on the dance team were blond, beautiful, and leggy. She wasn't tall, blond, or leggy. The band director insisted she try out anyway because the Cougar Dolls were short of team members. More importantly, he promised her she would still be able to march with the band and carry a letter if she failed the tryout. She was desperate for money at the time. She tried out and made it. She was on the team for two years. "So, I was the *chaparrita* (shorty) at the end of the line. I'm the last one on the end of the leg line. So, I kicked my way through pharmacy school."

Disaster hit while she was in her last year of pharmacy school in Houston. Her plastic knee gave out and she fell down a flight of stairs at school. Her plastic knee was a replacement for an injury she sustained two years prior while playing football. She had to withdraw from school and go home to recuperate.

Leticia's mom had a friend and colleague, a band director that had implemented the first *Mariachi* Band program in San Antonio, Pete Van de Putte. He came to visit her mom and re-met Leticia. She had met him before when she was sixteen. He was the band director for her younger brother and sister. Now she was twenty-three years old and began dating Pete while convalescing. They became engaged during a whirlwind romance, and three months later, they were married. But Leticia wanted to finish pharmacy school and transferred to the University of Texas, her dream from the beginning. She commuted for a year from San Antonio to Austin. "I mean, when you're young and you're married, you want to be with your husband every night. So yeah I drove back and forth because I wanted to be sleeping with Peter Van de Putte at night." She graduated in 1979.

She had always wanted two kids and her husband wanted six. They compromised on four, but they ended up having six children. She said labor and pregnancy were easy for her. Plus, she could take the babies with her to work because she owned the pharmacy and she made her own rules. The large family was not affordable on a band director's salary. Pete took over his family business, a flag company, in San Antonio.

About a week before her fifth baby was due she was elected president of the Bexar County Pharmacy Association. While operating the family drug store, she got involved with the downtown business owners. "I complained because there weren't any bathrooms downtown. I was tired of every morning when I opened the *botica* that I had to clean urine, because there were no public bathrooms for tourists even!" She was also involved with teaching catechism at St. Joseph's downtown. "I mean, you just get involved in life and the things that matter to you and your family. Well, then I bought my pharmacy in Loma Park. And my patients in the area, they always went to Rodríguez County Park. And there were big floods in San Antonio. And that park just didn't get refurbished." So Leticia got her facts in order and went to present before the Bexar County Commissioner's Court. "These are the facts; this is what you have spent at this; this is what you've spent. . . . It's blatant discrimination against Rodríguez Park that's only used by people in that community and a very poor community. And you are not willing to put the resources that you are in the other parts of the city." As a result, the commissioners appointed her to the County Park Board. Her political career was launched.

Leticia's family is politically connected and that also favorably influenced her career as well. Her *padrinos* are former state senator Joe Bernal and his wife, Esther. Her *compadre* (baptized her second daughter, Vanessa) and husband's former band director buddy is Paul Elizondo. He served in the state legislature and became a county commissioner. Another buddy is Charlie Muñoz, a former coach, and part of a political family. The three couples partied one evening in 1978. Leticia was a newlywed and completing her last year of pharmacy school. The men drinking outside in the yard came in to the house and announced they had decided to run Paul Elizondo for state representative. Pete was offered the opportunity but declined, given the family finances with Leticia still in school. Charlie also declined because as a schoolteacher he would have to resign to run. A teacher cannot run or be elected to a partisan government position in Texas. "You can't draw a salary from the state twice." Paul Elizondo was the candidate. He also was a popular bandleader and played at everybody's *quinceañeras* and weddings. Pete became the campaign treasurer, and Leticia and the other wives did the campaign work of hosting coffees, backyard barbeques, candidate forums, and knocking on doors while passing out campaign literature. Paul Elizondo was elected state representative. "In the '80s, I was always pregnant. I was building my business. Of course, we always helped my *compadre*, Paul, in any of his campaigns." Then something happened that got Leticia really mad and more involved in politics. Her grandmother, Memo, had suffered a stroke and lived with the Van de Puttes. At the airport one time, Memo had a humiliating experience that embarrassed her to no end. She needed a bathroom and the San Antonio International airport had no facilities that would accommodate a wheelchair. Leticia complained to City Hall and then-mayor Henry Cisneros. He appointed her to the Airport Advisory Board.

"Nineteen ninety rolls around. And our friend, who is our state representative, Orlando García decides to run for the Fourth Court of Appeals. He did. He made that decision between the primary and the general election. OK? When a vacancy occurs for state representative or any office between the primary and general election, then that party's executive committee, which in this case are the precinct chairs, decides who the replacement on the ballot is." Leticia was a precinct chair, and together with twenty-three other precinct chairs, considered all the candidates to replace García, but none made a strong impression on her. Her husband urged her to run for the office herself, if not to win, then to at least make people aware of the issues. But Pete underestimated his wife, or really didn't know her very well. She told him, "I just can't go into it half-assed. I mean, I cannot go into something thinking

I'm just going to do this. If I'm going to do this, I'm going to do it to win. I don't want to do this for show. I want to do this to win." Leticia jumped into the race with her own strategy. First she got her husband's pledge of support. The she discussed it with her children so they would understand that Mommy might be going away for hours and days at a time. Her baby Isabella asked why she was doing this. And before Leticia could respond, Nicole, her oldest daughter cut in, "She has to. Because there's not enough mommies there." With her family behind her, Leticia made her move.

Quickly Leticia had printed a little biography with her picture. She spent fifty-four dollars in this her first campaign. Then, she called every precinct chair and asked for their vote. She got one, plus her own. She then called every announced candidate to inform them of her candidacy. She then asked each one of them to support her as a fallback vote in case they lost in the early balloting. With everyone's second vote in hand, over a six-hour-long elimination round of voting, Leticia became the eventual nominee. All others failed to get the nomination in the first rounds and kept their pledge to support her in their second round. While each of them faded, Leticia gained more votes with each round.

As the Democratic Party nominee for state representative in the general election of 1990, Leticia faced another unknown candidate in the Republican column, Bart Simpson. Leticia campaigned pushing a stroller and other babies in tow. "Bring the kids. We'll put bumper stickers on the strollers. And we take off. And plus, block walking with kids is great. Nobody slams the door in your face when you've got a stroller." Leticia won. Simpson never had a chance. "It was a perfect district for me to run in because almost everybody either knew my family, my grandfather con la botica La Guadalupana, my other grandparent's from Roy's Ice Station, my mom who was choir director at Lanier, very famous in the cultural community, my husband, who was the band director in the neighborhood, me who had the pharmacy, our kids, our church." She also had the network of pharmacists across the county and all her contacts in the various boards she had been elected and appointed to over the years: Bexar County Pharmacy Association, Centro 21, Mayor's Commission on Women, Airport Advisory Board, County Parks Board, and Precinct Chair. Leticia had a full bank account of earned and saved social capital. And 1990 was the year Ann Richards sought and won the Texas governorship. Women voted in record numbers for Ann and Leticia.

Leticia was in heaven in the Texas State Legislature. "My first session, it was just getting used to it and I loved the public policy. I still love the public policy. That's what really drives me is the public policy part. Being able to put in the Children's Health Insurance Program (CHIPS); being able to do the lead screening program; being able to put in a lot of stuff that I was able to do because of my background in health, and as a pharmacist. I was able to do a lot of health care, a lot of children's legislation early on, the first six years I was in the House, because of that experience."

She had to learn how to become an effective legislator. She did learn quickly and began by hiring competent legislative staff such as Debbie Williams, former aide to Governor Bill Clements, the first Republican governor of Texas since Reconstruction. Debbie knew the legislative process. She said to Representative Van de Putte, "How are we ever going to get any of your bills passed? You don't hunt. You don't fish. You don't western dance. You don't play poker. You don't smoke cigars. How are we ever going to get your legislation passed?" So Debbie suggested, "We are going to have to go country western dancing. We're going to the Broken Spoke." That is where the boys hung out on Tuesday nights; all the chairmen, a lot of the members and staffers. So Leticia danced with Bill Carter, chair of a committee holding up her children's immunization bill and got his pledge to give her a hearing. That is all she needed. The bill made it to the floor. In order to get the bill passed she recruited another senior legislator by praising him, his floor-strategy skills, and acumen. He could not resist the lavish praise. He became her floor manager and helped pass the bill by letting other legislators know he was supporting the bill. Leticia learned that in the district, the voters are your constituency, but while in the House, other legislators are your constituency.

House Speaker Gib Lewis could not pronounce her name. Letika, Latricia, Latrina, Lutikia, anything but Leticia. So in exasperation, while introducing her, Speaker Lewis finally blurted out, "I'm just going to call you Representative Honey." Leticia heard the women in the chamber groan, but she goes up to the mike and said, "That's fine. You can just call me Representative Honey and I'll just call you Speaker Sugar." She adds, "I never felt intimidated. I just had to find a new way to work. Number one, if they would excuse themselves to another room, I'd walk in the door. I'm sorry. I would just walk in the door. And so, I have to tell you, it was just shifting methods of communication, and my success as a House member was that I worked the bills hard; I was always real well prepared; never ever, ever dissed anybody out in public. You know, treated everybody with dignity and respect. And asked for help when I needed it. Built up the personal relationships. Well, it is like going to the horse races and you don't know the horses, but you know the jockey. And I have to know a hundred forty-nine jockeys."

Often women have had a hard time in the public arena because of gender discrimination, but not Leticia. She claims it is an asset. "My gender, I think, has helped. I can say things and do things, though, that single women on that legislative floor can't. Just can't." She provides the example of Glen Maxey, first openly gay member elected to the Texas House of Representatives and the reaction of her House colleagues, "the Bubbas, the boys." They asked Leticia how they could help the Hispanic running against Maxey because they did not want a homosexual in the House. She rebuffed them. She even made fun of them by saying, "He'll be pissing in your bathroom, not mine." And when Maxey did win and made his entrance on the House floor, Leticia rose from her chair to welcome him. She approached him center hall and said, "Kiss me on the lips." Maxey was shocked. Leticia grabs him and, "I kissed him right on the lips. I am married twenty-some-odd years. I weigh two hundred pounds. I got six kids, you know. It set a different tone. And he knew then. . . . But a single woman couldn't do some of the stuff that I do. Simply because they don't have that shield of being married and, and having six kids, you know. It, it's just different."

Leticia served five terms in the House and two terms in the Senate. She moved up to the Senate in November 1999 with the death of State Senator Gregory Luna. Within a few months, she ran again in the regular 2000 primary election and had a difficult campaign against several formidable opponents, but prevailed. Now she represents more people than a member of the U.S. Congress. She also has to raise more money for her campaigns. "One mail-out to just consistent regular Democratic voters costs forty-five thousand." She believes that money doesn't buy her vote, only access. "They just want access. They want to be able to talk to you about their issue. And for me, I have open-door access to anybody whether it's money or not. There's a saying in the legislature when I got there. Of course, it didn't apply to me then, but it basically said of the lobby and the legislative relationship, 'If you can't drink their liquor, if you can't eat their food, if you can't _____ their women, and then have the balls to go out on the next day on the floor and vote against them, then you don't belong in the Legislature.'"

Senator Van de Putte was the chair of the Mexican American Legislative Caucus while in the House; chair of the Senate Hispanic Caucus, and since June 2003, chair of the Democratic Caucus. Leticia Van de Putte is the second-youngest state senator among the Democrats, and they chose her as their leader. In this leadership role, she has been tested to the limit. Leadership to her is "being able to have public value to whatever goal an individual is trying to obtain . . . to convince people collectively so that the outcome really adds public value."

As chair of the Senate Democratic Caucus she organized and executed a plan to deny Lieutenant Governor David Dewhurst a quorum. The House of

Representatives earlier in the 2003 regular session had broken quorum to prevent a re-redistricting bill from passage. Senator Van de Putte calls this re-redistricting because the process took place in 2001 and the judiciary implemented a plan in effect now, when the legislature was unable to pass a bill. There was a second attempt in 2003. The Republicans had a majority of House members, but a minority of Democratic members can break a quorum if they are not present and voting. The Democratic House members went across state lines to Ardmore, Oklahoma, and stayed gone until the regular session ended. The Republicans called a special session, and the House members passed a new re-redistricting bill.

The ball was in the Senate's court. Senator Van de Putte had to come up with a plan to break quorum. The Senate rules are different from the House's rules. In the Senate, a smaller body with thirty-one members, legislation is brought up for debate only if twenty-one or two-thirds of the senators agree. Eleven can block any piece of legislation. And two-thirds of the senators must be present for a quorum to conduct business. The Democratic senators refused to agree to call up the legislative re-redistricting bill. Lieutenant Governor David Dewhurst announced that the Senate would dispense with the two-thirds rule in a second special session to be called. The Democrats were on notice. The governor, with impetus from White House presidential advisor Karl Rove, if not President Bush himself, and Texas Congressman Tom DeLay, called another special session. Senator Van de Putte made plans for a fast exit before the Democratic senators were held hostage in the chamber and forced to be present while the Republicans passed their re-redistricting bill that would give them five to seven more congressional seats at the expense of minority and rural voters. The most junior Democratic state senator, Juan "Chuy" Hinojosa, was able to get friends to loan the Democratic Senators two airplanes with pilots to fly out of state. Under great secrecy and efficiency, Senator Van de Putte prepared the exit and instructed a staff member, Harold Cook, to conduct a dry run of the emergency exit plan. She asked another staff member to rent two vans and park them near the capitol building. A major concern in deciding the out-of-state destination was the health of a senator, Eddie Lucio (D-Brownsville) who had suffered a heart attack in May 2003. A Republican senator tipped off Senator Van de Putte that the lieutenant governor was going to end the session abruptly three days early and the governor was going to call another session immediately. The Democratic senators would be trapped in the Senate chamber.

Senator Van de Putte trusted her instincts and ordered the exit at noon. The senators had been instructed by her to meet at her Austin apartment once the plan was implemented. When she heard of the new special session in the making, she gave the order to exit. The senators gathered and were shuttled to the airport. The airplanes were on the tarmac. "And from the time we decided to break quorum to the time we were wheels up was about forty-five minutes. And they didn't know. . . . We were in the air and the pilots had filed a flight plan for Amarillo, and then we amended the flight plan. OK. We're going to Albuquerque."

Senator Van de Putte and her colleagues, every Democratic senator but one, Ken Armsbrister (D-Victoria), stayed in Albuquerque, New Mexico, for the entire special session. Every day at approximately 10:00 a.m., Senator Leticia Van de Putte would call the senators together for a press conference and conduct the briefing. She stood center stage surrounded by all male Democrats, black, brown, and white, plus another Chicana, Senator Judith Zaffarini (D-Laredo).

The Republicans, angry at their colleagues, levied unprecedented sanctions and fines on the Democrats while they boycotted the special session. It was estimated that each senator was liable for $55,000 each, plus their expenses while in Albuquerque's Marriott Hotel for the month. The Democrats filed litigation in federal court attempting to halt the Republican legislative juggernaut and lost. When the special session ended during the Labor Day weekend, one Democratic senator, John Whitmire (D-Houston), broke ranks. He was not returning to Albuquerque; instead he was going to attend the next special session. The Texas Eleven were now ten, and therefore short of the eleven votes to block. They surrendered and returned to Texas to face the Republicans.

Predictably, the Republican majority voted to pass the re-redistricting bill. The Democrats voted against. The governor submitted the plan for preclearance to the Department of Justice, because Texas since 1975 has been a covered jurisdiction under the Voting Rights Act. And as this writing is done the matter stands there. Regardless of the outcome, some Texas Democratic members of Congress may lose the next election to a Republican; others will not. Senator Van de Putte, however will remain in the Texas Senate for the time being and continue to lead the Democratic Caucus. She is the Chicana in charge.

~

# CHAPTER FIFTEEN

# Socorro "Coco" Medina

Socorro "Coco" Medina became the first female and the first Mexican county commissioner in Potter County, Texas, which comprises the city of Amarillo. But that was a small coup compared to her battle against a multi-millionaire businessman for ownership of a radio station. She beat out the businessman, and she and her husband established one of the first Spanish-language FM radio stations in Amarillo. In both of her capacities, Coco's goal was to inform and represent the Chicano/*Mexicano* population in Amarillo and to give them voice in community affairs.

Coco had come to Amarillo from Mexico when she was just a year old. She was born in Tacambo, Michoacán, where her mother was a pharmacist. After moving to Amarillo, Coco and her parents returned to Michoacán, Mexico, briefly, but they returned to the U.S. again when she was six. Her dad was an orphan and had left Michoacán in the 1920s. He hopped trains to *El Norte* (the North), got off in Amarillo to rest, and ended up staying there and working for the Santa Fe railroad as a coach cleaner. While he was a young man in Mexico, he had worked for a Mexican general, Irineo Rauda, taking care of his horses. He returned to Mexico in the 1940s and married the general's daughter. They had two girls, Coco and her sister, Lupe.

They sent the girls to Our Lady of Guadalupe Catholic grade school and St. Mary's Academy for high school and encouraged them to go to college. Coco attended the Rocky Mountain Art and Advertising Institute and later the University of Denver, where she earned her bilingual teaching degree. She became involved in the Chicano movement through working with

Corky Gonzáles and the Crusade for Justice in Denver, which was founded in 1966 to fight racism, poverty, and the chronic problems they created in the Chicano communities. While Coco was a member of the crusade, it helped to establish alternative schools for Chicano kids and organized mass walkouts of public schools to protest discrimination. "Denver is where I got, I guess, a taste of what it is to involve yourself in the community. And really work hard for the rights of people. And I really enjoyed it."

She taught for a while in Brush, Colorado, before returning to Amarillo. Once she was back home, she helped establish the Amarillo Rape Crisis/ Domestic Violence Shelter because she was very concerned about women's rights and health. One of the cofounders was Kim Pool, whose father was the county judge at the time. Once he got to know her, the judge nominated and named Coco to become the first female Mexican American county commissioner. It was 1968. "And there were several women that he had interviewed. And I was the one who was selected," Medina recalled. On the commission, her biggest achievements were getting a new courthouse built and getting a tunnel constructed between the new courthouse and the old courthouse. But her greatest accomplishment was learning the give and take of politics.

Coco learned quickly that to get anything done, she needed the support of a majority of the other commissioners. She would talk with them, learning about their concerns and building relationships. She noticed that women operated differently in politics than men. She asked a lot more questions than male commissioners did. She was always looking toward the future and weighing the costs and benefits of every move the commission made. There was only one commissioner, Eliza Demerson, who didn't communicate with Coco or the others. Later he would turn out to be responsible for ending her political career. After her two-year appointed term expired, she ran for election to the position but was defeated in a runoff election by Menny Pérez, who was supported by Demerson. Pérez went on to hold the seat for some twenty-eight years.

A few years after her unsuccessful run for county commissioner, Coco decided to run for the position of county judge against Demerson, whom she believed was out to divide the Mexican community

"I did it because I felt like there were a lot of things that Eliza was doing that I didn't think were right. I knew that I wasn't going to win because I was a woman. I mean, you have to be realistic. That was not the time. I don't know if the time is now for a woman to even try to be county judge, but at the time, it certainly wasn't the right time. But I felt like, you know, don't come mess with our community."

So she forced the election into another runoff between three candidates, and the white candidate won. But she saw this as a victory because she got Demerson out of office.

"Oh, you are the lady that always runs and never wins." And I was like, "Yes I won," you know. "I won. What I intended to do, I won." And if nothing else, I showed *Hispanas* in this area, young and old, newborn that now are young adult women that they can too. *Y que* (And that) somebody did it. I was not successful in becoming commissioner, but I was successful in being part of that pool." Another important lesson she learned was that Mexicans have to work with whoever wins the election.

"If you don't get the person you want *y si es Raza* . . . (and if they are Chicano), you make them what they need to be. It's your responsibility. *Ya que están allí.* (They are already there.) It doesn't matter *no le hace quien los puso* (who has put them there). You get in there and you say, '*Hermano* (Brother). You know, you gotta come down. *Y tienes que hacer por uno.'* (And, you have to do for us.) Because who else? And, and I think if, if we take the attitude that *no pos ése no sirve* (well, that one is no good). Oh, we are not going to worry about him. *Pa' la otra lo sacamos.* (Next time we'll get him out.) That's not that easy. We don't have that, that many people. And somebody who already has experience, don't let him go, you know. Work with him. And make him what you want him to be."

After her political career, Coco and her husband, Hugo, set up an immigration rights office. She also became a counselor at Amarillo College, helping to recruit and retain Mexican American students. During this time, she started an organization called *Los Barrios de Amarillo*, which promoted education for the Chicano/*Mexicano* community. The organization had a half-hour program on a local AM radio station on Sundays. They became very community oriented.

"For example, when there was an earthquake in Mexico, we went throughout the Panhandle organizing donations *con una* (with a) with a little van that we have. We used to call it *La Periquita*" (the little parrot).

The program was becoming a huge success until the station was sold and new managers changed the programming. This prompted Coco and her husband, Hugo, to try to start a radio station of their own. They thought they had a chance when the FCC approved a new FM station for Amarillo based on the 1990 census, and when they found a silent partner, a multimillionaire by the name of Kenneth Ramsey. He agreed to put up most of the money needed to start the station and to hire the lawyers to write the FCC application.

The millionaire had all the paperwork drawn up, including a contract that said he would take 80 percent of the profits and that Coco would take 20 percent, but she would have 100 percent control of the station's programming. She, however, would be listed as the applicant to the FCC, since she was a minority and a woman. The FCC was giving her preference because she had been a county commissioner, had run for county judge, and was a woman and a Mexican American.

"So, at first, you know, naive that I was, I thought: Bless his heart! *Pobre señor.* (Poor man.) He's going to put 80 percent of it. And he is trusting me with all this money. And here I am going to be the boss. The guy can't even approach me about anything. So, I called him back and I said, 'You know, Mr. Ramsey, I feel so bad about this. Do you realize that I . . . .' But he insisted on keeping the contract that way." After eighteen months of haggling with the FCC, they were granted the license. She called it Mandujano Communications, after her maiden name. Her next step would be building the station before it went on the air.

But the deal with Ramsey went sour, and Coco had to fight for the station. After she got the license, he basically disappeared. That would have been fine, except that eighteen months later, the FCC required that she file for an extension, and she needed Ramsey's attorneys and money again. He wouldn't return her calls, so she started looking for an attorney herself, and she found out that Ramsey was up to something. He had gone into business with eleven other women with the same 80-20 contracts, just in order to get the licenses from the FCC, and then had sold the stations from under them. Coco tried to contact the other women to try to sue Ramsey, but she could only find one of the women, and she wasn't interested in pursuing a case.

She went ahead and filed the application for a six-month extension herself, and the FCC granted it to her. Meanwhile, she still couldn't reach Ramsey. She finally located him, told him she was about to file a second application for another six-month extension, and asked if he would help, but instead, he tried to buy her out for $20,000 cash. Coco refused and told Ramsey, 'No. I never agreed to be a token. I told you I wanted to build this station. And I am for real.' He said, 'Well look, little lady, you know that you can't do nothing without me.' And I said, 'Oh, I think I can.' He goes, 'What are you going to do?' And I said, 'I am going to forfeit. I will forfeit before I let you have it.' Well, that's all he needed. A week later, I had a lawsuit. They sent it to me by a sheriff. He was suing me because I had put the, the license at risk. I had done those applications by myself. I was not an attorney. I just risked the whole thing, his money, my money, everybody's money I had risked. And so we went to court." The judge put the station into receivership, which is like bankruptcy. Before the judge decided what to do in the case, he let a third party, Bob Sanders, run the station to get it off the ground. Sanders had owned a very small percent of the station. He used Ramsey's consultants to help get the station started and then called Coco when it was time to go on the air, because it was Spanish-language programming, and he didn't speak Spanish. So Coco and her husband went on the air on the embattled radio station during a test mode, and then the station was closed down. The judge had decided to sell it to the highest bidder. But people had already become endeared to the station, and Coco decided to fight for it. Her husband was tired of the fight.

When they shut it down, people started demonstrating in front of the courthouse, People claimed ownership and pride in their first Spanish-language radio station. "It was like ¿por qué lo van a quitar? (Why are they going to take it away from us?) Why? This is the best thing we've had."

Coco borrowed enough money to buy the station out from under Ramsey for $600,000. Hers was the highest bid when the judge opened the sealed bid envelopes. But then the judge changed his mind and decided to auction it off publicly, which made it a lot more expensive.

"There were eight of us. And every one of the people there besides myself were people that were not buying it for themselves. They were experts. They were there to buy it for corporations. Consequently, they knew what they were doing. I didn't. I had never done this before. But I went for it. You know, I thought hey, you know, let's bid. And at the end, I got it at seven hundred and ninety thousand. The next bid was seven hundred and eighty five thousand.

"I did it. And then they gave me ten days to come up with seven hundred and ninety thousand. Ten days."

At first, the judge told her she needed a promissory note, which is like a loan. Then the day before the money was due, they told her she needed an irrevocable letter of credit, which is more like saying she had the money in the bank. She went to every bank in Amarillo and Dumas, and they turned her down. She then went to the richest, most powerful men in Amarillo and begged for the money. One of the men she approached was B. R. Barfield. She reminded him of the many times he had told her on the Amarillo Human Relations Council that he wanted to do something for Hispanics.

Coco told him, "I have the way of making Hispanics life better. I've got the vehicle to inform. So that we can get educated. So that we can mainstream, all of us. So that we can repair our credit, us Chicanos who have lost it. And become part of this system. I have got it." But no one would loan her the money. She got the judge to give her another ten days to try. Menny Pérez, her old nemesis, persuaded the judge to give her another ten days. And during that time, she went to her people.

"And so, the ones that came through were *pura Raza, pura Raza,* (just Mexicans, just Mexicans), just like me. People gave retirement money, special savings that they had, and we came together . . . *el señor Servin,* (Mr. Servin) who is a home builder. He put a signature for three hundred and fifty thousand dollars."

She got the money, and the station went on the air. And white business owners started advertising. They played *Norteño, Ranchero, mariachi,* and some Chicano music. "I consider myself a, a person who fought long and hard for a radio station. And all that I can provide is information. I am an informer. And if because what I inform them of causes them to do good, then good for me. And that's all that I can offer. Inform them to make choices, inform them so they can grow, and be part of what's here for everybody."

One of her major goals was to unite the Chicano and *Mexicano* communities—the recent immigrants with the Chicanos who were born in the United States and whose families were born in the United States before Texas was a state. Her approach to this was in helping to inform and mainstream the recent immigrants and to educate them about Chicano history and struggles.

"I think that if the new immigrants realize what we have been through, and how none of them have to worry about getting a haircut like a lot of our parents did, and how we were discriminated against, they will respect us," Coco said. She recalled the first time she felt the hurt of racism. When she was twelve years old, a shopkeeper refused to sell her donuts. She had gone to the store with her godparent's son, Jesse. "She didn't know how to come and tell us. She finally said, 'You know what? I can't sell any donuts to Mexicans.' And I thought I wonder why she can't? You know, to me, it didn't register. I thought: I wonder why she can't sell it to us? Are we a little special or difficult or what? But Jesse caught on to it right away. He said, '*pos mañana vay a traer la navaja* y (well tomorrow I'm going to bring a knife and) I'm gonna slash their tires.' And that's exactly what he did. And he did it. Foom, foom. Down, down they went. And we ran like heck. And I realize now, I think this is where the hurt began."

Coco said that one of her biggest dreams is to one day see a museum of the Chicano/Mexicano genocide, like the holocaust museum in Washington. "Because we have suffered. We need testimonies of what our parents and our *antepasados* (predecessors) have suffered. We've had it hard, but by golly, we have survived it y *todavía estamos sufriendo la opresión, todavía* (and we are still suffering oppression, still)."

~

# CHAPTER SIXTEEN

# María Antonietta Berriozabal

There are *dos Laredos*, the one on the Mexican side called *Nuevo Laredo* and the Texas city of Laredo. María Antonietta Rodríguez, much later Berrioza-bal, was born in Laredo, Texas. She is the result of the *unión* between two families, the Rodríguezes and the Arredondos. "My *abuelos* (grandparents), my mother's parents and my father's parents, were part of the biggest migra-tion into the United States from Mexico during the Revolution of 1910, and at that time, my, my mother's family lived in a little town near Monterrey, *una hacienda* (an estate) and they were workers, *trabajadores de los hacendados* (laborers for the estate owners). And my father's family was in León, Guan-juato, Mexico, and also *campesinos* (peasants) that worked also for the rich people there. When the Revolution came to Monterrey and both the *solda-dos* (soldiers) and *revolucionarios* (revolutionaries) raided the *haciendas* for food and supplies, they also violated the women. The rich landowners fled, leaving the *campesinos* to fare for themselves. So the peasant families came to the United States, fleeing for their lives."

Her grandparents crossed into the United States at *Nuevo Laredo*/Laredo. Her mother was four years old. But the family kept going; too many other Mexican families were settled on the U.S. side of the border. Both families settled near Lockhart, near Austin and San Marcos. "My mother's family came to a little area near Lockhart *que se llamaba* (called) Clear Fort. When I was growing up they used to call it 'Clio For.' And then my father, they came to Martindale and they called it 'Morondel.' Her dad was only ten months old at the time. The families grew up *en el mismo rancho* (on the same ranch). They met each other because the families grew up together, all the families, extended families, and all, and they met in the *fiestas*. They also met in school, my mother and daddy met when they were about twelve, going to school. They went to a Mexican school, *que se llamaba* (called) Prairie View. This was before the LULAC 1929 suit,[1] so that meant that they were separate and it was a *Mexicano* school."

Her Rodríguez grandfather died from tuberculosis when her dad was twenty-seven and married. "And this was when a big tuberculosis epidemic hit that area. And many families, entire families died. So his brother and his father died, so he became the, the, the man of the family helping my grandmother Sebastiana, who was *Doña Sebastiana*."

Her parents "were married in 1938 and they stayed in the *rancho* and they got their own *casa* as sharecroppers, too." But grandmother, *Doña Sebastiana*, wanted to return to Mexico. The family uprooted and followed the grandmother, but eventually settled in San Antonio. María was born in Laredo on one of those trips back and forth. Her brothers were all born in San Antonio in the 1940s.

Grandmother Sebastiana "went to Mass every day for about forty, forty years, never missed a day. *Muy religiosa* (very religious) but also a woman who was incredible. A woman that didn't like to do house things, like cooking and sewing and feminine things like that. I think a lot of my leadership skills and the vision of what it is to be a leader came from my grandmother because . . . she was the *presidenta de todas las asociaciones de la iglesia* (president of all the church associations). She was the president of the *Guadalupanas* (The Society of Our Mother, Guadalupe) and the president of the *Legión de María* (Legion of Mary), and the *Archicofradía del Sagrado Corazón* (Society of the Sacred Heart), and every association, she was the president." María Antonietta called her grandmother B, and she passed away in 1992. "And as I get older, I feel a kinship to her . . . the idea of a *mujer* (woman) being in her community, being a leader, being active, doing, *hablando* (talking), is nothing new, and I am not the only one. I mean, this is very much in our people, *la mujer fuerte* (the strong woman). Taking her family and nurturing her family, even when the man wasn't there anymore." *Abuelita Teresita*, the maternal grandmother, and *abuelito Melisio*, had stayed near Lockhart on the *rancho*. They died there. *Abuelita Teresita* was most feminine. She liked to "have crocheted things in her house and she like to cook and she made the best cheese spread and she was a very soft, always smelled very good, and she gave me little presents that were like little soaps and little sweet smelling things, you know, she kind of nurtured the feminine in me. And so I got a good combination from both grandmothers. One is like the strong woman that does things outside, but another one is also a love of the home and beautiful things that women can make." And to María, "being feminist, it is, I think two different things. Feminine is *cosas femeninas* (feminine things), you know, language corrupts sometimes, but *cosas de mujer* (things of a woman). Feminist is a political, a political designation, you know, I am a feminist and I am feminine, too, you know."

María and all her brothers and sisters attended Christ the King, a private Catholic school. Her dad worked in the San Antonio area with the Maselli Construction Company until he got injured while working on the Hemisphere '68 job for Lyda Construction Company at age fifty-nine. He was never the same after that. Frank Maselli had a daughter that must have been the same size and age as María because "they would give us hand-me-downs. I remember a pair of velveteen shoes with rhinestones stars from Frost Brothers. Sometimes I had the fanciest clothes of anybody at school." But María was moved by the tragedy of her father's accident. She decided to help her father somehow. As a young girl of fourteen, she was allowed to go to the main city library downtown and read. "I read the biography of Margaret K. Smith. I don't know how I got to her. But she was the first senator (woman) of the United States and I was very impressed with Margaret K. Smith for some reason, and then there was a little sentence that, where she was talking and she said that her first job was as a secretary and that being a secretary is a good stepping stone to any career, and I said, I want to be a secretary."

She went to work right after high school graduation from Providence High School at age eighteen. Her first job was as a clerk at the local S. H. Kress store. But a former teacher nun spotted her, "We didn't teach you all that, that we taught you to work at Kress, so we are going to get you a job at a law office, so I went to work at a law office as a legal secretary for these two attorneys. They were terrible. And I left." She took the civil service test for federal employment and got a GS-4 rating, potentially earning $3,200 a year. She was not hired at Kelly Air Force Base, however, for lack of experience. She found a job during the Christmas season with the Salvation Army typing and stuffing envelopes. She stayed in that job for seven years and started college classes at night. Her bothers, Felix, Louis, and Miguel, had attended St. Mary's University. Her two sisters attended Our Lady of the Lake College. María was helping her father by working. "I went to college at night for seventeen years and it took me twenty years to get my bachelor's degree."

After tiring of the Salvation Army, she was offered a job by John A. Daniels. He was the Bexar County Democratic Party chair and legal counsel for Hemisphere '68. María gives much credit to his strict and precise management style.

Among her responsibilities was typing contracts between Hemisphere '68 and foreign governments, state of Texas, concessionaires, exhibitors, and the U.S. government, as well as translating documents from Spanish to English that arrived from Mexico and Argentina, for example. She quickly realized how valuable her bilingual abilities are. "I put value for the first time on speaking Spanish." She would also attend, take notes, and transcribe lunch meetings between Daniels and his associates. These meetings allowed her to meet many officials, listen, and learn a great deal. Every Friday Daniels would have María call the major, white power brokers in San Antonio and a few *políticos* from the West Side *barrio* for a "pow wow" at the Chameleón Room at Joskie's: Bob Sawtelle, John Scovel, Bill Sinkin, Milton Guess, Blair Reeves, Val Mora, Ruben Munguia, for example.

Mr. Daniels was forced out of the Hemisphere '68 project as a consequence of the statewide battle between liberal Ralph Yarborough and closet-Republican John Connally for control of the Democratic Party. The Connally forces, conservative Democrats, wanted Daniels out. And so María Antonietta Rodríguez, with her strong sense of loyalty, felt compelled to also leave her job. But Daniels just shifted her name from one payroll account to another. He hired her as his executive assistant at the local Democratic Party office. Daniels was running the Hubert Humphrey presidential campaign in 1968. María became the de facto campaign manager for the Humphrey campaign in Bexar County.

An acquaintance and political ally of John A. Daniels was Blair Reeves, the Bexar County judge at the time. When Humphrey lost the election, María was hired by Blair Reeves to be his executive secretary at the county courthouse. She worked for Judge Reeves for seven years and credits much of her career advancement to his mentoring. The scope of her responsibilities included monitoring the social services provided by the state in the county and legal work of issuance of certificate of waivers to birth and marriage certificates. Although she enjoyed her work, her proficiency was hindered by hostile work environments, which included racist coworkers. Older white women would say bad things to her personally and treat the people, Mexicans particularly, with disrespect. She threatened to quit her job; it was that bad. Judge Reeves convinced her to cope, find a way to get through it, continue to help the people; and so she stayed.

Meanwhile, she was involved with community projects and educating her neighborhood on such things such as politics, education, social services, and labor issues. She began aligning herself with local Chicano activists such as members of La Raza Unida Party: Rosie Castro, Mario Compeán, Fernando Pinon, and Gloria Cabrera, to name a few. María had always been politically active in getting out the vote in her local precinct "when Joe Bernal was running or when Henry B. was running or whoever . . . I know that we worked our precinct and delivered it, you know, and we would used to take credit for it, for delivering our precinct. Because we knew the people from church and those were the ones who vote. People in church vote and we knew the *familias*, you know, so I was involved in that politics, so I knew who Joe Bernal was and I knew who Pete Torres was and I knew political people, so then when we were having lunch, and they were talking about political things and about GGL things, and I knew GGL stuff, too, it is like, my eyes started opening."[2]

She worked for Judge Reeves for seven years until 1975 when she married. "I had a mission, remember. I was earning money, and I was helping my father send my brothers and sisters to school. No clubbing, no *bailando* (dancing), no *novios* (boyfriends), no *nada* (nothing). I was very committed to doing something for people, and I loved, loved working at Hemisphere, loved working at the courthouse, I mean, at the, well, particularly with the Salvation Army." The mission was over. "So in May of '71, my last sibling got their degree. I was thirty years old, and not ten months later, I met my husband. And I knew the evening I met him that I was going to marry him, the very evening that I met him." It took three more years, but she did marry him in 1975 at age thirty-four.

She met her husband through the priest at Our Lady of Guadalupe church, Edmundo Rodríguez. Bishop Patricio Flores, the first Chicano Catholic Bishop appointed in the United States, called a meeting to discuss plans for the Mexican American Cultural Center (MACC) to be built by the diocese. Manuel Berriozabal was in town looking for a teaching job at the newly established University of Texas, and Reverend Rodríguez brought him to the MACC meeting. Berriozabal was born in San Antonio but not raised there. His life was spent in Kansas with his mother's German relatives. His first tongue was German, then English, then Spanish. He attended Notre Dame University and obtained his doctorate in mathematics at the University of California–Los Angeles. The problem with Manuel Berriozabal was he still lived and taught at Tulane University in New Orleans. María moved to New Orleans. It was not until this move, that Mrs. Berriozabal got the chance to attend daytime college courses.

Her husband suggested she finally finish her degree while in New Orleans. She had accumulated many general credits over the many years of night school without declaring a major. His advice was to pick something that interested her. She decided on political science as her major, not a big surprise. After nine months in New Orleans, the couple moved back to San Antonio.

Dr. Berriozabal began teaching math and María finished her degree at the University of Texas at San Antonio (UTSA).

While at UTSA she had the opportunity to intern with Councilman Henry Cisneros, who was her representative on the council from the old family neighborhood. Upon graduation in 1979 she took a job with the San Antonio Census Bureau office just beginning operations. The decennial census of the population was around the corner. Ultimately, María became the office manager in charge of 1,400 employees and got to experience firsthand the politics surrounding a bureaucracy.

Her work experience with John Daniels and Judge Blair Reeves made her well suited for this job. Her familiarity with election precincts, neighborhood districts, and her work with the Chicano community provided the many contacts and necessary political clout to take the 1980 census of population in Bexar County. During the count, she learned firsthand the effects of Urban Renewal, or Chicano Removal, as some militants labeled the program. Many formerly high-density Chicano neighborhoods had declined in population from the 1970 census to 1980. Washington bureaucrats called her to recheck her count for the "missing Mexicans." She knew the undercount was not a mistake or intentional negligence of the enumerators, it was Chicano Removal by city planners.

With the census complete in 1981, she was now looking for work. Her plan was to volunteer for Henry Cisneros in his bid for mayor. Many of her friends had other visions for María. They saw her as the next council member for San Antonio. But running for office was the last thing on María's mind. Her plans were to get another job and start work on her master's degree. While at UTSA, finishing her political science major, she had done research for Professor Richard Gambitta, chair of the political science department. The research question was: Why were few Mexican American women in public office? The survey research instrument they administered to Chicanas focused on six factors, ranging from their understanding of their roots to religion and capacity as a leader. The survey revealed that religion and political awareness were inversely related. The more political a woman saw herself, the less religious she was. The more religious a woman, the less political she was. María's experience in her Catholic upbringing was different, her people voted. María never concluded the research, but the work she did for it allowed to her to gauge her own political, religious, and career aspirations. María knew she could be political and have a religious conscience.

The fire was lit inside María's heart to run for the vacated Henry Cisneros council seat, but there was still doubt in her mind. She sought the opinion of respected political scientists from local universities. She was told by several professors, Charlie Cotrell at St. Mary's University and John Booth at UTSA, that running for election required large amounts of money, about $10,000. They doubted she could raise it. "Particularly Charlie Cotrell, he was really, *no me animaron*, and I went home totally feeling very good. I said, I don't have to run. They said I can't do it. I don't have the money. What a wonderful excuse. I can't do it. Political scientists say I can't." She took the advice initially as an excuse for not running. Another major problem against her candidacy was that the position on the city council paid a measly twenty dollars a week in salary. Her husband would have to support her; she was not used to that.

Several events, however, propelled María into the public arena. Al Peeler, former police officer, announced his candidacy for District 1. She viewed him as an outsider, a carpetbagger. The thought that that someone like Peeler who lived and raised his family in Inspiration Hills, a north-side suburban community, could move into her district and decide what was best for them caused her outrage. Ms. Berriozabal came to the conclusion that her thirty-nine years of living, serving, and knowing the people in her community made her best suited for the job, not Peeler. Then, her friend Irma Martínez wrote her a letter, "this is your first contribution and there will be many more." A check for one hundred dollars was enclosed.

That started the money flowing, and soon others were contributing. "To me this was an omen. You know, I said, 'I have got to do it.'" The last straw was lifted from her burden of indecision by a retired lieutenant colonel, John García. He invited her to lunch and asked that she bring her resume. His wife and he interviewed her. They were both very impressed. He called the next day and volunteered to run her campaign office, five days a week, 8:00 am to 5:00 pm. She called another retiree from Kelly Air Force Base, John Alvarado, to manage her campaign. He accepted. A grassroots campaign was in the making. A friend got a former candidate to donate his leftover volunteer cards. Another friend, Sylvia Rodríguez loaned her a book from the Women's Campaign Fund on what to do in a campaign. She began to read the how-to book and tossed it a third of the way into it. Instead she relied on her instincts and developed her Chicana version of the highly successful Emily's List political action committee. "So what I did, I got my wedding list, wedding invitation list, my Christmas card list, and then I sat down and made a list of every person that I could remember since I was a little girl, that I knew and that I had done something with, either went to school with their children at Christ the King, the Mexican American VFW; by then, my husband and I had become active in the neighborhood association movement. People in the church, priests, nuns, anybody that I could think of, and I came up with a list of 800 names and I gave them to Dolores to type them on the little card."

She called a meeting of volunteers. "I scheduled a meeting. *Sociedad de la Unión* (Society of the Union) was the only place that I knew then because the church wouldn't lend you the facilities, right? I didn't even try." At that first meeting fifty persons showed up from the volunteer card list. She organized them into committees. "One committee was going to be, like block walking, another committee was going to be fundraising, one committee was going to be, I forgot what the committees were." With the help of her parish community, neighborhood organizations, the various women's groups she belonged to, and the former activists of the Raza Unida Party, she was able to enlist all 800 people on her volunteer cards and mobilize them in political walks, rallies, fundraising, and the tasks necessary for an effective campaign. Luz Escamilla, founder of the Mexican American Business and Professional Womens' Club became her fund raising chair. Additionally, what María may have lacked in political campaign experience she made up for in determination. The thought of being the first elected Chicana councilwoman in San Antonio was a motivating factor for her.

The idea of bringing politics to new people was a great source of pride for María. Her campaign was a success. "I was told by Cotrell and Gambita that I needed to raise at least ten thousand dollars. I raised thirty-nine and I had money left over. I had money left over at the end." She made the runoff with Peeler. He got 46 percent of the vote to María's 44 percent. In the runoff election, she trounced him with 55 percent of the vote. María Antonietta Rodríguez Berriozabal became councilwoman for District 1 in San Antonio.

Becoming an elected official where she grew up and knew both the people and their concerns was a wonderful ideal. "To be an elected official is a noble thing. It is an honorable thing." Her tenure as councilwoman spanned just over ten years. Her stance against the water reservoir and nuclear projects made her an enemy of the business sector and the neoconservative politicians. Applewhite, a water reservoir, was defeated with her help. Businesses had already invested several hundred thousand dollars to start the project, only to get defeated. To this day, these two issues divide the city of San Antonio. She judges her success on what she accomplished on the city council and what she learned from both success and failure.

She was successful because she gave political legs to constituents who otherwise had been crippled by the political process. She reached out to her constituents and felt it her duty to educate them and empower them politically. She failed in that she isolated herself from other *políticos*. She chose to be with the poor people, not the business interests. This posture did not help her bid for mayor.

President Clinton was considering Mayor Henry Cisneros for secretary of Housing in his first administration, and he was appointed. Henry while on the city council or as mayor was not a housing person. "It is funny. When Henry got anointed by Clinton to be secretary of Housing, they had a party for him at the palace, the governor's palace. And my husband and I were invited. I hadn't seen him in a long time and when he looks at me, he says, 'María, can you imagine,' and both of us at the same time said, 'housing?' He says, 'there is nobody . . . is there anybody that know less about housing than me?' I said, 'I know, that is what I was thinking.'"

The mayor's seat was going to be up for grabs. The seat of mayor was a natural progression for María. It would allow her to serve her district and broaden her reach to the rest of the city. Her grassroots campaign was still strong. She still had lots of support from the community. She had a new, strong finance manager in Frank Herrera, local millionaire attorney. Lionel Soto, the advertising guru, was eager to help María with her campaign for mayor. Lionel Soto had experience doing political advertising campaigns for Ronald Reagan, George Bush, and other Republicans. He became her campaign manager and a major financial donor as well.

María ran for mayor on a platform of economic development and human capital investment. By this she meant investing in the community, both in people and infrastructure. Improvements in education, neighborhoods, and community involvement, which were mainstays of her tenure as councilwoman, were now resonating in her campaign for mayor. Professor Richard Gambita became her pollster. Lionel Soto came up with a simple, direct, campaign logo and theme: María for Mayor.

The reality of running for a bigger office is that you must appeal to big business as well as to grassroots constituents. She raised $400,000 in her campaign. Frank Herrera loaned her $50,000 and Lionel Soto $75,000. An ophthalmologist delivered a $10,000 check, others $1,000 checks. The opposition, however, raised $700,000 and spent it going after María. She got free media on Spanish-language radio and television with her friends Mateo Camargo and Marta Tijerina. The opposition bombarded her via the English-language media with their messages of ominous warning about "María for Mayor." In her earlier race against Peeler she had marched against the police murder of a man named Santiscoy. The paid media advertisements reminded the voting public once again of her antipolice role. The paid media also reminded voters that María opposed Henry Cisneros in most projects, such as the nuclear plant, Applewhite, Fiesta Texas, the Alamodome, for example. "It was like those were all their votes, all their successes, all their big wins, and I am on the other side, you know." Unfortunately for María, while being on the other side, she had made enough enemies in the business community that it cost her the election for mayor.

When Henry Cisneros decided to run for District 1 in the 1970s, he was endorsed and supported by the Good Government League. Mayor Lila Cockrell, the first woman to hold that position in San Antonio, mentored him while on the city council. When Lila stepped aside it was Henry that got the endorsement of the remnants of the Anglo political machine, the GGL, and Lila Cockrell. Then, when Henry decided to vacate the mayor's seat, he nods in the direction of his old political *madrina*, Lila Cockrell once again. Three major political figures and some minor players square off in the mayoral race: María, Lila Cockrell, and Nelson Wolfe, plus six others. The charter amendment calling for term limits is also a ballot measure. The voters will turn out.

"So it was just one Mexican and all of these Anglos, men and women, and boy, you talk about an education in my city and racism. The first question and a big gathering, a question to Mrs. Berriozabal, 'Do you think you will be capable of representing the whole city?' Then I answered, 'oh yes.' And then afterwards I said, 'are you going to ask the question to all of us?' I am the only *Mexicana* and I am the only one that is asked can I represent the whole city. We are 56 percent of the population."

Term limits passed and María received 30 percent of the vote; Wolfe received 26 percent, and Lila Cockrell received 24 percent. María was in a runoff election for mayor against Nelson Wolfe. In the second election, María only received 47 percent of the vote to Wolfe's 53 percent. María claims to this day that people who voted the first round for her were tricked into not voting for her during the runoff. At the polls they were told if they had already voted for her once, they could not vote for her a second time. Many of the Chicano political leaders, men, and "Hispanic Chamber types" did not support her. Instead they cut their deals and supported Nelson Wolfe. She names names: Ciro Rodríguez, now a U.S. Congressman; Henry Cisneros, now a convicted and pardoned felon developing private sector housing projects; Yolanda Vera; and Frank Wing.

María is humble about the loss for mayor and proud of her career in politics. Today, she continues to focus on her desire to mentor the women leaders of tomorrow. She has passed the leadership mantle in the organization she founded, Hispanas Unidas, to a younger woman lawyer. She organized a tour of the city, "María's Social Political Tour of San Antonio." "It is a six-hour

tour and I started it at the missions and I ended up in Fiesta Texas and before it is over, you know who runs the city. Seventeen white men who run the utilities, who have the biggest businesses, who run the television stations, the newspaper, the developers, you know. They run it and they decide who gets elected."

María gave politics one more try in 1998 when she ran for the vacant congressional seat left by Henry B. González, the Twenty-first District. In the hotly contested Democratic Party primary election seven candidates filed, including three formidable persons: State Representative Christine Hernandez, former city councilman Walter Martínez, and District Judge Charlie González. María made the runoff as did Charlie González. However, María lost to Henry B's son, State District Judge Charlie González, in the April 14,

1998, Democratic Party runoff election. María garnered 37.86 percent of the vote.[3] The powerful interests may still run San Antonio, but the María's of the world are giving them a run for their money. Life has been good to María. She served as president and board member for the National League of Cities. She also was a representative at the United Nations Fourth International Women's Conference in Beijing, China. Ms. Berriozabal is affiliated with the Center for the Study of Women and Church and Society at Our Lady of the Lake University. This university has begun an archival collection of her public papers. Friends circulated a paper she wrote about San Antonio politics, "In Keeping Secrets," which was eventually published in La Voz, a publication of La Esperanza Peace and Justice Center.[4] She has taught at Harvard University. A former Harvard student is now teaching at Palo Alto College in San Antonio and is on the fast track running for public office.

She believes that mentoring young Chicanos gives them an edge. She had to learn firsthand about politics, through experience and trial and error. She has had to overcome many barriers and stereotypes because she was one of the first Chicanas in the public arena.

Ms. Berriozabal founded the Santuario Sisterfarm, a space in the Texas Hill Country, which has been created by women to promote a holistic understanding of justice, which embraces social justice principles, cultural diversity, and biodiversity. In addition, she serves on the board of the newly created AGUA of San Antonio and is part of a cadre of citizens, including many young people, who are promoting principles of sustainable development, human rights, economic justice, and values of cultural diversity. María regularly speaks before groups, particularly Latinas and students, and continues her mentoring of young people. María spends the major portion of her time on her family life with her husband, Dr. Manuel Berriozabal, professor of mathematics at UTSA. She has helped him defend programs he initiated at UTSA.[5]

She is primary caregiver for her elderly parents.

## Notes

1. LULAC is the acronym for League of United Latin American Citizens. LULAC was organized in those years. Some historians peg the founding in 1927 in Harlingen, Texas, while others 1929 in Corpus Christi; regardless LULAC did not file suit in 1929. Mrs. Berriozabal probably is referring to the litigation styled *Guadalupe v. Bastrop* (1939) that attempted to end the segregation of Mexican children in the Texas public schools.

2. The GGL, Good Government League, was the white power structure in San Antonio politics for decades. During this time the head was Mayor Walter McAllister, also owner of the San Antonio Savings Association (SASA).

3. See www.sos.state.tx.us for returns of state and local partisan elections. Go to 1998 Democratic Party Run Off Election.

4. See www.esperanzacenter.org October 2003 for edited version of her article on San Antonio politics.

5. See www.saveprep.com.

~

# CHAPTER SEVENTEEN

# Trini Gámez

At a young age, Trini felt obligated to help people and to fight back against racial discrimination. When she was a ninety-eight-pound teenager, short and skinny, she helped advocate for a group of Mexican workers who had been cheated. "I was walking downtown and I saw—This must have been in '52—a bunch of *Mexicano braceros* (temporary workers named for their arms because they did manual labor) that they would bring to pick cotton. And they ran into me and they asked me if I spoke English and I said, 'Yes.' And they said, 'Well, we have this check and we can't cash it. We don't know what to do.' Well, the lady had not signed the check. And they, they all had a check. So it was just, I don't know, intuition. I don't know what took me into the attorney's office because I didn't even know what the attorneys did. I didn't know anything about the law. So I just walked in there to Cowsert and Bybee. I saw Attorney At Law. And so I walk in there and I said, 'Look, this, this lady gave these people their checks, but she didn't sign them. And they can't cash them.' So they looked at the checks. And they knew the lady so they called her up right away. And, so they went back and got their checks cashed."

That same lady rancher made a habit of not signing checks. She hired undocumented people from Mexico and kept them on the ranch for months working for no pay. A year after Trini's first run-in with the woman, she had another. This time, her father-in-law sent her husband and her brother-in-law at about three in the morning to pick up a family from the woman's ranch because the woman would not let them come into town.

Trini, a tenth-grade dropout, learned that she had a little bit of power to make things right. "I learned something there, you know. I learned everything the hard way just working with the people. I would run into problems and I would try to help them solve their problems. And I learned a little bit all the time."

Trini's family were migrant workers. Her mother, María de la Luz Sánchez, was from Silao, and her father, Roberto Hernández, was from León, both cities in Guanajuato, Mexico. Her parents crossed into the United States in 1928 before she was born. Trini has four sisters and a brother. She was born in Yorktown on May 1, 1929. But she was raised in Mount Column about twenty miles east of Waco. The Hernández family lived in San Antonio for a couple of years, beginning in 1945. Trini lived with her family until she met Refugio Gámez. Refugio's father, Baldomero Gámez, was a crew leader. The Gámez family also were migrant workers. They were from Saltillo, Mexico, and had crossed into the United States earlier in 1921 or 1922. Their oldest son was born in Mexico, but all others were born in the United States. Trini quit school and eloped with Refugio in 1947. She traveled the migrant stream with her in-laws and husband. "My whole family were migrants and my in-laws were migrants, so that was how I got to Hereford."

The migrant Gámez family settled in 1955[1] in Hereford, Texas, in the Panhandle. Trini Gámez lived there for the rest of her life. Trini and Refugio had nine children. "Juliana, Juan Francisco, Cecilia, Baldomero, Américo, Alma Belia, Carlos Eduardo, Horacio, Patricia Angelica are my nine children." The kids worked in the fields also. "My five, first five, all worked in the fields. The last four were the ones that didn't work much. My kids were migrants for a little while until I decided to stay home with them for them to go to school." Little by little, she started getting involved with the school system by becoming a room mother and a member of the Parent Teacher Association (PTA). "Then, I was hired by the school system as a teacher aide in the late sixties when bilingual education programs started." Parents would seek her out and "they began to use me because I was bilingual." Her experience with the schools opened her eyes to injustice. "That taught me a lot. I could see perfectly what was happening." Children who had come to school so bright and enthusiastic, speaking two languages, would suddenly become school dropouts in the seventh or eighth grade, because of the oppression they were subjected to in the school system.

"There were times when we had 80 percent *Mexicanos* in the school system. And out of 80 percent of two hundred graduates, *Mexicanos*, but only two of those would go to college. And all the others would end up working as cashiers at a grocery store or custodians or something like that. What does that tell you? That they were not prepared for anything. It was just, it's pathetic. And that angers me. That used to anger me. It still does because it is still happening."

In her young adulthood, she was asked to contribute a paragraph for a little history book about Hereford, where she grew up. "I wrote for my family and I mentioned that those were the best days because it was a peaceful time. We were a peaceful people. We were working people and we lived happy at the labor camp. And so they quote me as saying that." But then the authors added their own words and meaning to what Trini had described. They said that the peace Trini was describing was contrary to what others believed about the labor camp being a place where crime was harvested. "So, they were labeling us since way back when. Since we came as migrants. And when I found that, I thought, you know, this is why there is so much anger in me." That kind of anger prompted her to do many things.

"I could do a lot of things if I, if I had the, the things to do it with. The money and stuff like they have. It's, it's, it is just frustrating. Very frustrating. And it's more frustrating because I don't see enough people that care. That care enough about it to, to get up and do something: Holler. This is enough!"

The people that ran the school system where she was a teacher aide also used her. She explains, "They were friendly and asked me to do a lot of favors. And during campaigns they wanted me to help register people and get the people out to vote and all. And since I was a Democrat, well I was used. I know I was used because when I decided to do it myself, I had no friends to vote for me. That's when I understood all about politics." The problems she had seen in the school system and the fact there were no *Mexicano* political representatives are what prompted her to seek public office. Trini ran, unsuccessfully, for many positions. "I ran twice for the school board. I ran once for the city commissioner, and I ran for county judge in '94. And, but all this time, I, I knew I was not going to win because I could see the people just, you know. I don't know if they, they didn't care or they just, maybe they didn't know enough about politics. And they tried to save their jobs. That's mostly what worries people even today." It is hard to believe that in this day and age in the United States people are afraid to vote for fear of economic retaliation by their employers. Trini insists this is the case in Hereford. "When President Clinton ran for office, Holly Sugar told their employees that if they voted Democrat, they wouldn't have a job the next year. So, the people didn't vote."

Trini wanted to change the school district. She knew that as teacher aide she would lose her job in order to run, but choosing to lose a job is different from being fired from a job for voting, and voting against the employer's wishes. Both times she ran for the school board, she lost. "I was seeing all this all this time, but my friends couldn't see it. We would talk and they would say, "Yeah, we will support you. We will support you." She tried organizing volunteers, but no one would show up to the meetings she called. She turned her organizing efforts, instead, to redistricting so that *Mexicanos* would have more voting power in their neighborhoods. Elections for school board and the city commission were at-large, meaning that the whole city would vote for each position, rather than being divided into neighborhoods or districts that would elect their district representative. There were no single-member districts in Hereford. Voter fear and lack of opportunity to run in single-member districts caused Trini's defeat time and again. The Voting Rights Act of 1975 required single-member districts, but Hereford refused to comply with federal law. Because this was happening in several parts of Texas, a group of Chicano organizers decided to meet in Lubbock to come up with a plan. Trini met with Paul Abalos and Froy Salinas, then a state representative, and with Willie Velasquez of the Southwest Voter Registration Education Project (SVREP).

Trini's sons, three of them, had joined the navy in the seventies. In 1978 Américo, her third son, returned home from the navy with an honorable discharge. He drove Trini and friends to the gathering in Lubbock. Life would change radically for all of them as a result of this trip. "When we started hearing all of these things, you know, we were excited. This was the first time we had ever heard anything about gerrymandering and how the lines were drawn and all this, you know. And then, when the speakers were finished, then they said, 'Well, OK, we want to know if you are ready to go, you know. We want plaintiffs.' So everybody was real quiet. And Américo just looked at me. He knew I wanted to do something. And, so I asked him, I said, 'Will you do it?' And he said, 'Sure.' I said, 'Go ahead. Go for it.' So, then they warned us that there could be retaliation and all. So the heck with it, you know. You live at home. You know, we can eat beans the rest of our lives. I don't care, you know."

That day three plaintiffs from Hereford were signed up to file a voting rights lawsuit forcing the governmental entities to redistrict for single-member districts: Américo Gámez and Cecilia Gámez, both Trini's grown children, and Oralia Guzmán, her friend. Both Oralia and Trini were single parents. She and Refugio had separated that same year, and she was raising her younger children by herself. He opposed her political involvement. "He was totally against everything I was doing. I think that's why we finally separated. Because we just disagreed on everything. It was, well, he, he is illiterate, you know. And that's a big gap between us. He just couldn't understand me. And

I couldn't make him understand and, and the kids, it was hard for the kids. He just finally, slowly moved away from home." Trini and Refugio remained legally married. Trini said she didn't have the money to file for divorce.

SVREP filed the single-member redistricting lawsuit. The suit made headlines in the local newspaper in April 1979. Américo's name was on the front page along with the names of the other plaintiffs. Since his return from the navy, Américo had gotten a job with the county government as a surveyor, gotten married, set up a household, borrowed money to furnish the home, and his wife was expecting their first child. The county fired him the day after the newspaper article appeared because he was a plaintiff in the litigation.

Trini had to find a job. The city and school district would never hire her in any capacity; she was always running for election to their governing boards. Now her son and daughter were suing them. She was not going back to the fields to work. She had to find something else. She had to help support her family and Américo's new family until he could find another job. Meanwhile he went back to the family tradition of working in the fields picking potatoes and onions. Finally, he took a civil service test and after nearly a year of migrant work, got a job at the post office. He was a Vietnam veteran with college courses, yet unemployable in his hometown. He was almost run out of his hometown.

Trini was very fortunate that the Texas Rural Legal Aid, a legal services program, opened a branch office in Hereford. She found a job with TRLA. "And that's what saved my life because otherwise I wouldn't have lived in Hereford. No one would have hired me. Working for TRLA I learned a lot about the law. And all the attorneys that I ever worked with were great. They were great. They helped me a lot." Trini remained with TRLA until retirement in 1997.

Secure in their new jobs, together the Gámez family pressed on with the redistricting litigation. They succeeded in redistricting the school board and city commission boundaries in Hereford. Trini turned her attention to the county government. It was the county that had fired her son. It was the county that would not hire her daughter. The Deaf Smith County Judge, Bill Simons, a four-term incumbent, had been a radio announcer and a former disc jockey. Trini believed she knew more about the law than he did. She ran for his office in 1994.

The *Mexicano* community in Hereford, Deaf Smith County, had organized a political chapter of the Mexican American Democrats (MAD). *Mexicanos* had been involved with politics since the Viva Kennedy movement days in 1960. Voter registration grants from SVREP, successful litigation against the school and city and county on employment practices, and the impetus from MAD had produced other electoral victories. Trini called a meeting of Chicano leaders in the area to discuss the county races. They had succeeded in getting two *Mexicano* county commissioners elected, Lupe Chávez and Tony García. Trini wanted there to be a third so that they would have a majority on the commission, plus she as the county judge. At the meeting, Trini asked Commissioner Chávez to run for county judge, but she wouldn't. So Trini did it.

Filing for county judge also turned into a nightmare. Trini now worked for TRLA in Plainview, assisting the Texas Farm Workers Union, and lived in Hereford, two different cities, thirty miles apart. On the last day for filing Trini picked up her voter petition with two hundred names supporting her candidacy and sped to the courthouse only to find it closed before 5:00 p.m. Trini and her volunteer, Delia Griego, pounded on the door of David Ruland, the district/county clerk. He opened the door but refused the petition and filing application. He told Trini she needed to file with the Democratic Party chair, not him. The Democratic Party chair was in another city, Wildorado, near Amarillo. They zoomed over to file properly and timely but the Democratic Party chairman also denied the petition and application. The signatures on the nominating petition had not been notarized, a legal requirement. He said, "I tell you what. You go back to Hereford, get that notarized and bring it back. I don't know it." So Trini drove back to Hereford for the notary seal and signature, drove back to Wildorado and filed properly, and somewhat timely. Nobody checked their watches for the time.

"In '94 when I ran for county judge, we were, we were going great. And I had two women who were just great women. They would work to the hours of the night registering people. They would go door to door during elections. Well, what happens? They were indicted for fraud." The local district attorney, in order to stop the Trini Gámez campaign, charged Delia Griego and Grace Gonzales, her main campaign workers, with registering noncitizens, bribery, intimidation, and forging voter signatures on registration cards. Eighteen counts on their indictments. They broke the community spirit to fight. "A lot of elderly said, 'Look, I don't want to talk about this. I don't ever want to vote again. I am not used to this. It scares me to see these people come into my house. And, and threatening us like this. I don't want to go to jail. I have never been in trouble in all my life.' They regressed us twenty years."

Delia left town for Albuquerque. Grace left for Austin. "Everybody left. Because they were so demoralized that the people didn't support them. They didn't want to do anything for them. They didn't want to testify. They didn't want to give any affidavits or anything. And so Jeff Blackburn told them that, that he was plea bargaining for them." Jeff Blackburn was a local attorney that took their case on a pro bono basis. Trini's opponent, County Judge Tom Simons was the judge hearing the case. Delia and Grace without a defense, pled guilty. Each one paid a hefty fine of $1,500 each and accepted probation. They also left town. Grace says, "she will never do that again because *la Raza* (the Mexican people) is not supportive of anything." And Delia "tried to commit suicide. She took a lot of pills because of all the pressures, not only from the, the *gringos*, *que también* (that also), you know. It was her own people, her own relatives telling her how dumb she was. It, it almost broke the marriage." Even after the election the local authorities tried to return them from Austin and Albuquerque and jail them for violation of probation by leaving town without express court permission.

Trini lost the election for county judge.

When elective office didn't pan out, Trini turned to the legal system to fight for justice on other people's behalf. She poured herself into work, becoming a Spanish-language interpreter and advisor with the Texas Rural Legal Aid office in Hereford. She helped the farmworkers in organizing a labor union in Plainview. She assisted with many cases. A most memorable case involved a young woman who had been raped by a local feedlot operator, a rancher. She became pregnant as a result of the rape but was afraid to tell her husband. They had only one child and were not planning on more yet. She told Trini the story of how the rape happened instead. She said the rancher walked into where she worked early one morning when she was alone and raped her. She tried to get the rancher to admit the baby was his, but he refused. The rancher did send her flowers to the hospital. Her husband thought the baby was his until the boy was about six months old. She finally told him the truth because she saw that that baby was looking more like the rancher boss than her husband. He didn't speak to her for a couple of weeks. Finally they talked it over. Her husband loved the child as his. He was concerned that the rancher could claim the baby as his at any time and they would not be able to afford to fight him. Her husband told her, "He's my son. And I am not going to give him up." Trini advised the couple to hire an attorney and file criminal and civil charges against the rancher. But Trini also warned them that the attorneys on both sides of the case would ask a lot of questions they might not feel comfortable with answering. "This man needs to pay. You should do it not only for yourself, but for all these other women that are coming. No telling how many other women he has done that to. Someone needs to stop him." The couple did not press charges or sue. They left town.

Trini's daughter, Alma Belia, has come back to Hereford from living in Chicago. She wants to follow in her mother's footsteps. "She is going to continue where I may leave off, you know, someday pretty soon. Who knows? I am sixty-nine years old. So I don't think I have too much longer to live. But I am going to work as, as long as I can." And Alma Belia is in the thick of organizing a trucker's association to defend their rights before the major growers, feedlot operators, Holly Sugar Company, and others that use them to haul produce and livestock. She is also contemplating running for public office.

When Trini retired from work with TRLA in 1997, she made more time to spend visiting her mother. At the time of the interview, Trini's mother was eighty-five years of age and lived alone. Trini and her daughter Alma Belia had also organized a support group to keep *La Picosita*, the only Spanish-language radio station on the air. And Trini also organized a nonprofit organization to provide services to persons that the legal services program could no longer perform. The legal services programs came under attack beginning when Ronald Reagan was governor in California and continuing when he became president. Legal Aid programs such as TRLA are precluded now from many aspects of litigation, such as advocacy for renters, class-action litigation, Voting Rights Act violations, wage and payroll collections, the stuff of Trini's fights since she was a teenager. The board of directors of this new nonprofit organization named it the Gámez Center.

By the 1998 elections, the Chicano voters in Deaf Smith County had replaced Lupe Chávez on the commissioner's court. Margaret Del Toro was elected the tax assessor-collector and Joe Brown Jr., a Mexican American, was sheriff.[2] And by the 2002 elections, Armando Gonzalez and Sammy

Gonzales had been elected as county commissioners, but Tom Simons was still the county judge.[3] The Hereford City Council now has two Chicanas serving among six city commissioners: Angie Alonzo and Martha Rincon.[4]

Trini has been one to live by the proverb spoken by General Emiliano Zapata, during the Mexican Revolution of 1910: "*Prefiero morir de pie, que vivir de rodillas*" (I prefer to die on my feet than live on my knees).

## Notes

1. Dates, places, and events mentioned in this profile do not match with those cited in Yolanda Romero, "Trini Gámez, the Texas Farm Workers, and Mexican American Community Empowerment: Toil and Trouble on the Texas South Plains," in Emilio Zamora, Cynthia Orozco, and Rodolfo Rocha, eds., *Mexican Americans in Texas History* (Austin: Texas State Historical Association, 2000), pp. 143–55. Also, her name appears as both "Trini" and "Trine."

2. Texas State Directory, Inc., *Texas State Directory, 2000*, 43rd edition (Austin, TX: State Directory, Inc., 2000), p.329.

3. *Dallas Morning News, Texas Almanac, 2002–2003* (Dallas: Belo Corporation, 2001), p.472.

4. The Hereford City Hall phone number is 806 363 7101.

# PART IV

# TWENTY-FIRST-CENTURY
# *ENTORCHAS*/TORCHBEARERS

The twenty-first century is upon us, and the torchbearers of this era are forty years removed from the generation of *adelitas*, the warriors. The collective work of generations in between, Chicano/a movement activist and middle-class, middle-aged Hispanic women, established a solid foundation for the torchbearers. Anthropologists and students of ethnic politics, among others, point out that the third and fourth biological generations tend to reacquaint themselves with their ancestral linkages. This is certainly true of the group of women in part IV. They alternatively identify themselves as Chicanas and Latinas, sometimes Hispanic. They earned degrees in higher education or are near completion; some are single women such as Norma Chávez, a state representative, and Lupe Valdez, the sheriff of Dallas County; some are single mothers such as Diana Flores, a community college trustee, and others are married but childless, such as Gloria De Leon, a talent recruiter, and Lena Levario, a former state district judge. Elfida Gutiérrez, Rosa Herrera, and Norma Villarreal are the ones with a traditional family structure. These women like others before them have also learned to handle the obligations of family, job, community involvement, and of being the influential one in the relationship. They light the way for family and community as the prototype of Chicanas in charge.

Diana Flores began her involvement as observer of the Chicano movement while a student, then housewife, at Texas A&I–Kingsville. Birthing children and putting her husband first in his career/degree track caused her to postpone her higher education several decades. As a single mother and head of household, when a son got involved with the juvenile justice system she joined others in organizing and hosting issues summits for Chicano high school and community college students. These youth summits helped her acquire organizational skills and resource gathering, not to mention supervising, budgeting, mentoring, leading, advocating, and even making food and cleaning after the events. The success of these youth summits gave her notoriety, and she became much sought after by politicians needing expert campaign managers and organizers. She joined the Mexican American Democrats, worked precinct-level get-out-the-vote campaigns, electing the first Chicano officeholders in North Texas, particularly Dallas. She finally ran for public office herself.

Norma Chávez, unlike Diana, is single, but she also had to experience a personal tragedy to get deeply involved in the public arena. In her case, new regulations promulgated by the state over gasoline stations, the family business, caused her grief. The family would lose the gas station. She lobbied and campaigned tirelessly to repeal those rules. Then she realized she could make the rules, and a new political figure was born. She ran and was elected state representative from El Paso County. She is prominent within and a leader of the Mexican American Democrats.

Lupe Valdez struggled with poverty from childhood in the *barrios* of San Antonio and managed to complete college after much effort. She found a home in law enforcement. After a long career with various federal agencies, she sought public office. The odds were against her winning the office of sheriff of an urban Texas county. Dallas has been a conservative Republican bastion comprised of wealthy whites and home to the largest minority group, primarily Latino nonvoting immigrants. Dallas County was an unlikely place for a lesbian Latina to seek such a historically stereotyped macho public office. Her family opposed her decision to run, but run she did and won. She has become the poster woman for Lesbians and Gays nationally and earned the respect of her deputies at home for her competence, stamina, guts, and feminine toughness. Her candidacy and victory has made Dallas County a tightly contested area for Democrats in the years to come.

Corruption and allegations of drug dealing by county officials prompted Norma Villarreal to run for county judge in Zapata County. She was a recent law graduate, but not licensed, when she ran. The election was stolen from her twice, and she had to fight in court for every vote, eventually winning the position. Reform, however eluded her, given the entrenched nature of the system in Zapata County. Norma Villarreal lost her reelection bid as county judge for Zapata County, Texas, again because of opposition from male Chicano Democrats. She has been one of only five Chicanas in Texas to reach that position and none of them were reelected.[1] Only in the 1990s was Dolores Briones of El Paso County elected and reelected as county judge, a clear example of the foundation that Alicia Chacón laid in that county from the 1960s to the 1980s.

Lena Levario was the first in her family to attend college and obtain a law degree. She became a public defender and volunteered in local Democratic Party politics at every election. Ann Richards ran for governor of Texas in the early 1990s and became the second woman to win. Lena worked day and night on her election. She donated money and got others to back Ann. When opportunity arose in Dallas County for the governor to appoint a district judge, she named Lena. But in the 1990s, Dallas County was a Republican stronghold with Latinos and blacks beginning to have the impact of their numbers in the Democratic column. She lost reelection and lost a subsequent try in 2002. Once again she is the Democratic nominee for district judge in 2006. Another Chicana Democrat, Dennise Garcia, won over a Republican incumbent for district judge in Dallas County in the last general election in 2004. With these victories had by Chicanas, Dallas County is becoming Democratic Party territory once again.

All of them, except Gloria De Leon, are holding public office or recently held such a position. Rose and Elfida lost their reelection as school board trustees in Fort Worth and El Paso, respectively. Elfida is now an associate superintendent in the El Paso school district.

All of the women in part IV are active in Democratic Party politics, locally and statewide, Sheriff Valdez being the most prominent and sought after as speaker. In the case of Diana Flores, Rose Herrera, and Norma Chávez, they are also active and hold office in the Mexican American Democrats of Texas. Gloria De Leon has never sought public office; she recruits and trains future Hispanic leaders with the National Hispanic Leadership Institute (NHLI), encouraging them to seek election to public office and make policy. Several of those students have done just that, such as Dolores Briones (NHLI Class of 1988–1989) mentioned previously. These women will continue to carry the torch of leadership and set the example for those that follow into future decades.

# Note

1. See José Angel Gutiérrez, "Experiences of Chicana County Judges in Texas Politics: In Their Own Words," *Frontiers: A Journal for Women* 20:1 (Spring 1999).

# CHAPTER EIGHTEEN

~

# Norma Chávez

Norma Chávez's story is one of identity development. Becoming who she is was a process that unfolded over many years and accelerated when she bought her first house—a real fixer-upper. As she rebuilt her house, she rebuilt herself. Like the house, she had a solid foundation, from her parents, but she and the house both needed buttressing. Everything was there, but it all needed repair. She could easily have gone home and lived a quiet, middle-class life with her conservative parents, but she felt a need to really establish herself as a whole woman of color.

Norma's parents had been raised in that era when they were punished at school for speaking Spanish. So they didn't teach their own children Spanish and tried to fit them in to the middle-class in El Paso, Texas. Born in 1960, Norma attended racially mixed schools. There was no overt racism, but there were undercurrents. For example, she knew she couldn't count on the white students to vote for her when she was nominated in popularity contests. But there were enough Chicanos in the school that she won pretty often. She played softball, volleyball, and ran track. She was also on the student council. She led this sort of idyllic high school life. The Chicano movement of the 1970s completely passed her by.

"I think that my activism was late compared to most of the young people from El Paso. At sixteen and seventeen years old, I was playing volleyball and softball and in a middle-class high school that I didn't feel was divided by racism.

"I was fighting at that age to be within the system that they have and they created. You know, it was not an all-Chicano campus. It wasn't an all-black campus. It was very mixed and we all had to fight for our positions within the high school, and then being a natural athlete, I think that gives the gift of learning how to compete and how to lose, you know. I worked so hard but I could have lost and understood."

Even in college she stayed away from any kind of student activism. She never set foot in a Chicano studies class. College at San Angelo State University is when she first started noticing racism and discrimination. There were no popularity contests to win, so she just became this dark-skinned girl in a sea of mostly white students.

She shared a dorm with a white girl from Lubbock who would tell her, "You don't act Mexican. You don't look Mexican." Norma would tell her, "Look at me, I'm pretty darned Mexican."

The dorms, the local bars and nightclubs were all segregated. She went through a phase of actually feeling inferior and of being embarrassed of her parents.

But college was her way of breaking the umbilical cord with her parents. The custom then was to either get married after high school or go to college. She chose college, even though she wasn't prepared academically and she would be the first in her family to go.

She left San Angelo to attend UT Austin, but then fell really behind academically. She flunked out and decided to stay in Austin selling real estate. This was her way of striking out on her own again, against the wishes of her parents, who wanted her to come home. In Austin, she bought her first house. It was in the *barrio*, and its foundation was sagging. All the plumbing and electrical wiring had to be replaced. Her parents, especially her mother, disapproved tremendously. But bit by bit, with help from her dad, her uncle, her neighbor, and her Chicana friends, she rebuilt it. By doing so, she became empowered and sure of herself for the first time since her sheltered days in grade school.

She had had a streak of bad luck and had overcome the obstacles. The guy she hired to reframe her house ran off with the money. She wrecked her car. Her real estate income was vanishing. Around the same time, her grandmother, Rosa, died. Norma began longing to learn who she was as a person.

"I missed what I had in my grandmother, you know, the Spanish, the culture."

She had always been made to feel ashamed of being dark skinned. Her dad's family had always treated her and her mother differently because they were dark. In her high school yearbook, she was one of the darkest skinned. She had a very good friend who was also dark skinned, and they would talk about how racism begins in their own families.

"I think that when you talk to *morenas*, you have to go through this process and now I love my color."

The process, for her, was buying the little *casita* and fixing it up to make it livable. Brown became beautiful. "It was my struggle and I fought for something, for pride. It was my own pride that it was just not going to be my downfall. I was not going to let my parents have a foreclosure. I was not going to have us lose the house. It was just my thing and it is my Chicana friends that pulled me through, that pulled me through that house. It is Yolanda and Elena and Jeannie who pulled me through."

Buying the house and rebuilding it was a cataclysmic event in her life. It symbolized much of the identity crisis she was undergoing—the not telling her parents how bad the situation was, living with no bathroom and thinking it was normal. It was like living in denial.

"In the process of rebuilding my identity, the house becomes me. It is a rebuilding of myself. The people who really came around and helped me were the, you know, I had moved back into the *barrio*. I had moved back to my roots, even though they weren't in El Paso and it was a real invention to me that our common struggle was right there."

The mural in El Paso of the *mestizo* holds special significance for Norma.

"I think the mural that we have here in El Paso, where it had three images of three faces really is perfect because we come into this world *Mexicanos*, dark, and then as we move into our adulthood, we are confused because society makes us be something that we are not. And then as we go through the circle, we end up with the final product, which is Mexican American. You know, our culture, our ideology, and who we become as a whole and that is kind of what happened to me."

A latecomer to the Chicano movement, Norma began becoming politicized by working as a real estate agent and helping Mexican immigrants to buy homes after they had been granted amnesty in 1985. She saw that many *Mexicanos* were still being discriminated against, even though the amnesty law was meant to protect them.

After fixing her house, she moved back home to El Paso to help her parents. Her father had had a heart attack and couldn't be a truck driver anymore. She helped them buy a gas station, which had always been one of her father's dreams. She helped run the station and after two years, decided to go back to school to finish her degree right there in El Paso.

She started getting involved in local Chicano organizing activities. She had missed the Chicano movement in the 1970s, but was drawn to the funeral of César Chávez when he died.

She saw 40,000 to 50,000 Chicanos there, mourning the labor leader, and felt moved to start working for her community more. She started going to Chicano art shows and was really impressed with Carmen Lomas Garza's work, which shows a lot of images familiar to Chicanos, such as *fiestas* and *piñatas*. Her love of this art became a political statement when she stood up for it in the newspaper. The director of the museum had called the work an embarrassment, which riled the Chicano community. She wrote a letter reaffirming the work. Her outspokenness won her a place on the Friends of the El Paso Museum's board of directors.

"With the Carmen Lomas Garza, what becomes my interest is that she helped me heal my wounds." On the Friends of the El Paso Museum committee, she was the dark one—the token Mexican American representative. Through her appointment, she became principal organizer of a lowrider parade to open the CARA exhibit.

"I think that I have always fought for my identity and my struggle. I used to hate my color. I used to hate how I looked and I think it is because of what they make us feel, you know, she is, you are dark. And I was like, in the other Hispanics that are in this little progressive group, the Friends of the El Paso Museum of Art, they are upper-middle-class Hispanic people and then Norma kind of comes in and is part of this issue and I am organizing around it. We were always treated different because we were dark."

The lowrider parade drew 10,000 people. Some 4,600 walked through the doors of the museum. The museum had never seen so many Chicanos. She organized it by going to the Whataburgers, where the lowrider clubs met, and the lowrider softball tournaments, and talking to all the club presidents. She brought them all to the museum.

"Can we have [sexy girls on the cars] and I said, no, no. I was like, I am not going to exploit the women and me organize that parade. No way man! Because you know how they always have these babes and I said, they have got to be dressed, you know, you can have them, but you have got to have them in shorts and maybe a T-shirt and everything." She got the image of the girl for the flyer from a calendar pin-up her dad had in his garage. She painted a blouse on the girl, and put the image on the flyer. She invited the Chicano Elvis impersonator to be in the parade, and a local Chicano activist to be the grand marshal. There were *folklórico* dancers, children and seniors, floats and lowriders, and a Chicano color guard. A *Mexicana* sang the national anthem.

Meanwhile, by accident and circumstance, she became one of very few Chicana lobbyists in Austin while trying to save her father's gas station, which had added auto emissions testing to the business. She successfully lobbied against bigwigs and in favor of an amendment to the Texas emissions bill to make it possible for small businesses like her dad's to stay in business. During these activities, she was being eyed for political office and for training as an organizer. Through all this, she came out a strong Chicana role model and one of the few Chicano state representatives in Texas.

Organizers approached her from the Industrial Areas Foundation, a Saul Alinsky-inspired organizing network. Through IAF training, she learned the ins and outs of politics, the benefits of dramatizing political power struggles, and of using the media strategically. She put what she learned to use when she volunteered to work on José Angel Gutiérrez's U.S. Senate campaign in 1993.

"We became kind of the red-headed stepchildren of the Democratic Party," she recalled. She was organizing the campaign along with several young people in their early twenties. She was in her early thirties and still idealistic. But they were all in for a rude awakening. Not even fellow Mexican Americans welcomed Gutiérrez's candidacy with open arms. The group came up against the Mexican American political machine in El Paso that was run by Alicia Chacón and Paul Moreno, a longtime state legislator.

"You know, I am not in this political process that they are going through and understanding the machine that they have organized. All I understand is that we have young, young people with a lot of *ganas* who are trying to work on a campaign and we were being blackballed all over town. We were being treated badly. We couldn't raise any money. Nobody wanted to have a check tied to them to your name, you know, because it would get back to the governor and that was kind of new to me," Norma recalled. The "machine" denied Gutiérrez access to the Democratic Party headquarters, even though he was a Democrat, to hold a press conference. Norma turned that rebuff into a very politically cunning campaign move.

"And so the young students, you know, Sylvia, Renee, and Laurie, Laurie's father had a van and I said, go, you know, put the van up against the Democratic headquarters and put José Angel bumper stickers all over it. And then I called the press and I said, they are defacing, they are defacing the Democratic headquarters, they denied José Angel access and they are defacing it, right. We weren't defacing it, but so and then I remember the Democratic Party had a donkey, you know, and I said, come on you guys, go put a bumper sticker on the butt of the donkey, José Angel Gutiérrez."

The campaign couldn't have paid for advertising like it got. It was great. "You got known. People started questioning. I remember even some of the

Democratic old guard, I don't remember who for sure, but there was talk between the Democrats that why were you denied access?"

The old guard's position was that Gutiérrez didn't have a chance of winning. But Norma saw the issue differently. He was already the candidate, so why not take it as far as they could, and learn something from and teach the young people that were motivated to work on his campaign. "Why didn't they allow us to have the passion? We were making their MAD (Mexican American Democrats) meetings very lively, you know? Why didn't they allow us to have the passion and then after you lost, pull us in? They didn't do that, you know, they polarized us, and we actually lost some of the students who never got involved in politics in the end and I really hated that. That, to me, was the biggest failure that we had in your campaign is that some of those students felt that the democratic process, or politics was not worth it. And they were good leaders. They didn't understand the old guard shutting the doors on you."

This experience led Norma to really question the rise to power of the old guard Mexican American Democrats. "What is the purpose of the MAD if it is not to empower our people? If that is the Mexican American political machine, then why do I want to be a part of it? We did not get rid of the patrons, right, to be controlled by the Mexican patron mentality. I mean, we felt like we should all be at the table. And of course, I have gone through this new leadership training (IAF) and I am sitting there saying we should all be, you know, here at the table and kind of figuring out what is best."

After Gutiérrez's unsuccessful campaign, Norma went on to work with the United Farm Workers union. She started after César Chávez had died. She was the public action coordinator, whose job it was to mobilize public support and be part of the press team during the time the UFW had a pressure campaign against Coca Cola, as the parent company of Minute Maid, which was the employer of Florida orange pickers.

The UFW launched the pressure campaign at company headquarters in El Paso. Norma was making $287 a month, but was learning a lot that she would use later in her own campaign.

"In the process of working with the Farm Workers, I learned how to develop the message, and how to keep the message simple. . . . What is it that you want them to do? Call 1-800, Coca Cola," she said. "The UFW is a master of delivering a message with no money, you know, and I know that because I have witnessed the UFW with minimum budget do miracles and move mountains."

As an organizer, you don't get a corporate office. You have to organize to get desks, chairs, and other resources. She enlisted volunteers to help make

flags and posters. After two years, she moved on to her own political campaign when an old college buddy who was working for the Speaker of the
House of Representatives approached her about a representative's retirement. A reporter put Norma on the spot, and in the heat of the moment, she
announced that she would run for this political office.

"The reporter said, 'Nancy McDonald announced her retirement. Are you
in?' And I said, oh, you are crazy. He says, 'Norma, she just gave me, for the
record, she now has announced her retirement. Are you going to run?' And
I said, yes, without even thinking about it. And I think the reason I said yes
is because I didn't want to say no, you know. But I didn't really know why I
was saying yes."

It was 1997. A friend gave her this piece of advice about running: "Make
a list of 200 people that will support you to run for office and if you can't
come up with 200 people, you have no business running. Because that is going to be the rank and file that you are going to try to organize." To make her
list, she went through all the friends and contacts she had made over the
years—as a member of the museum board, the Chicano artists and their supporters, the IAF folks, the UFW friends, the gas/emissions contacts.

"I call a meeting. I say, OK, I am going to make *menudo* and we are going
to have a meeting at Lucy's house to discuss my campaign. I mean, I don't
know what the hell I am talking about. So, we are going to have this campaign and I want to be real community based because I am a community candidate."

"I tell all my family and I tell my mother. You know, OK, I am going to
run for office and they don't know what it means. Right, my parents, and
then I just say, and she is just like, oh, well, I don't want to get involved in
this and that. And I sat her down and I said, mother, I said, I have never been
married and if I were to get married, you would have to organize from the day
one until the day that I got married and I would have to have my parents
there and I have to have you there, you know. I mean, I may never get married. This is it, you know."

Her campaign manager was a young, twenty-something recent college
graduate. She and Norma had very different approaches, at first. The campaign manager had all the plans on a computer disk, but Norma had to see
it, on butcher paper, up on the walls. She took all the pictures off her living
room walls and started taping up the tactical plan.

"I would put up a sheet for the money. OK, who am I going to target
money? Who is going to do the invitations? OK, here we are going to have
my announcement. We need *frijoles*, we need this and that and I had it up on
the wall and I went off to go to do something at the gas station and the next

time that I came back, my mom had filled in names, you know, and my mom understood. So, my mom became in charge of the food committee and we are organizing an action."

She established a core team, mostly of close childhood friends and family. Then she approached one of the members of the old guard, just to test the waters. Since she had not sought or obtained the anointment of Alicia Chacón, the matriarch of El Paso Mexican American politics, she was rebuffed. In fact, the old guard tried picking off her team, and gradually, some of the team bowed out of her campaign.

"It was, my philosophy was that we needed to clean out the weeds, you know, so that the grass could grow," she said. She was up against a deeply entrenched member of the old guard. She raises her filing fee by having a margarita party. She approaches the gas station owners and lawyers for the big donations. She puts on a good fight, raises the money she needs for a grassroots campaign, and wins the primary with 4,899 votes to her opponent's 4,687, forcing a runoff election.

"And everybody is floored. Nobody thought, everybody knew I would be in a runoff. Nobody thought I would lead in a runoff. And so, Dr. Nan calls me, he goes, 'oh yeah, by the way, your dad Norman, he won.' So, my dad, he won for precinct chair. It was real great and, you know what was funny when we did the precinct analysis, what was even more funny, but not really funny, is that my dad got more votes than I did."

In the runoff, her opponent went on the offensive on the radio and accused her of tax evasion, called her a lesbian, and used her UFW organizing history as though it was a negative strike against her. It was an ugly fight. "We have to do a strategy against the negative radio and what I learned is that you attack at the medium they attack you. If they attack on radio, you come back on radio. You have to inoculate. They attack you in the mail, you have got to attack back on the mail." And so the radio spot went like this: "Have you heard the radio ad about Norma Chávez? Nacho says Norma doesn't own a business. Guess he forgot the Chávez' Texaco at Trollbridge. He says she doesn't pay any taxes; it is because she doesn't owe any. What is wrong Nacho? Scared that we might remember that you abused taxpayer funds while sitting on city council? It is time we said No to Nacho. For honesty, integrity, and Norma Chávez, she is 100 percent committed to finishing the job."

She and her opponent had a televised debate. The timing could not have been worse. It was Holy Thursday, before Good Friday, and the debate was on Spanish-language television, and her opponent attacked her for being pro-choice. He dug his own grave, however, by also coming out against educating undocumented children. He tried to rile Norma. "Everybody had told me, 'Nacho knows that you are a hot head. Everybody knows that you are a hot head and they know that that is when you are weak and they are going to go after you to lose your temper.' So, my campaign manager was there looking at me like, don't lose it and I had prepared my twenty seconds, right, and I was furious and all I said is. I asked them for their vote. And that was it. And I left and he and I never talked, we never talked. We were not friends, not alliances, nothing, and I got off and I was furious. Everybody was furious and everybody was freaking out. We didn't know what the implications were going to be. We didn't know, there is no way in Spanish to say pro-choice other than to say, you know, abortion is different. It has a different term in Spanish and we just didn't know, you know. And so, it was Thursday, Holy Friday was Friday. I think that the politics in Texas suffers because whoever sets up the system knows that Mexicans' Holy Week is a Holy Week and politics is not on the agenda, nor is it on the mind. It affects early vote. Good Friday, I wanted to campaign and I couldn't. I couldn't campaign on Easter and the election was on Tuesday. So, we just didn't know.

"My mom is a Christian and pro-lifer and we struggled with that issue and I felt real bad for her because I knew she felt bad about it and I don't budge on being pro-choice. And so, I told Lena, I said, what if I lose tomorrow, you know? And she said, then you be gracious because you have participated in the greatest, greatest thing that the American people have is the right to a collective vote and the voting rights and you be happy because they have spoken and I have been on both sides. And if you lose, you be gracious, you tell Nacho, you know, the best to him, it is the voice of the people. And you remember this experience."

But as it turned out, Norma won, by the largest margin of any candidate in that election. "I just beat him so bad. He concedes. He never calls me. And I take him 64 percent, 6,665 votes to his 3,400." She became the first Mexican American woman elected from El Paso to the Texas State Legislature, and the eightieth woman elected to the Texas Legislature in the history of the state, compared to 4,000 men who have been elected. "I think that that in itself is an empowerment of ourselves and then for Latinas or even somebody like a Chicana."

# CHAPTER NINETEEN

~

# Diana Flores

Diana Flores is a very plainspoken woman. In her opinion, the lack of independent wealth among Chicanos is the chief reason that leaders like her risk becoming co-opted. They rely on funding and jobs from organizations that maintain the status quo. Diana says she has kept from becoming co-opted by remaining poor. She was last working as an ESL instructor while she held the unpaid position of trustee on the Dallas County Community College District Board. Diana is as candid as they come. Code switching[1] between English and Spanish, she tells the story of being inspired by her parents and being motivated in college by her *Raza* in the Chicano movement. But like many Chicanas, she took a long break before becoming involved in politics. During the "break," she raised five children and worked for a living, as well as earned her college degree over an extended period of time. She was the first in her family to do so. Her role as a college trustee has largely been to make that opportunity a reality for the thousands of Chicanos and *Mexicanos* in North Texas.

Diana Flores was born on May 23, 1951, in Palacios, Texas, a small town located on the Gulf Coast. She was not the first generation to be raised in Palacios; both of her parents were born and raised there as well. Diana's parents tried to move away a couple of times, but their hearts brought them back, as the familial ties were just too strong to keep them away. In Palacios, both Diana and her parents lived with institutional racism. They were sent to the Mexican school. Her mother made sure that she learned English at home because she didn't want her children to face the same discrimination that she had faced when she entered school speaking no English.

The greatest problem that Chicanos faced at the time, and still face, is that of low graduation rates . . . or put differently, the high "push-out" rates.[2] Diana cited her family as a prime example of this: "I was the fourth of five [children] and I was the first one to graduate." Her older siblings were: Jesse, who lacked half a credit for his high school diploma; Lucy, who eloped when she was sixteen years old; and Mary Ann, who also married by age sixteen and did not graduate. Lucy's elopement sent her mother into such a shock that she became physically ill and laid on the sofa for days crying over the incident. Diana's mother and grandmother never stopped stressing the importance of acquiring as much education as possible.

For one thing, she was trying to prevent her daughters from doing the same thing she had done, getting married and dropping out of high school in her junior year. For another thing, she wanted her children to have better employment opportunities than most Chicanos/*Mexicanos* had in Palacios. Nearly everyone worked in the shrimp factories, including Diana's father. She remembers it being "a real stinky, dirty, smelly job" for her father, and for the women who worked processing the shrimp. At one point, her father was captain of an offshore oilrig, which meant he would be away from home for weeks at a time.

Diana remembers that her father was the one who instilled in her a fighting spirit—one that demanded that she be treated with dignity. He would tell her that he never wanted his children to feel inferior to others simply because of their Mexican ancestry. Diana remembers her father recounting "stories about how *se peleaba con los gringos* (he would fight with the racist whites)." She also remembers how skin color was such an intense issue in Palacios. Since she and her siblings were light skinned, she remembers being able to feel the difference in school. Lighter-skinned Chicanos had an easier time with the larger community than darker skinned Chicanos. This did not mean that light-skinned Chicanos got off easy . . . because they were definitely treated differently than Anglo students. If an Anglo student did something wrong they would be given a reprimand, but a Chicano could be expelled or even beaten for the same infraction.

Both the black and Mexican populations were literally raised on the "other side of the tracks," as the town was separated by railroad tracks. Diana remembers how blacks couldn't attend the same schools as Mexicans or whites, until she was in junior high, when desegregation started in Texas. When black and Mexican student bodies combined at previously all-white schools, they often forged alliances. At the time, there wasn't much tension between blacks and Mexicans. Instead the two groups would band together to support a candidate for class president (either brown or black). Their candidate would make it to the runoff election, but inevitably would lose once in the final vote against an Anglo. It was rare for a minority to be popular with white students. It was more the norm that minorities would vote for a white candidate. Usually people within minority groups, especially children, will adopt various aspects of the dominant group they are confronted with.[3]

In Texas, many Mexican children acquired a Texas twang accent, some of them more so than others. Diana tells about her older brother: "Jesse is real funny *porque* (because) in terms of our particular branch of the family *somos gueros* (we are light skinned). So you can pass somewhat. Jesse can, if you're among *bolillos* (white people), especially because of how he dresses, carries himself and talks. I mean, he's got that real heavy Texas twang, real heavy." Her sister Lucinda, has resided in Dallas since the early 1970s; Mary Ann, who is married to Serafin Alvarado, lives right around the corner from Diana; Jesse now resides in Freeport.

She remembers how her father would curse a great deal when telling his stories. Another defining memory was a hurtful one—of her father as a real womanizer. This experience would later impact her adult relationships.

Children swear that they won't make the same mistakes as their parents. But often history (and patterns) tends to repeat itself. Within a little over a year after graduating from high school, Diana enrolled at what was then known as Texas A&I University, now Texas A&M University–Kingsville (TAMUK).[4] Diana was not prepared for the major changes college would bring. She was the first in her family to attend college. She did not know how to plan her degree. Her only comfort was that A&I was filled with *Raza* students, where in Palacios, she had been a distinct minority. She loved the new environment, except for an experience she underwent when the *Raza* students made fun of the way she pronounced her name—Die Anna, such as the princess, rather than the Spanish pronunciation, Dee Ana. After a few teases, she never pronounced it in English again. Diana was at A&I during the rise of the Chicano movement. Ethnic pride was abundant everywhere. She was very active in various organizations, including the Political Association of Spanish-Speaking Organizations (PASO) and Teatro Atahualpa de la Quineña (a guerilla theater group that would travel and perform in different parts of the Valley). Becoming involved and falling in love took its toll on her grades. Diana dropped out of A&I with a GPA of only 1.6.

She married her college sweetheart and moved to Houston. The pattern of her father repeated in her husband, and the marriage ended, but not before three children were born: two daughters, Quetzal and Angelita, and a son named Eliazar. He was nicknamed Maco by his grandfather, who called him *Chamaco* (Little Boy). Flores had supported her husband financially while he finished pharmacy school at Texas Southern University by working night shifts at a hospital emergency room in Houston. She saw things there that changed her outlook forever. When her husband finally graduated, he told her he was no longer in love and wanted out of the marriage. This was shocking to Diana since she was raised to believe that a couple should try to make a marriage work. But she felt there was little she could do. Once he left, she had to take him to court several times to obtain child support.

The struggle of being a single mother and raising three children would later become compounded by a second failed marriage in Dallas. This husband was emotionally and verbally abusive. From this marriage, Diana had two more children: Robert Eric and Diane, her namesake. The older children left the home. She said they tired of the stepfather's verbal abuse.

Diana believed she had to endure the abuse for the sake of the marriage and the younger children. But when she realized the degree to which her husband's temper was affecting her and the children, she found a way out. Leaving her second husband was not easy. She had to save money for a deposit on a rental home and until then she had to bide her time. She had asked her husband to move out, but he refused. So when Diana had enough money, she called a few friends who sent over some moving trucks to help her with her furniture. She left and never looked back. Her ex-husband found her and came begging for forgiveness, but Diana remembers telling him, "I'm not a ball. I don't bounce back and forth. You were warned many a time; you didn't take it seriously."

Raising five children was no easy task. She put her education and her activism on hold in order to raise her children. "Everything comes to a stop, I think especially for a woman, because the emphasis has to be on the home and family and well, work." The time she spent in her second marriage after her older children left created a wedge that was hard to overcome. She lost control of them during critical teenage years. Her oldest son became involved in a gang; her two daughters ran off with their boyfriends and married at a young age. So to keep her sanity, Diana went back to school in 1985 on the advice of a friend. She took a job that served dual purposes, as a secretary at the El Centro College where she was attending classes on her breaks. By 1994, Ms. Flores graduated with a college degree from Dallas Baptist University. She finished the coursework for her bachelor's degree with a 4.0 grade point average. "I had to make up for the horrible GPA I had at A&I and I did!"[5]

During that time in her life, the gang problem in Dallas was intensifying, and she worried for her eldest son. "That was when I started getting politically active, was back in the early '90s as a result of what happened

with my son and not wanting to see that happen with other families." She started volunteering with the City of Dallas Gang Intervention Program. She also became involved with Mothers Against Gangs in Crime (MAGIC) and met other people through that association. It was through her work on gang prevention that Diana slowly began to encounter other organizations where she felt she could assist.

Flores networked with other Chicanas, including Maricela Aguilar and her sister Nita during a Chicano and African American Youth Summit. The women clicked and from then on worked on other projects together. One project was a Hispanic Summit in the early 1990s. People from the community came together to discuss the issues that were of most concern to Hispanics in the Dallas area. The issue of showcasing Latino art emerged as a priority, and Diana volunteered to help get funding included for the art displays through an upcoming city bond election. City Councilman Domingo Garcia assured the community that bond money would be appropriated to the project. But his support turned lukewarm when he announced his candidacy for mayor—a citywide election that would require a majority vote—and the majority were white. Naturally, Ms. Flores and others got on the telephones to mobilize their supporters to attend an evening city council meeting. Because of the vast network of contacts she and others had amassed, over 200 people attended, some with picket signs. They all expressed their support for a Latino cultural arts center. In the end, the center was funded through the bond election. Garcia ultimately took full credit for the center. This convenient turnabout would fuel Diana's next political moves.

Diana defines leadership as "being able to take the ball and run and make the changes necessary." One of the ways that she took leadership was in bridging the gap between the Chicano and Mexican immigrant community through an organization called GAILA: *Grupo de Apoyo para Inmigrantes Latino Americanos* (Support Group for Latin American Immigrants), which has since gone defunct. It formed around the time of California's Proposition 187,[6] when activists in Dallas decided to organize before a similar anti-immigrant measure hit Texas. Diana worked for gender equity within the group, which had been controlled by men. She and others forced their way into the decision-making circle of GAILA and prevailed. Women began making suggestions for action and initiating projects for GAILA. The group held a mock election in 1996 for the Mexican presidential election, as a symbolic vote to show that immigrants do care about politics and they would be active if they had the ability to vote from abroad. GAILA and other groups were somewhat effective in tearing down some of the barriers between Chicanos and recent immigrants. Intermarriage has also helped.

Another place where Diana has shown leadership was in her job at CMAS, the Center of Mexican American Studies at the University of Texas–Arlington (UTA).[7] She remembers the exact date she started working there: September 23, 1995. That date would become important later when she became embroiled in a controversy surrounding CMAS. As soon as she came on board, Diana was assigned to organize the Tejano Student Unity Weekend Conference. Her job was to make sure that everything for this statewide conference came out smoothly. She had less than two months to get everything coordinated and ready. Despite the short timeline, the conference turned out to be the largest and most successful, based on student evaluations. After that, she coordinated at least one major event each month. She said the days felt like eighteen-hour days, and the weeks often required six days a week. But it was worth it, because Diana sensed the importance of what the center was doing: "preserving our history—preserving the history of Chicanos in North Texas and statewide."

But that idealism came to a sudden end. The CMAS controversy began when the president and provost of UTA decided to reorganize the center, remove its director (José Angel Gutiérrez), and eliminate Ms. Flores's position. Accusations and innuendo began flying about misappropriated funds from various programming events and mismanagement of university time and computers. Diana recalls that the UTA administration even went so far as to have the "UTA police break into my office that Saturday and take everything." The meticulous records that Gutiérrez insisted on keeping regarding any and all CMAS activities eventually cleared the accusations—that and Diana's computer disks, which showed the dates of certain documents. The administration had accused Diana of using university computers and time to perform her own political activism: including her campaign for the Dallas Community College District (DCCD) board of trustees. Their proof, they said, were the confiscated disks. However, "lo que no se fijaron los pendejos (what these dummies did not take notice of) was that everything they cited predated my official hire date at the university." Although Ms. Flores had proof of her innocence, she was still out of a job. She filed a lawsuit against the university, but court battles are long fought. And it turned out Diana had bigger fish to fry. She had to defend herself against accusations of election fraud filed by her old nemesis, Domingo Garcia, who was now the lawyer representing her college board election opponent Bill Velasco.

Diana won the June 1996 election with 840 votes in the runoff; compared with Velasco's 786 votes. He filed an election contest, alleging voter fraud. A local attorney, Robert Wightman, agreed to represent her pro bono. Diana believed the intent was to deny the will of the people by abusing the law and court procedures. "In this country if you don't have the money for a legal defense, you lose even though you are not guilty of anything, and it is possible to steal an election through the courts if you cannot afford legal counsel." Flores was fortunate to have a volunteer lawyer, because she didn't have any money to pay one. The trustee position was unpaid, so she was scraping by teaching English as a Second Language (ESL) classes. She had rejected settlement offers from the university, hoping to hold out until the truth came out in court. But she had bills to pay and finally was forced to settle out of court. "I'm just sorry that I couldn't hold out and make them, in court . . . show them for the liars they were." She used the settlement money to pay off some debts and to live off of, but had to continue working.

She and Velasco settled the election contest finally, just before her 2002 reelection campaign. He signed a settlement agreement that gave up all his claims to any voter fraud or illegality in the 1996 trustee election.

Her goal as a trustee has been the same since she first decided to run for the office. During her ten years as a secretary, she had tired of hearing high-level administrators "talk the talk but not walk the walk" when it came to increasing student and faculty diversity. She embarked on a very grassroots campaign, making calls, walking city blocks and passing out literature. She had very little campaign funds and did not have money to mail out campaign literature. She raised about $3,000 from contributions and loans. Instead of direct mail, Diana went directly to the voters, meeting and greeting them at early-voting locations such as the Dallas Multipurpose Center and the Beckley Sub-Courthouse. Diana also had the support of the incumbent Steve Salazar, who had left the DCCD position to run for a spot on the Dallas City Council. He assisted with her campaign by working with people he knew in the West Dallas area.

Her next bid for public office was for state representative against her old adversary, incumbent state representative Domingo Garcia, the former Dallas city councilman. Diana decided to challenge him because of the public outcry against Garcia's style of leadership. Flores was able to raise $35,000 to $40,000 dollars, while her opponent had to take out a $50,000 loan. "It's a testament to how disgruntled people were with his leadership." Her campaign felt confident they would win, if by a small margin, because of the feedback they were receiving from the phone banking. "But come election day, it was the total opposite." The vote share for Ms. Flores was 1,340 (39 percent) while the incumbent would take 2,094 (61 percent).[8]

Flores put all her energy back into her work as a college board trustee—this time fighting an admissions requirement that prospective students divulge their immigration status, plausibly for the purpose of determining residency for tuition rate purposes. "We're not the INS (Immigration and Naturalization Service). We're an educational institution and it seems as if we're asking primarily Hispanic students. That's like selective enforcement." After a great deal of educating fellow board members and others about this issue, the board of trustees in August of 1998 decided to strike the residency questions from the admissions application and, further, to charge all county residents the same tuition rates. This board policy went into effect in the spring of 1999, but was not fully implemented until later. Trustee Flores closely monitored implementation to ensure follow-through. This reform later became state law in Texas and elsewhere, and it was subsequently endorsed by the U.S. Senate Judiciary Commission under the legislative bill acronym D.R.E.A.M Act.

Diana's focus on increasing student, faculty, and administrative diversity also paid off. In 2003, the DCCD was cited by the Texas Higher Education Coordinating Board for having the largest increase (48 percent) in enrollment of Chicano/Latino students compared to all other colleges and universities in the state.[9] With these accomplishments on her record, Flores won her 2002 bid for reelection. She will continue to champion her educational equity causes.

She also continues her broader political equity work. In 2001, she was one of several organizers who formed People United for Representation and Equality (PURE) to work on redistricting in Dallas County. The group met monthly and monitored the redistricting processes in the city of Dallas, the county, Dallas Independent School District, the state legislature, and U.S. Congress. Members of PURE formed committees to monitor each governmental unit. The members provided testimony, submitted proposed maps to all of these governing bodies, and found money to bring a lawsuit against the school district. Their efforts resulted in an additional Hispanic city council district. The lawsuit against the Dallas ISD is challenging that institution's failure and refusal to provide additional Hispanic representation on the school board. Chicano and Latino students are the majority of the student body. Chicano and Latino parents are the majority minority population in the school district, yet only two seats come from majority Hispanic districts. The group's goal is to guarantee equal representation by 2010.

Diana Flores is a woman who has struggled in almost every aspect of her life, but who has been able to maintain the spirit of a survivor. It is her unique ability to laugh at her circumstances that helps her maintain her sanity during tough times. She not only keeps herself motivated but also motivates others in the process. Her endeavors and their legacies are a testament to her tenacious character and her enduring courage.

# Notes

1. Florence Barkin, *Language Switching in Chicano Spanish: Linguistic Norm Awareness: Social and Educational Issues in Bilingualism and Biculturalism* (Washington, DC: University Press of America, 1981); Margarita Hidalgo, "Language Contact, Language Loyalty, and Language Prejudice on the Mexican Border," *Language in Society* 15:193–220.

2. The interviewer (José Angel Gutiérrez) and the interviewee (Diana Flores) used this term during the course of their discussion.

3. G. Roysircar-Sodowsky and M. V. Maestas, "Acculturation, Ethnic Identity, and Acculturative Stress: Evidence and Measurement," in R. H. Dana, ed., *Handbook of Cross-cultural and Multicultural Assessment*, pp. 131–72 (Mahwah, NJ: Lawrence Erlbaum, 2000); G. R. Sodowsky, E. W. Lai, and B. S. Plake, "Moderating Effects of Socio-cultural Variables on Acculturation Attitudes of Hispanics and Asian Americans," *Journal of Counseling & Development* 70:194–204.

4. Texas A&M University–Kingsville: http://www.tamuk.edu.

5. Telephone interview, Nov. 7, 2003.

6. California Voter Foundation: http://www.calvoter.org/archive/94general/props/187.html; CNN: http://www.cnn.com/ALLPOLITICS/1998/03/19/prop.187/.

7. University of Texas–Arlington: http://www.uta.edu.

8. Dallas County Elections Department http://www.dalcoelections.org/archived results/primary2000finalcum.rtf. The quotes attributed to Ms. Flores in pages 210–211 are from the telephone interview cited above in note 5.

9. Preliminary report on progress toward the participation and success goals of *Closing the Gaps by 2015* presented at the April 2003 board meeting of the Texas Higher Education Coordinating Board, Austin, TX.

# CHAPTER TWENTY

~

# Gloria De León

Gloria De León is the youngest of five sisters born to Juan and Herlinda De León on December 16, 1952, in McAllen, Texas. Her father was born in Robstown, Texas. This side of the De León family came to Texas in 1924 from Matamoros and Adelfonso, Mexico, in 1836. Her mother's side of the family came from Doctor Arroyo and Saltillo, cities in Mexico. Ms. De León spent most of her childhood in the Rio Grande Valley.

Her parents worked *en las bodegas* (in packing sheds) and did seasonal work. Her father sacrificed so that his daughters received a high school education. He wanted them to have indoor jobs in offices, not working in the fields like him. Most migrant families withdrew their children from school in the late spring and made the trek to northern states in search of work. Juan De León went alone. He was not about to interrupt the girls' schooling. He picked cotton in Floydada, Texas, and fruit in California. Her father worked and sent money to the family. The De León dream came true; eventually all of the girls graduated from high school.

Being the youngest, Gloria was in high school when her older sisters were married with families of their own. Her older sister interceded with the parents about sending Gloria to college. Her sisters and their husbands were having a hard time making enough money even though they were working full-time jobs making minimum wage. They knew that just having a high school education was not enough in this society. They encouraged their parents to send Gloria to college. The turning point in Gloria's life was Operation Service Employment and Re-training (SER), a joint job training program of the American GI Forum and the League of United Latin American Citizens (LULAC).

The SER programs included prevocational training for students that were in high school or had dropped out of high school. By the time Gloria graduated from high school in 1971, Operation SER had started a program for high school graduates. She enrolled in that summer program and got involved with two individuals, Anola Cantu and Frank Castellano. They took an interest in Gloria. They thought she had potential. She didn't have plans to go to college, however. Her family, along with the teachers with Operation SER, encouraged her to enroll at the University of Texas–Pan American. She attended this college from 1971 to 1974. She loved the learning environment in the School of Social Work and took classes year round without summer breaks and graduated early.

Her first job was with the Regional Planning Commission for the Lower Rio Grande Valley Development Council. She met the political elite of the region: county judges, county commissioners, and mayors. They were the members of the board of directors for the Lower Rio Grande Valley Development Council. She got to meet a lot of them: Michael Allen, Buddy Ruiz, and Greg Montoya, for example. She also met her husband, Wayne Ewen, in 1976 while working with the Development Council. He worked with the Texas Commission on Alcoholism as an educational specialist. She was the regional coordinator for alcoholism and drug abuse with the Development Council. That's how they met. They married six months later and relocated to Austin. The marriage did not last long, not even a year. Wayne was very violent. She left him quickly and divorced.

She remained in Austin and sought a government job with the state of Texas. She landed a position working at the Department of Community Affairs. Her second husband, Ernesto Nieto, worked there also. Unlike Wayne, Ernesto was an older man with four kids from an Anglo wife. He was also divorced. Her family objected to this relationship, but after they got to know him they realized that he was a very different kind of man than the first husband. The family accepted him.

Gloria never took on her husband's name. As a child she had promised her father she wouldn't. All girls and no boys in the family meant no De León offspring to carry the surname. So, she kept her own De León name. Besides, by the time she married Nieto she had already bought her house, established her credit, and enjoyed a professional life as Gloria De León. She felt that marriage was a status, not an identity. Ernesto Nieto, as husband had became a part her life, but first and foremost she was the child of her parents. Together, Gloria and Ernesto have developed a fantastic leadership training program called National Hispanic Institute (NHI).[1] It was Ernesto's brain-child but Gloria's unpaid labor and money that brought the program to fruition.

In 1979 through 1981, Ernesto developed a management-training series for young, professional Hispanics coming to find work in Austin. Ernesto felt his skills and ideas were not utilized effectively by Anglo managers working in state government; that frustrated him. He had also been fired from his job and found the experience demeaning and depressing. In doing the management-training programs for young professionals he focused on dealing with the various sources of stress they endured and encountered. Many of the Hispanics coming to Austin were from the Rio Grande Valley, and first-time managers in state government. They were going through culture shock, because they didn't quite seem to fit in, neither in Austin nor state government. They didn't have the ability to be seen, to be integrated or accepted into what they were doing. There were no peers or mentors, and staff looked to them for leadership. Ernesto thought he had the handle on how to overcome these barriers and developed a training model. While Ernesto began these training programs, he sought out a variety of individuals to help him and Gloria bring organizational shape to what they were doing and a strategic plan of where they wanted to go with the organization.

One key individual was Dr. Roberto Jimenez, a psychiatrist from San Antonio. He urged them to really think and experiment with what they proposed to do for the Hispanic community. Those enrolling in their early program were young adults in ages ranging from twenty-seven to thirty-five, who were burned out and pretty much set in their ways. They had developed a very clear understanding of whether or not "the system" was going to be accommodating to them or allow them to integrate. Anger had set in, and they became almost disabled. They were unable to mobilize themselves into being effective community leaders.

Those programs were the founding of NHI more than twenty years ago in Austin, Texas. Gloria and Ernesto recruited sixty students for the Young Leaders Conference and about thirty young professionals in 1981. The following year the young professionals assisted in the training of high school students. "The culminating event of the Young Leaders Conference that year was a three-day program called the Lorenzo de Zavala Youth Legislative Session; the first LDZ, as we called it, was actually in 1982. The students went to the state capitol for two days to do a Youth Legislative Session." Gloria has been the director of the LDZ program ever since. This component of NHI now processes hundreds of students per year in various states and Mexico. "We replicated it in 1988 in New Mexico. We went to Colorado State University, the Colorado LDZ in 1990. In 1991, we experimented in the Midwest with the Midwest LDZ, which was the following year; because it was in Iowa and there was difficulty traveling in and out of Iowa, we moved it to Chicago and renamed it the National Lorenzo de Zavala Youth Legislative Session." Next they started the Collegiate World Series, a weekend program that trained students in a hands-on dry run with the college admissions process. The result was better prepared students.

Colleges and universities began to take note of NHI's work. NHI was identifying and training Hispanic students to attend college while colleges and universities were paying recruiters to accomplish the same thing. It seemed like a relationship could be worked out between NHI and national higher education institutions. Gloria and Ernesto worked out a plan where NHI features eight different leadership programs that operate both nationally and internationally, mostly Mexico, and serve up to 4,000 students a year. NHI's primary goal is to provide high school and college-level Hispanic youth with key learning experiences that will enhance their leadership skills.

Among the most distinguished characteristics of the NHI is in the kind of work it conducts and the manner in which youth are trained. Gloria and Ernesto personally interact with the students involved on all the NHI programs. Programs of the National Hispanic Institute include the Young Leaders Conference, the Lorenzo de Zavala Youth Legislative Session, the Collegiate World Series, the Mexico Language Program, the Student Support Services, the John F. López Community Service Fellowship, the Community Leadership Councils, and the Collegiate Leadership Network. The College Register and the Graduate Consortium work to enroll and graduate NHI students at member institutions and are actively involved in developing Hispanic leadership. The College Register is a members-only consortium of postsecondary institutions that are committed to developing the Latino college campus community. Since its founding in 1989, NHI and the College Register have developed programs that create new recruiting techniques for Latino students, increase register member notoriety in the Latino community, and cultivate strong and effective leadership among Latino students on college campuses.

NHI resists the approach of passing down someone else's blueprint, because such an approach would not remain relevant, given current conditions. The NHI helps encourage young people to learn what's going on in the rest of the world around them. Gloria and Ernesto also encourage students to keep up with the technology and the growth of America as it is seen today. Gloria says she doesn't advocate that students become "Americanized," but that they do keep up with everyone else. In so doing, Gloria stresses that they shouldn't forget about their culture, their language, and most of all their community. She encourages students to take what they've learned and regenerate it back into the community. She stresses the mantra, "Don't forget where you came from." Gloria believes that leadership is a learning experience and it has to do with how you empower people to actually become enabled. By enabled, Gloria means that people have the ability and responsibility to create, motivate, and energize in order to bring about a change. It has to be personal and come from within.

Another program of the NHI is the John F. López Fellowship program. The purpose of the John F. López Fellowship program is to provide college-age young men and women with a means to share their developing knowledge and expertise with others. As counselors, research specialists, trainers, and planners, interns gain direct experiences that enable them to critically examine the needs and capacities required for future leadership. Ten John F. López Fellows annually convene at the National Hispanic Institute in the summer to share an experience of growth and personal development. They are Latino college students selected for their leadership potential, willingness to face challenges, and ability to share talent and skill with the Latino community. Named in honor of John F. López Jr., the López Fellowship is designed to elicit qualities of spirit, creativity, and talent exemplified by its founder. Of the 40,000 NHI alumni, John F. López made the greatest contributions to the growth of the institute. He served as a student participant in the first statewide LDZ program in 1983, volunteered eight successive years to NHI programs, served as an NHI full-time professional, and now is a member of the NHI board of directors. He also founded the idea of the College Register and the NHI fellowships.

Another program developed through the NHI is the Mexico Language program, which actually came about from the desire of parents. They realized that all the great kids in the NHI were losing language. The students could understand it, but no longer speak it. Some of them could not even communicate with their grandparents. So the parents suggested that they would like to send their son or daughter to Mexico to be immersed in the language and to learn more about their culture. They contacted friends and families who were in universities in Mexico for assistance in getting the program started (particularly el Tec [The Tech] in Monterrey, Mexico) and were able to start the Mexico Language program. The program is for college students who have completed at least one year of college. The students study in Guanajuato, Mexico, and receive a college credit for their participation in the program.

The NHI recruited most of their students by going into high schools and developing relations with their high school counselors, principals, and superintendents. Since academics are criteria for getting into the NHI, the school will help determine if the student is qualified. According to De León, former students who have gone through the program personally recruit 50 percent of their students. The primary recruitment is by word of mouth.

The NHI has five staff members. The NHI also has about forty-two community leadership councils run by community volunteers. In order to support the cost of the students in the NHI, the organization has developed partnerships with individuals and institutions that share an interest in the students.

Gloria De León can't imagine herself doing anything else but working with the NHI. She grew up in a community where she saw involvement and participation, not just from family and friends but a relationship with the people she interacted with every day. She thinks that it is very important that their children grow up with the same type of environment. She uses Austin as an example of the *Mexicanos*/Latinos as being scattered. They have to figure a way of creating new *barrios*, new connections, and new associations. De León is inspired and driven by her community. She has always believed that her community is the best in the whole world. She feels that it's something unique about who they are that makes them so precious, decent, and spiritually committed. "They have so many things about the qualities, whether it's rich or poor, qualities of who they are, so intricate to what the fabric of America should be in the future. America is going to elect a Latino president."

De León thinks that the most pressing issue in the Hispanic community is the loss of culture. She believes that the inability to connect with an identity in becoming American is the biggest threat. Another challenge is the tension between Chicanos and *Mexicanos* that she experienced on a trip to Mexico with her husband. She said that the Mexicans called them *"pochos"* (white wannabe's). She said that a Mexican stated that she and her husband were better than Mexicans because they speak two languages, they have professional careers, and that they are more advantaged. De León believes that Chicanos, *Mexicanos*, and other Latinos should see themselves as one community.

## Note

1. See http://www.nhi-nrt.org.

~

# CHAPTER TWENTY-ONE

# Lena Levario

Because Lena Levario was such a strong-willed child, her father always told her she would grow up to be a lawyer. Coupled with a strong sense of justice and a knowledge of her people's history, Levario did become a lawyer, and a judge on top of that. Her father had recounted to her the battles that Mexican Americans, blacks, and the poor had to face in Pecos, Texas, where she was born. She became very knowledgeable about the politics of the past, having relived them through her father. Although she could never trace her ancestors back to Mexico (four generations were born in the West Texas area) she drew her culture and pride from Mexico.

Lena's father believed that the only way to correct the injustices suffered by the Mexican people in West Texas was through the judicial system. He believed Lena would return from college and fix what was wrong with the system in West Texas. That geographic area of Texas is hard. But the Mexicans, as laborers, proved time and again that they were a hardy people. West Texas is barren, not a tree is visible to the naked eye. Water is scarce. The summers are insufferably hot. The winters are bone-chilling cold, and windstorms are a fact of life. The area is also chronically poor, where Chicano workers are often unemployed. Racism is as abundant as dust.

Lena was born on August 7, 1961 in West Texas in a town right off the Pecos river: Pecos, Texas. It is located approximately eighty miles south of Carlsbad, New Mexico, and ninety miles west of the Midland/Odessa area. Pecos is too far from El Paso and not near enough to Lubbock. Nevertheless, that is where her family stayed. Pecos and West Texas was Levario's world.

Lena recalls that it was her father's goal to make sure that his children would receive the best education possible. Unfortunately this was not feasible in Pecos. The public schools were segregated, even until the 1960s, into "Mexican" and "Anglo" schools. There apparently were no blacks around. Lena attended a school on the East side of town, "over across the tracks where all the Mexicans lived." She recalls how her grades were very low. She had no incentive other than to pass to the next grade level.

Part of her problem at home was her dad; the same man that inspired her, taught her, supported her, also hurt her. He was an alcoholic. He drank all his life. While he battled alcoholism throughout her childhood, it was difficult for her father to maintain a job. He supported the family financially as best he could as a laborer in the oil fields. He held jobs as often as he lost them. Despite his alcohol dependency, her father "decided he was going to buy a house in a district where we could go to the white schools." He knew the white schools had better teachers, better facilities, and better opportunities, including academic challenges for his bright kids, Lena being the first. He managed to move the family.

In the sixth grade, Lena began attending the white schools. Her grades improved. She remained on the Honor Roll for most of her middle-school years. The promise of "separate but equal" had been anything but equal. Her improved grades were a reflection of the superior education she was receiving in the white school. But along with the superior education came extreme racial prejudice, which only grew worse upon entering high school.

While there were many instances that she described as the "most painfully obvious" of racism, one among many stands out. When the high school was determining the list for who would be placed on the National Honor Society, Lena and a friend were amazed their names were not on the list. Both met the qualifications requirements. In fact, they exceeded the qualifications. The two decided to be proactive. They investigated the matter further. What they learned was that all of the Mexican American students that qualified to be on the National Honor Society were left off the list "accidentally." Had it not been for their proactive stance in wanting to know what had happened, why their names were not placed on the list, what the school authorities were going to do about the omission, nothing would have been done. In fact, their investigation uncovered that it was not two but twelve Mexican American students who were not placed on the list.

A second incident that Lena recalls all too well was when she wanted to be a part of the staff on the *Annual*, the high school yearbook. The process for being eligible and selected was to have those on the existing yearbook staff vote for new additions to the staff. The tradition had always been to have white students on the staff. The process was a matter of white privilege and maintaining a closed society. It was difficult, if not impossible, for anyone not an Anglo to be selected. The white students were not going to vote for a Chicano student. Lena became very upset at this racist, exclusionary tradition. Again, she decided to take matters into her own hands by organizing a petition. Almost all the Chicano students signed her petition. She met with the principal with petition in hand. And she was able to pressure the school principal to change the way in which the *Annual* staff was selected.

A year later the new rules were instituted. Chicanos were able to join the *Annual* staff. By then Lena had lost interest and decided not to join. She learned that the catalyst of change is often not the beneficiary. Her consolation was that being the oldest of four children, she was ensuring, through her actions, that the future would be brighter for her siblings.

Four years after Lena was born, her brother Ruben came into this world. Then her sister Gloria arrived. And finally, fourteen years after Lena was born, Gabriella "Gabby" became the youngest member of the family. With such tremendous age differences between the first and last child, Lena noticed that the first three children had the value of education instilled in them more so than Gabby, the baby of the family. The eldest three would be punished if they did not make the Honor Roll. Punishment meant being grounded or prohibited from participating in an extracurricular activity. Punishment never meant physical abuse. "My parents didn't believe in hitting us, so we never got hit." Gabby on the other hand did not face the same type of punishment. Her mother, tired of living with an alcoholic, had kicked their father out of the house by then. Lena said this "made Gabby grow up in a much more relaxed environment, less stress." Her baby sister became very lackadaisical about studying, and her career options began to narrow as a result.

As the oldest child, Lena feels that she was more motherly than protective when it came to her siblings. "They didn't like me a lot because we would go grocery shopping and they would want to get cereal that was sugar. I would say, 'No, you have to get the stuff that doesn't have all that sugar.'" Levario looked out for the welfare of her younger brothers and sisters in part to assist her mother. Her mother now was supporting the family. She had to find work, and while she was working she couldn't always be with her children. By the time she graduated from high school, Lena was ready to take flight from the family home and head off for college.

She was fleeing the role of surrogate mother and wanted to fulfill her father's dream for her. Her father's words and stories were still vivid; his career vision for her had become her goal. Given her exemplary grades, she applied and was accepted at Texas Tech University in Lubbock.

During her years at Texas Tech, there were no Chicano professors or staff members to encourage her to accomplish her goals. She was alone. But her eyes opened at meeting so many different people from various backgrounds. "There were people from all over the world there. And I studied things and learned things that I never was aware of, and so, I really liked that part of it." College was a time of exploration. Lena discovered political science and sociology. These subjects became her major focus in academic studies. At Texas Tech, she put her past and the blatant discrimination of her hometown behind her. Lena made her experience at the university a positive one. She joined the United Mexican American Students (UMAS) chapter on campus. The most valuable gains she made at Texas Tech were the friendships she made. Even though the Chicano movement was in full stride elsewhere, the UMAS chapter at Tech was not very politically oriented. Instead it was more social in nature. The campus lacked a political edge. Chicano militancy could not find a haven in West Texas or at Tech or Lubbock. But Lena held on to the goal of becoming a lawyer and championing causes for those who could not defend themselves.

After she graduated with her bachelor's degree, Lena remained at Texas Tech to pursue her law degree. Her proven academic strengths and strong work ethic, plus discipline, helped her in law school. The ability to perform under pressure and speak before an audience is not an automatic talent or a character trait. A person must develop those skills and Lena did. Not all of those graduating from law school learn or acquire those skills. Lena had been debating in high school for four years. She developed a healthy self-esteem as an undergraduate, facing that world alone without a mentor. These additional factors allowed her to graduate and pass the state bar exam in the same year, 1986. She wanted to become a civil rights attorney after graduation but "there's not a lot of work to be a civil rights attorney out there . . ." since "they don't have firms that just do civil rights." So she did the next best thing, she left West Texas and relocated.

Lena accepted a position as a public defender in Dallas County, one of the few programs in the state. She was going to be paid to defend poor people accused of crimes before the state prosecutors. She was going to be the champion of the defenseless, standing between them and loss of liberty, a jail sentence. As a public defender she was in court almost every day. She handled hundreds of cases. She tried cases against the best and worst prosecutors and judges in Dallas County. What better way to earn a living than by doing something you enjoy. And by also "providing a good service to the people that don't have money to hire an attorney."

Through all of the trials over the years, she not only accrued a great deal of practice but expertise. Public defender Lena Levario won most of her cases. Lena's talents did not go unnoticed. When Governor Ann Richards looked around to fill a vacancy anywhere in the state, she looked for women and minorities. Governor Richards took special interest in the appointee for a Dallas County criminal judge bench. Dallas County was a Republican stronghold. All the judges were Republican, except for two lower court justices of the peace. She sought out Lena to appoint her. Lena accepted the opportunity.

There is a formal process that a candidate for appointment has to undergo. A person must be recommended to the governor. A governor cannot be expected to know personally all the eligible persons available in any given area. The potential nominee must be politically acceptable and qualified. A lengthy application must be filled out. The governor's staff interviews the prospective candidate and gives a thumbs up or down. Criminal District Judge John Cruzeau encouraged Lena to make her intentions known to the Democratic Party leadership in Dallas County and submit the paperwork. He was a Republican. The governor was looking to appoint a Hispanic judge, and the Democrats were looking for such a person. Lena, with her experience and ability, fit perfectly. There were other candidates who were being considered. In the end, Lena received word from the governor's office, via telephone, that she was chosen for the appointment. Public defender Levario became State District Criminal Judge Lena Levario. Her investiture as judge was a family celebration.

Lena did not formally get to meet the governor until her reelection bid for the position, but she finally met Governor Richards, and Judge Levario describes it as a fun encounter, "She had me laughing at all these funny stories." In fact, Lena was left with a quote from the governor that is her favorite. "Politics in Texas is a full-contact sport."

While politics is indeed a full-contact sport in Texas and any state, the experience of being a judge was actually easier for Judge Levario than being a lawyer. "When you're an attorney for either side, either you're advocating for either the state or for the defendant. When you are a judge, you're not advocating for anyone. You're just there as a referee of sorts." Being a judge allowed Lena to formally be in a position in which she could make sure that people were getting a fair trial. It is something her father had always advocated. Through this appointment she was able to serve on the side of justice.

Judge Levario's docket was a criminal one, whose jurisdiction encompassed all of Dallas County. She had her work cut out for her. She encountered difficulties in meting out punishment. This part had been easier as a public defender; she tried to minimize punishment for her court-appointed clients. Now, as judge she had to weigh how someone found guilty would be punished. If the case was tried without a jury, she also had to rule on innocence or guilt. The benefits of serving as a judge, however, outweighed the burden. She was dispensing justice, not just being a cog in the process.

She also welcomed the opportunity as judge to appoint attorneys to represent defendants who could not afford to pay for an attorney. It is a fundamental right the accused have in the United States. Lena had learned in the years as public defender that some judges would often appoint their friends as lawyers on behalf of indigent defendants. This practice is not always in the best interest of the client. Texas and Dallas County had been mentioned in the statewide media as being very poor in the defense of poor people charged with crimes. The State Bar of Texas had issued a report condemning the practice of judges appointing defense attorneys, and the major dailies in the state had editorialized against the continued practice in favor of an expanded public defender program. As a judge, Levario was very diligent in appointing qualified attorneys to handle cases in her court.

Levario had long held strong beliefs on how the legal system could be reformed. One reform that she implemented was in setting qualification standards for court-appointed lawyers. While this reform was in the right direction Levario said, "Unfortunately, some judges, most judges in Dallas County, have chosen to ignore that and do not appoint lawyers off the wheel, and don't use the system that's been developed." Reform is hard to come by, and when it does occur, the implementation and enforcement processes remain a constant struggle. Other issues, such as our current immigration laws, leave Levario a bit disheartened and aggravated. "I think the immigration laws in the country are a joke because they are applied differently, depending on which country you come from, and there's not a fair way of allowing people to come in this country." To make matters worse, Levario sees that big business, especially in Texas, has encouraged people to come work illegally for low wages.

The interesting aspect about Lena Levario becoming a judge is that she never really had the desire of becoming one. She felt that her qualifications were not strong enough to serve on the bench. It took her husband of twenty-five years, Mark Matos, an engineer with Sysco Systems, to point out to her what she said arriving home from work every day. Lena frequently would complain about how ignorant so many of the judges were. When he repeated her words, she realized that she could be a better judge than some. Her experience and knowledge actually had made her better qualified than most of those already serving on the bench.

Having been appointed to fill a vacancy was an honor. But she could only retain that position through a subsequent election. Lena was in unknown and uncharted waters in electoral politics. The domination of Republican judges in the state of Texas was such that Democrats were a rarity, especially in Dallas County. Levario observed, "There have been no Democrats that have been judges since 1995, which is the last year that I was judge." Levario knew that the Republican judges who presided over the Texas courts had become too comfortable in their positions. They were not working as hard as they should. Republican judges in Dallas County did not want to report their work hours to the public. A most blatant example of relaxed professionalism came when the state Criminal Court of Appeals, all Republican judges, ruled that an attorney who had fallen asleep during a death penalty case was not guilty of "legal malpractice" nor "ineffective counsel." Fortunately, a federal appellate court overturned that decision and ordered a new trial. These types of incidences created a deep frustration in Levario. As usual she put these frustrations to good use.

Levario decided to stand for election on her own right as a Democrat in Dallas County. There were twenty-four other Democratic candidates, not all judicial candidates, who also threw their hats into the political ring in 1994. They all lost. Lena returned to private practice and began a successful career as a self-employed criminal defense attorney. In 2002, she sought a judicial seat once again. The Democratic candidates campaigned long and hard. The top of the Democratic Party ticket included Tony Sánchez running for governor; Ron Kirk, former mayor of Dallas and an African American; John Sharp, a former statewide officeholder; and Linda Reyna Yáñez, a candidate for the Texas Supreme Court. But in the end, only one Democrat in Dallas County won a judicial seat. All the statewide candidates went down in humiliating defeat. The sole judicial candidate who won her seat was previously a Republican incumbent judge who had been ousted by another Republican candidate in a prior election. This led her to run as a Democrat, but did not represent a change in her political philosophy. The candidate that Levario lost to was accustomed to showing up for work around 10 a.m., but during the campaign, made a point of starting court at 8:30 a.m. Levario knew she was feeling pressure. This created a greater passion and determination in Lena to win the position. Her issue-oriented campaign did bring her closer to winning the position, but elections are won by one vote. She lost by less than one percentage point to the incumbent Republican candidate.

Lena has not let her narrow defeat discourage her from remaining active in the legal arena. She serves on the Grievance Committee for the State Bar of Texas. This committee examines complaints against lawyers, such as violations of rules or ethical codes of conduct. Criminal defense attorneys have many grievances filed against them. Oftentimes, the complaints are from convicted felons attempting to find a way to reopen their cases or to blame a scapegoat for their conviction. Levario also serves on the Civil Rights Committee of the League of United Latin American Citizens (LULAC), of which she is also a member. Lena is also the legal counsel to the national LULAC organization. Levario is a member of the Hispanic Fifty, a group of women whose mission is to "educate the community about the economic situation of Hispanic women in the Dallas area." Members of the Hispanic Fifty meet with government officials and business heads to advocate the hiring of more Latinas within the public and private labor markets.

On top of all these activities, Lena also manages to serve as a mentor to high school students. Drawing from her childhood, Lena recalls her mother being a devout Catholic and father who would encourage his children to assist others who could not help themselves. Mentoring was a natural part of Levario's childhood; she remembers serving as a mentor to other students while she was in high school. Today, students come into her office for about an hour a day to learn about the legal profession firsthand. During her time on the bench, she mentored four local students. Helping children is something that comes naturally to Lena, as she has served as a representative of children who are placed in Child Protective Services. These are generally cases where children are removed from their parents' home. The court attempts to find what is in the best interest of the child. Former judge Levario tries to mentor as many children as she can. She has developed a juvenile criminal defense practice as well.

Levario defines a leader as someone who has sincere beliefs and does something about them. This is the type of leadership that Lena admires most. Her definition and life examples make her live by her own set of grounded principles. The local and statewide political scene is hard for Levario to accept. She sees too many self-interested individuals in public office. She believes many politicians are missing the point of their position, which is to serve the people. These individuals instead, as Lena puts it, "are in it just for themselves so they can acquire power or money and a different life." She is as critical of Hispanic political leaders at the national, state, or local level as she is of other politicians. Lena does not think we have effective leaders on the national radar screen. In her opinion, the Hispanic Fifty has the most selfless local leaders making changes in such areas as education, health care, and voting rights. These women are fighting for the rights of others and hoping to improve the chances for future generations.

As Lena sees it, the greatest problem facing Chicanas today is the economic condition that many women find themselves in. When Chicanas do not control their own economic destiny, then they are at the mercy of others.

Levario encourages young people to pursue careers that will provide them economic freedom. She believes this freedom will allow students to have a greater voice in the decision-making processes in the halls of government and business. Looking toward the future, Lena does not see parity in wages coming anytime soon. "I think that within a hundred years women will probably be making equal amounts of money to men." Levario believes that Chicanas have recently had more opportunities open to them, but does not deny the impact of racism on their ability to progress.

Lena believes that Mexican Americans with lighter skin may not face the same barriers that darker-skinned individuals have when applying for a job or trying to advance in other areas. However, a barrier still exists that many cannot easily overcome, and that is the stigma attached to Spanish surnames. For this reason and others, Levario believes in the need for affirmative action programs. "I know all too well how you can get a job or a position based on who you know. And it's always who you know, you know." A bookkeeper position is coming up. The person in charge calling one of their friends to apply is probably the standard operating procedure. The white majority is in power. They always have positions available to them. This scenario creates an inner circle of privilege, an unspoken program of white affirmative action. How then is a Chicano or black candidate able to get their foot in the door? For Levario, the only way to create opportunities is through affirmative action programs. "I'm for affirmative action because it gives other people that have been historically deprived of those positions the opportunity to have them." The problem lies within racism that has evolved into internalized oppression among Hispanics and African Americans. Hispanics and African Americans have both internalized the racist beliefs about others; they are products of the same system—educational, political, and social—that produces these belief systems. Instead of worrying about protecting their piece of the pie each group needs to come to the table and think not only about their group but about other groups.

An internal mechanism within Lena keeps her constantly wanting to bring more people to the table. It is from her upbringing in a small West Texas town raised by a father, flaws and all, who instilled in her a strong sense of justice. In many ways this has been the driving force behind her pursuit of a legal career and her involvement in organizations and associations that advocate for the community. Levario has lived her life by a set of principles and values that are unbending and in this vein has taken on challenges that aren't always the easiest. For example, her last bid for public office was only unsuccessful in terms of winning versus losing. Overall, it serves as an illustration of the dedication of one strong vibrant Chicana who keeps pushing those doors open for the rest of us. She never stops pushing.

# CHAPTER TWENTY-TWO

~

# Elfida Márquez Gutiérrez

Elfida Márquez Gutiérrez was born in 1950 in Fort Hancock, Texas, about fifty miles outside of El Paso. Her mother, Josephina Peña, was from Chihuahua, Mexico, and her father, Jose Márquez Carillo, was from Gran Morelos. They had come to Texas with their parents in 1948 as migrant farmworkers. Elfida grew up picking cotton. Her father always encouraged her to go to college. She went to Sul Ross junior college in Alpine, Texas, where her older brother was a student, then got married, and finished her teaching degree at UTEP. She quickly earned her master's degree in bilingual education a year later, and began teaching in the Ysleta School District. She became the first Mexican American principal of Hueco Elementary in Socorro, Texas, a school that is 99 percent Mexican. After nearly twenty years as an educator, she was appointed to the El Paso Community College Board of Trustees, and later was elected to that post, which she uses as a springboard to fight for equal educational opportunity for Mexican students. She continues to reside in a *colonia* (unincorporated area) outside of El Paso near her students.

Elfida got her first taste of racism while a student at Sul Ross. She was one of only a handful of Mexican students and was not welcomed into sororities or other white-only student circles. This was a major departure from her experience in high school, where she was a cheerleader and student council member and graduated third in her class. The exclusion from sororities served her well, though, by forcing her to concentrate on her studies. She got another dose of discrimination when she moved with her husband, Gilberto Gutiérrez, to Lubbock for a year for his first teaching job. This was even worse than her experience at Sul Ross because at least then she was accepted as a college student and was seen as educated. But at the doctor's office in Lubbock when she took their child in for care, she was ignored and treated like a second-class citizen. It wasn't until a third experience, back home in the El Paso Valley that she finally spoke out against the racist treatment she and her family were subjected to. This was the beginning of her political activity and outspokenness.

Elfida Márquez Gutiérrez had been conned. She and her husband and parents had bought a piece of stripped farmland in the desert countryside outside of El Paso, Texas, to help her parents build their own home. The developer who had stripped the land of all its drought-stricken cotton plants had promised them water lines, gas pipes, and electricity service within six months.

"It was a lie," Elfida recalled. "People in my culture value people's words. If you are selling something to me and you tell me that there is going to be utilities here in the next few months, I'm going to believe you, you know, because we value people's word and integrity. And we were taken."

This was how many of the *colonias* along the Texas-Mexican border came into being. "They (developers) were just getting rich off of people who they would sell half an acre, a lot, a lot for a mobile home, and they were not providing anything. And so, therefore, we have a lot of *colonias* here in this area," she recalled. "It was the rich people who did this. And they got rich by selling off farmland. El Paso went through a drought; the cotton fields were not going well anymore. And this was another way for them to, you know, to keep the money coming in for them. At the expense of a lot of people, you know, who maybe didn't know how to read English, maybe didn't know how to speak English, and they had somebody translate and say look, buy you a piece of land. Water, sewage, gas is coming."

Her dad had bought two acres and gave Elfida and her youngest brother each a small piece of land. Her aunt and uncle did the same for their family. And now Elfida and her husband have done the same for their oldest son. Altogether, they bought four acres on which to build their homes and live together. It was the American Dream, Mexican-style, with extended family living in close proximity. That's when reality set in that there were no utilities.

So Elfida, then a bilingual education major at UTEP and a member of MEChA (Movimiento Estudiantil Chicano de Aztlán), took the lead in holding the developers, and the county government, accountable. She got a bunch of neighbors together, made signs, and started attending all the Public Service Board meetings, demanding services. Once, she tried to hold a meeting at the local public high school, but the principal refused, so she held the meeting in the parking lot of the school, standing atop a pickup truck with a megaphone. Elfida's mother took care of her sons while she was going to school, and later when she was organizing in the *colonias*. Her husband was busy building houses and working and was supportive of her community activism, but not involved. Taking cues from watching MEChA organize on campus and from watching the United Farm Workers union activity, she began to organize the *colonias* to demand services and accountability from the developers. She had also learned about increasing community involvement from her father.

"I remember my father working the polls and carrying people out to vote and I thought how exciting because I always used to ride with my father because I was his interpreter. My father did not speak English, so he used to carry me around. I was, I think, in fourth or fifth grade, and he used to always carry me with him. Why he didn't take my brother, the oldest, I don't know. But he would always take me and I would always sit by him and, and interpret the news for him and so I knew that my dad had high expectations of me back then."

Like her father had done years before, Elfida took families down to City Hall. She also called the media. Next, she started visiting with Rogelio Sánchez, who was her county commissioner. "He was elected and he was responsible to us to make sure that those developers did not do this to other people who maybe didn't have, like my parents, a daughter that was going to do these kinds of things for them. And so, that's when they started looking, you know, at not selling undeveloped land, you know, that way to people. And now, I mean, it's very sophisticated. Before a developer sells any kind of property, he must make sure that the streets are paved and, you know. I feel so comfortable with that. And, and I know that this started, gosh, it was in '75, twenty years ago when we first started looking at what developers were doing, you know, to people."

After eighteen months of organizing and demonstrating, her *colonia* did get water, and they went on to help other *colonias* do the same. "It took a lot of work for us to politic and go and harass that Public Service Board and our commissioner to get those utilities there. So we've got our water, we've got paved streets, but we still don't have sewage."

Now, Elfida is a respected educator in her community of Socorro, Texas. She sees in her students herself as a little girl, very bright, but labeled slow because she spoke mostly Spanish and came from a low-income family. Like her family, they are mostly migrant workers or recent immigrants trying to make a better life for themselves and their children. They are pursing the so-called "American Dream," trying to buy a piece of land, build a house, and send their children to public school to learn English and get ahead.

"I mean, it reminds me of me, my generation, you know, thirty years ago. This is what we have in this community. People who are just starting out and I certainly relate to them because I had that dream, my parents had that dream, and I am here to make sure that a lot of those dreams come true." Elfida always believed that becoming an educator would be the best way to help her people. Her elementary school is south of I-10 where the majority of the Mexican American students reside. She chose to work there because she wanted to help her community. "I've always worked in bilingual education with migrants. My school now has 96 percent of low-income students. Ninety-nine percent Mexican American, limited-English-proficient students.

"I worked all of my life in the cotton fields. And I knew that I wanted to do other things as I was growing up," she said. "I've always had this desire to work with students that need understanding and models and all those kinds of good things that I feel in my heart that I can provide for them. I knew that I wanted to get educated and then I knew back when I was nine years old that I needed to get into the system."

Her father had left the farm to work with a Hudspeth County commissioner, working elections. He did this for six or seven years until the commissioner lost his race and her father lost his job. Elfida wondered back then why good public officials lost.

"I guess that was my first taste of what I thought, you know, needed something to be done with elected officials. But then, I kind of lost that and went on to school and became an educator," she said. "My parents had been very, very caring people and, and I did have some very good teachers along the way that were very good models. And I knew I wanted to do many things for the community. And I thought since my parents' valued education so much, I knew that that was the way to go. And I saw the difference. Once I became an educator, got my degree, I was able to buy things that I never had when I was growing up. I can remember just being so poor. Buying one pair of shoes, you know, for the whole year. Buying one or two dresses and my mom would make all the rest of our dresses. We were very, very poor. So I always wanted to have a better life and help my parents. I've always helped them and they are my neighbors. They live right next door."

As an administrator, Elfida worked to ensure that the predominantly Mexican schools were equal with the white schools in terms of quality programs and teachers. She also started working with Head Start, a federal preschool program for low-income families. She offered parenting classes and citizenship classes for adults at night. All the while, she was registering people to vote.

"As an educator, I've always concentrated on the whole family because there is no way that I could take a child and say you got to come to school and learn. And you know, I always did home visits and I saw the conditions, you know, of my students. And I knew that something needed to be done for those families. And so, I've always been involved in community.

"I knew that they needed to be voting for elected officials that made decisions for them on what kind of parks they got in their area of town. And so all during my senior year and even my first couple of years of teaching, I taught classes at night for adults. And I think they paid like six dollars an hour, so it wasn't for the money. I enjoyed working with adults. Whether I was teaching ESL or GED, whatever, I always had my voter registration cards there. And then I taught citizenship classes and had my first graduation of citizens and right after that they all registered to vote. And I remember back then when a lot of our people back in Ft. Hancock when I was nine or ten years old and our beloved commissioner lost and how they weren't registered to vote. So I knew the power of voting back then and then."

Elfida became involved in local politics after some fifteen years of teaching—when Socorro was becoming incorporated as a city. She was appointed to the zoning committee, where she worked to protect the *colonias* from commercial and industrial encroachment, and then with various local political campaigns. It was through an appointment to the El Paso Community College Board that she first became involved in campaigning for office. She did it by registering people to vote and by walking the district and encouraging people to vote who hadn't voted in a long time. She also wrote a letter to all the parents in the school district who knew her as a principal and told them what she hoped to accomplish as a college board trustee.

"I wrote to my community and I told them, you know, I am here; this is what we've done; this is what we need to do; and I, I had a lot of support from my parents, from all of my different campuses. And they came out to vote. The numbers that show here, you know, with seventeen hundred votes, are people that had not voted here in Socorro in a long time. My reputation as an educator in that community said she does good things for us. We want her over there. So they came out to vote and it's sad to say, but even one of my staff members here in the office hadn't voted in six years. She came too and brought ten people. Cousins and relatives and whatever. So the turnout for this position in the past had been like four hundred votes."

Elfida campaigned on things the community needed, such as a campus and transportation because the distance between the *colonia* and the nearest campus is forty-five miles. She proposed the college district establish a *rutera* (a route pickup bus like they have in Mexico) to pick up students. On the day polls opened, she saw people carrying the letter she had sent to parents. "And they came and they said, '*Vote por Elfida Gutiérrez.*' (I voted for Elfida Gutiérrez.) We said yeah. They said, '*Recibí su carta.*' (I got your letter.) And so, writing to my people was the best investment, I think, of my campaign." Some people said Elfida was new to the political world. "Maybe I am new to politics, but I'm not new to working with community projects and working on, with our people, to working on empowering them and giving them a better place to live. So, all those people that I've known, that I've worked with on projects, that we've brought services out to, they came out. '*Ay, vamos a votar por la Miss.*'" Her opponents received 312 votes and 475 votes, respectively. Elfida had 1,783.

"Don't underestimate the strength of this community. That has been my biggest glory. Winning is, of course, wonderful, but the biggest thing for me was to see our community is not dormant. And they've got all of this voting power, so you better listen to them. Furthermore, people I had met in political functions called me. I got a call from the mayor pro tem, 'Elfida, congratulations. Wow, what a showing.' And I go wow, that's pretty nice. I get calls from very important city and county officials. Why? Because of the votes. Not Elfida. But because of the people that came out. Hey, I have two thousand votes and so they better listen because we can vote somebody right out of office."

Elfida believes that women have to work a lot harder for their positions. "They work hard, period. So I think it's an asset to our community to have women in, in politics, in significant places because they've worked hard all of their lives. In our culture we have worked hard all of our lives. In our culture, we have to take care of our families, take care of everything, and do anything else that we want. I don't have the luxury of having anybody helping me at home. So, guess what I did yesterday afternoon? I celebrated my husband's birthday, but I also washed and I cooked supper and I cleaned the dishes after the whole *familia* (family) came over to celebrate the birthday. So we, just by nature, you know, have to work really hard and I think it's an asset to our community, you know, to have hard workers there. You've got a hard worker already in place, I think, by having a woman."

Her experience as the first Hispanic principal in the school district was a real eye opener. She felt as though she had to be much better prepared than her colleagues in order for them to treat her with any respect.

"I think it's an asset to have a woman in a leadership position because usually she has worked so hard to get there. And Hispanic women maybe even more because of the nature of our culture."

~

# CHAPTER TWENTY-THREE

# Rosa Herrera

Rosa Guerra, now Herrera, was born August 20, 1954, in Gonzalez, Texas, located approximately ninety miles southeast of San Antonio. Her family draws their Texas roots from both sides of the U.S.-Mexico border. Her maternal grandparents, Plutarco and Andrea Guerra, were born and raised in Texas. Her paternal grandmother, the only such grandparent she really knew, Teresa Castro, was brought up in Mexico. Rose's parents, Pauline Guerra, native of Seguin, Texas, and Cleofas Castro Olmos, originally from Piedras Negras, Coahuila, Mexico, moved to Fort Worth, Texas, in 1956.

While Rosa was born in a small town, it would not be the place in which she was reared. In fact, the family moved to Fort Worth, after a little less than two years in Gonzalez. Fort Worth is home to her, and her family continues to reside there today. Rose recalls her childhood in Fort Worth as being "just the norm" with "no thrills or frills." Rosa is the youngest of eleven children, six girls and five boys. From eldest to youngest the siblings are: Teresa Olmos, Pete Olmos, Carmen Olmos Cruz, Zenaida Olmos Sanchez (aka Sandy), Cleofas Olmos Jr., Evangelina (aka Angie) Olmos Guerrero, Maria Elena Olmos Mendez, Jose Manuel Olmos, Adan (aka Danny) Olmos (who is deceased), Raymond Olmos, and Rosa herself. She keeps in frequent contact with many of her brothers and sisters, as they live in Fort Worth also. In fact, they usually stop by to visit her if they see her car parked at the house. Rosa and her sister Mary shared many childhood experiences with one another. She was the sister Rosa went to when she needed advice. Sister Sandy, however, is her "biggest cheerleader" and has always pushed her to reach her greatest potential. Everyone in the extended family has a hectic schedule, but they keep in contact by phone and in person, with others like Joe and Pete on special occasions and holidays. Her family, which has always been large, keeps growing, not only with children but also grandchildren. Today, their children and grandchildren are better off financially than they were during their own childhoods. Rosa's childhood was not one of money and privilege, but it was one that provided her with the tools she needed to become the woman she is today.

In order to make ends meet Rosa's father did "basically anything and everything, mostly he was a hauler . . . he had a big truck and he hauled, you know gravel and things of that nature, dirt and soil." Rosa's mother, on the other hand, was a homemaker who spent her every waking moment running the household and caring for the children. She remembers being raised in a strict household where playtime meant staying in your own yard, "[w]e had no business being down in the neighbor's house or whatever." Sadly, her father died when Rose was four years old. Her mother never remarried. Fortunately, most of the older siblings were grown. Rosa's mother is ninety years old and is still working around the house.

Rose attended Sam Rosen Elementary on the north side of Fort Worth. The north side of Fort Worth is the historic Mexican neighborhood, adjacent to the stockyards. Sam Rosen elementary was the feeder school to J.P. Elder Junior High and then on to North Side High School. She only attended high school for one year. Rosa was part of a pilot program that was established in 1969 in which ninth graders were sent to North Side High School to see how they would adjust. Prior to this time, the Mexican students were tracked into a vocational program. Ms. Herrera recalls that at the time this new program was instituted many in the community were skeptical about the effect this would have on the students. The reality was that "most of the *Mexicanos* went on to Trimble Tech and we felt that we didn't belong at North Side because it was predominately Anglo." For Rosa, the question about the new program working was beside the point; she merely wanted to be around her siblings at Trimble Tech. Ms. Herrera remembers that a group of students, who were being transferred, decided to "take matters into their own hands." The students were aware of the hazing that many of the freshmen received from the upperclassman so they decided to stick together. When Homecoming rolled around, in order to show solidarity, many of the transfer students wore Trimble Tech mums and adorned Trimble Tech colors (green and white). According to Rosa, "[i]t was an interesting day and an experience I will never forget."

Rosa transferred and graduated from Trimble Tech High School, the school her brother Raymond was attending. Her brother was a year ahead of her, and they hung out together during breaks in class. That experience with her older brother was positive for her; she recalls seeing her brother during passing periods, riding to football games together, and watching him perform in the marching band. Once, another brother, Joe, came to her rescue during her sophomore year. That was the year she wanted to try out for the Junior Varsity cheerleading squad, but her mother was against it for economic and gender-role reasons. Mother Pauline was a single parent with no job. Rose wrote a letter about the situation to Joe. He was stationed in Taiwan at the time, but he wrote back telling her to try out. If she made the team, he would assist her with the expenses. Rosa tried out, made the team, and Joe kept his word. Her mother remained very upset with one of her daughters being on the cheerleading squad. "She was of the belief that girls were not supposed to be out of the house after dark and most certainly not at a football game."

All in all the memories of Trimble Tech have stayed with her and she says, "I was glad I was able to transfer to Trimble Tech. When I transferred and attended the first day you really felt that you belonged there, that you were accepted!" Ms. Herrera believes that the vast majority of students are not prepared to take on the responsibility of being in an Anglo high school. She would like to see the creation of sixth-grade centers that would give students the opportunity to transition and would also like to return to the junior high method of schooling in which seventh, eighth, and ninth graders are placed together before entering high school. Her feelings are that "the biggest problem we have now is losing so many of our students through the cracks because they are not ready."

After high school, Rosa was ready for the job market and college. She worked and took noncredit college courses on such topics as insurance, personal injury law, and liability. Her interest in becoming a legal assistant was sparked after working as a receptionist at a medical clinic. Ms. Herrera assisted with interpreting whenever injured workers with limited or no English-speaking ability came into the clinic. Rosa witnessed the injustices occurring to the workers while at the clinic. This inspired her to pursue work at local law firms, but they just wouldn't hire her. So instead, Ms. Herrera applied and received a job at Southwestern Bell (SWB) as an information operator. Of course, the odd shifts and long hours took their toll on her, and she again looked for work in the field of law.

This time the work experience she had garnered from SWB was what allowed her to be hired as a receptionist at a law firm. Rosa moved up the ranks from receptionist to secretary for the senior partner, before finally arriving at her current position of legal assistant. In this job, Rose manages from 150 to 200 worker's compensation client files at a time. Over the years she has also attended various conferences such as Mental Legal Institute and the Trial Lawyers Association. These trainings have assisted her with adjusting and negotiating claims. Her previous experience as interpreter has also paid off as a translator at legal hearings and conferences. Rosa's passion for her work grew as she gained more experience, "I became even more motivated and worked harder when I would see the results were advantageous to the clients and not the insurance companies."

Family has been and continues to be an integral part of her life. She married Albert Herrera over thirty years ago. Albert Herrera is a Fort Worth native. Their two children, Albert Shane Herrera and Malica Elaine Herrera, have given her and Albert four grandchildren. Sunday mornings are usually reserved for family breakfast visits, in which the entire family can catch up with one another on what has been happening in their lives. Aunts and uncles drop in. Pauline, her mother, is visited or taken out, and Albert's parents and family are another clan that keeps family life busy.

Public office takes its toll on personal time. An officeholder often laments not being able to attend all family events. However, Rosa realizes and values the importance of preserving tight familial relationships, and she tries as hard as she can to keep her weekends free, especially Sundays. Face-to-face personal interaction is how bonds are formed and maintained. Ms. Herrera prides herself on the ability to maintain free time to nurture those bonds. Rose believes some people attribute a *Mexicano* family's clannish appearance to their small-town roots and Mexican ways, but it has more to do with a personal, internal mechanism that drives preservation of strength and unity of family.

Ms. Herrera has been shaped by her education, but it really was the education of her son, Albert Shane, beginning with elementary school, that motivated her to become more deeply involved in her community.

The Parent Teacher's Association (PTA) was a way in which Ms. Herrera felt she could help her son and also the community. She wanted to help the teachers with "whatever we could do." Rosa continued this civic participation through the education of her younger daughter, Malica. However, Ms. Herrera has one regret. Between her son's high school years and her daughter's, Rose was elected to the school board. She could not volunteer as many hours at the school; plus, teachers had a difficult time separating her position on the board from her role as a parent. Ms. Herrera wanted to take an active role in her daughter's educational experience. But, "I was always wearing the hat as a board member and it's like, oh, there's a board member."

Ms. Herrera never dreamed of being on the school board. She credits her husband and the North Side High School principal at the time, Mauro Serrano, for encouraging and supporting her entry into the political arena. Once in the PTA, her high level of activity in the organization was noted, Principal Serrano asked Rosa to become a member of the Site-based Management Team, a new concept in parent-teacher-student shared leadership. This team included the principal, teachers, students, and parents all working to better the educational process by determining what were the most salient needs of the school. Ms. Herrera accepted the responsibility and juggled that with also being president of the Baseball Booster Club. Rosa felt she was "just doing, doing, just because it needed to be done." But others like Principal Serrano saw that her participation on all these various activities had prepared her to run for a vacant position on the school board. Ms. Herrera was a bit shocked at this proposition, "I had no intentions ever to get into this arena, none whatsoever; that was not something I ever aspired to do." While Mr. Serrano was influential in her decision to run, Rosa gives the majority of the credit to her husband. He told her, "You're always saying people need to step up and try, you know, voice your concerns and fight for other people and so here's your opportunity." However, she jokes about her husband's support by saying, "I don't know if I should give him credit or if I should be mad at him."

The position of School Board Trustee of the Fort Worth Independent School District, as well as any other public school district, including the community college districts, are elected positions, but unpaid. The candidate must be able to afford to run, and more importantly, able to afford to win and serve. The position requires a lot of time, usually after normal working hours attending meetings. Time and resources to afford to serve are in and of themselves a great deal of responsibility. Imagine the displeasure of an employer with an employee elected to serve who must be gone from work to attend to school board business or go out of town to conferences. Then there is constituent service. Parents and others call the school board member with their concerns, problems, complaints, and needs, not the superintendent. The public feels they elected the school board member, not the superintendent.

Ms. Herrera's single-member district has twenty schools within the boundaries. "I represent the north end of Fort Worth, and basically it's our responsibility to oversee the superintendent for one, managing the schools and making sure that all the schools have the things that they need, the tools that they need in order to educate our children." The tasks that must be undertaken with this position range "from budgets to bond elections . . . making decisions on personnel matters; it's a variety of numerous, numerous responsibilities." Since the school board position is unsalaried, Ms. Herrera works as a part-time legal assistant.

Rosa has run for the position of school board trustee three times. The first time out it was a last-minute plunge into the race. She recalls filing about ten minutes until the official deadline. It seemed as if the race was going to be a tight one, since two others had also decided to run. Ms. Herrera remembers walking into her place of employment and her boss wanted to strategize how she needed to run her campaign. While Rosa was getting coffee and sat with the boss, word was received that the two other candidates had withdrawn from the race. Mrs. Herrera would win as an unopposed candidate without need for a strategy. Her first bid for public office was a breeze. Rosa's second bid for office was done much in tune with the first bid. She waited until the last minute to see if any other candidates would throw their hats into the ring but went unopposed for her reelection bid as well. Would her third bid for office be as charmed as the first two?

Three times is not always a charm. For this next election bid, a retired schoolteacher entered the race. Rosa's reelection, because she was the incumbent, could have been easy. However, campaigning is demanding, costly, and difficult, and it could not be avoided this time around. In fact, this campaign became a difficult one. She had to meet the voters and ask for their renewed support; some of them did not believe in her educational agenda. During the campaign, tragedy struck. Ms. Herrera's mother-in-law became very ill and did not recover from her illness. The sickness, death, and wake took valuable time away from the campaign. The burial took place just before election day. The family concentrated on grieving for their loved one, including Rosa. She did manage to post a few yard signs promoting her campaign in the neighborhoods. In fact, her campaign basically consisted of family members going out the morning after the funeral to put up as many campaign signs as they could in the neighborhoods. Ms. Herrera felt as if she had let some of her constituents down. Her inability to campaign caused her to feel pangs of guilt. Rosa waited at home election night with her family for the results. In the final vote returns, Ms. Herrera won by roughly 45 votes. Incumbency gave her an advantage, as did name recognition by the voters, but her dedication to her community was the ultimate reason for her reelection. "I feel I'm pretty much supported by my community because they know that I put them first and that I will fight for them." However, she also gives credit to friends that carried the campaign in her absence. They also took people to the polls to vote. Rosa did not regret the decision to stay by her husband's side in his time of need. Family always comes first for Ms. Herrera.

Beyond the school board Ms. Herrera has been involved in numerous organizations. "One of the things I'm very proud of is the fact that I'm one of the cofounders of Centro Cultural de las Americas." The Centro has a fine

arts after-school program for latchkey kids. They can engage in creative ac-tivities instead of going home from school to an empty home or idling away hours in the street after school.

The community has been so impressed with Ms. Herrera that Diamond Hill High School named a new wing the "Rose Olmos Herrera Centro de Bellas Artes" in her honor. Ms. Herrera's attitude toward community and ser-vice involvement is one of altruistic merit. "If somebody needs my help and I see it as a worthy cause, then . . . I'll help out." This is displayed by the many organizations, boards, and committees Rosa has served on: Gang Task Force, Mexican American Democrats where she served as Treasurer, KERA Latino Advisory Committee, the Hispanic Salute Committee, the Hispanic Cham-ber of Commerce Board, the Latin Arts Association Board, and she was ap-pointed by Fort Worth Mayor Kenneth Barr to serve on a committee in-volving the renovation and reuse of the Modern Art Museum.

A particularly fond memory that Ms. Herrera has about her involvement in the community is embedded in a familial moment. When Rosa was honored with the Hispanic Salute Award in Dallas, Texas, most of her family attended. Each of her sisters, mother, husband, her children, and some very close friends, politicians, and colleagues were in attendance. As she reached the podium to give her acceptance speech, she looked down and saw her mother. Rosa remembers that her mom was "standing at the head of the table with so much emotion telling me how proud she was of me in tears and ready to snap a picture." It was an unforgettable evening for the entire family. The accomplishments mentioned above are but a few of the many activities Ms. Rosa Herrera has been involved in.

As a committed and working member of each organization she is affiliated with, Rosa participates in their events and activities. The Latin Arts Association holds an annual Louis Zapata Menudo Cook-off. Mr. Zapata was the first Mexican American elected to the city council of Fort Worth. Mr. Zapata asked Rosa to enter *menudo* (stomach lining soup with corn) made from her family recipe into the contest. She thought it couldn't hurt to enter but did not expect to garner any prizes for her entry. In fact, she jokes, "I don't consider myself a great cook but nothing's happened to my family to date!" So on the morning of the cook-off Ms. Herrera prepared the *menudo* entry from a special recipe of her own. When it came time for tasting, Rosa was far from nervous, she had only entered because Louis Zapata had asked she do so. She was not truly vying for the top prize. Three judges each took their turn sampling the *menudo* entries. A judge was a restaurant owner. After the initial tasting, they compared their notes. Rosa Herrera's *menudo* did not take the top prize, but she placed in the competition. Ms. Herrera, in both politics and cook-offs, does not worry overzealously about the end result. Confidence has paid off well for her. Cooking is a fun thing, but Rosa keeps the majority of her attention on more serious matters.

While she has always concentrated on the education of her children, currently at the forefront of her mind is how to provide the best educational opportunities for other children as well. The major problems surrounding the schools in Fort Worth and in her district are familiar scenarios that occur all over the United States. "The major problem is there's not enough funding." Beyond the funding issues that plague school districts in Texas and throughout the country, Rosa has heard from many parents in the district "that there are not enough teachers [who] relate to them culturally." Ms. Herrera feels very strongly about the issues of parents feeling welcomed in their children's school environment. She is especially concerned about the lack of attention to those who may not have acquired a formal or higher education and are thus relegated to the lower tiers society has placed them in. Teachers, Rosa believes, are an integral part of this process of making not only the parents but also the students feel welcomed and cared for. When teachers cannot relate to their students and do not form some type of bond with them, a problem is created. These children are seeking out role models, and if no one is there to lend a hand, they may fall needlessly through the cracks in our system. Ms. Herrera points also to the lack of male teachers in some areas and how this affects the young men in school. The only answer to this problem is just to keep working at it, according to Rosa. The lines of communication need to be opened up so that the administrative staff can create venues for those teachers who feel passionately about assisting students before and after school. Unfortunately, budget cuts have hindered the ability to provide outside draws for students such as art, music, and field trips. In light of the financial cuts that nearly every school district has been taking across the country, what other areas does Ms. Herrera believe can assist our students?

Rosa believes other opportunities are possible. She recalls during her first election to the board how numerous members of the community wanted her to push strongly on the issue of naming new schools after Hispanics, if the issue should ever arise. In order to begin the process of changing a school name, a petition with at least 250 signatures of residents within the attendance school zone must be obtained. The first school name change Ms. Herrera dealt with was when a petition was received to change Denver Avenue Elementary to Rufino Mendoza Sr. Denver Avenue Elementary was originally built for only Anglo students in Fort Worth. When the subject of the school name change occurred, several members of the Anglo community called to complain. In addition to this opposition, Rosa also received phone calls from a few Chicanos in the community who felt that naming a school after a Chicano really did nothing to contribute to the neighborhood and the education of their children. With the assistance of another board member, Rachel Newman, the item was placed on the agenda. Two new schools in Fort Worth Independent School District were named after Dolores Huerta and César Chávez, famous for their leadership roles in the United Farm Workers Union (UFW). The new school names have not been without controversy. Anglo residents of the Diamond Hill area, where the new César Chávez Elementary is already being constructed, have complained about the new name. Ms. Herrera was the strong advocate on the school board for naming these schools in honor of Chicano heroes such as Chávez and Huerta.

Schools are such an integral part of our everyday lives: educating our children, providing a haven for community-based endeavors—from meetings to polling locations—it is a great honor to have this epicenter of neighborhood life have names that reflect the names of the people in the district itself. The naming of these Fort Worth schools after two historic figures in Chicano history is a testament to the nature and drive that Rosa Herrera has in serving her constituents and her people by placing them at the forefront of decisions made on the school board. Ms. Herrera realizes that there are many items within a school district that must be attended to, and she has expanded her service to networking on behalf of and for the needs of the community.

While the state and local coffers for such initiatives have been tight, Ms. Herrera and other members of the school board were able to secure new funding sources by asking local businesses to give back to the community by providing funding for some of these programs. Joint ventures with the business community have not only allowed the school district to gain additional financial resources for some of their proposals but also have given the school district a source of mentors for at-risk students. Some of the businesses will lend their professionals to the schools to serve as mentors for students. One such program in which students can receive a sneak peek at potential jobs is called Vital-Link. With Vital-Link both students and teachers are able to spend up to a week on a particular job site in order to learn the ins and outs of that profession. Students have observed occupations ranging from banking to running railroads. It is but one success story that Ms. Herrera can point to during her tenure.

Another great program that may have the opportunity to evolve into something greater is Success High School, an evening alternative high school. This program allows students who need to work during the day the option of continuing high school by attending courses held in the evening. Courses are offered from 3:30 p.m. to 10 p.m., allowing students to catch up with any missed or needed courses in order to graduate. In order to enroll in this program students must be either sixteen years old (having earned less than ten credits) or over eighteen years old (having earned less than fifteen credits). The semesters are spread out over four nine-week periods in which students may take up to four courses, which allows them to obtain two credits a semester. If they are denied credits because of absences, they can make these up during classes that are offered on Saturday mornings. Success High School originated as an alternative high school, but because of its achievements the school district asked the Texas Education Agency (TEA) for permission to make it a full-fledged high school. They are awaiting their decision on the matter. With so many remarkable accomplishments during her two, now going on three, elected terms as a trustee, many would wonder if Rosa Herrera has her sights on accomplishing more in a higher elected office position.

There have in fact been rumors that Ms. Herrera might seek a spot on the Fort Worth City Council, but as of yet those rumors have not come to fruition. Rosa has been asked multiple times to run for city council but has not done so to date. When asked about her future political plans, including a bid for a council seat, Ms. Herrera discusses how one of the biggest hurdles is the financial investment it takes to run a strong campaign. Rosa does see herself as pursuing higher office one of these days, just not right now. Her concentration is on her current position as school board trustee.

Ms. Herrera talks about being grateful for having had the opportunity to contribute in a positive way to her community. Rosa feels that the "school trustee position is not only the most important . . . but it is also the most thankless position, but someone has to make the sacrifices and do it for the children!" Her mission ever since her days as a PTA volunteer has been assisting the children, and that is where her current concentration stands. She is not ruling anything out, and from the looks of her ability to serve the public, from her elected position to her community involvement, let's hope she never rules any of those options out.

CHAPTER TWENTY-FOUR

~

# Norma Villarreal Ramírez

When Norma Villarreal was in junior high school, she lost the contest to be homecoming queen. The loss was such a blow, she vowed to never lose an election again. And she didn't. Against very heavy odds and a well-entrenched political patron system, she managed to become the first female county judge in Zapata County. But her career in politics turned out to be disappointing, she says, because she came to realize that not everyone in office was as honest as she was.

In junior high and high school, she had been a cheerleader and served on the student council as secretary, treasurer, vice president, and later as president. She also was the first chair in band playing the saxophone and went to state as a twirler in the marching band. She never dated. She was too involved in extracurricular activities. She wasn't an outstanding student. But she did keep her grades up and knew that she would go to college. Her mother, Dolores, made sure of it. Her older brother and sisters also influenced her a lot, since they were all attending college when she was in junior high. Her father, Derly, was perhaps her greatest influence. He was the youngest county commissioner elected in Zapata County at the age of twenty. From him, Norma got the idea that she could also run for office and help a lot of people that way. In addition, her government teacher, Teresa Lopez, influenced her and helped her go to a special summer civics program for girls called Girls State. Her mother was very pleased that Norma was being exposed to so much more than she had been when she was a girl.

"My mom tells me that, in those days, they would never stress education, especially for the women. It was sort of like, finish school if you can, if you don't, get married, and let the husband support you; and that is basically what happened to my mother. And so she made it a point that we would do more things than she ever did, and if it cost her, uh, her life, whatever it would be, she would assure that we would have an education. Because she has always told us that if there is one thing that nobody can take away from you, it is your education."

Her most memorable high school experience was going to Girls State where she was elected municipal judge of Cookie Monster County, her first taste of politics.

"By then, I knew that I was going to be involved in politics sooner or later. I greatly admired, and admire, my dad for all the work that he did as the commissioner. Very down to earth. If he had to take food away from our table to help somebody else, he would do it. And that is where we have an ingrown, what would you call it—desire to help people, no matter what."

At Texas A&I University, she was in the band and in *ballet folklórico*. She also served as secretary in the Young Democrats organization. But she wasn't nearly as popular as she had been in high school, because Texas A&I was a lot bigger, and a lot more segregated. For the first time, she noticed that black people, whites, and Chicano/*Mexicanos* didn't mix socially.

At first, her goal was to major in psychology, like one of her sisters had, so that she could teach in high school, but she realized psychology isn't taught in high school. She got her bachelor's degree in psychology anyway and her teaching license. Then she decided to go to law school. She thought she could help more people that way. She even thought about one day running for office as a state representative.

She attended law school at Reynaldo Garza in Edinburg for about a year, and then took time off while she got married and moved to Houston with her husband, Javier Ramírez, who was the first man with whom she'd had a serious relationship.

"What attracted me the most was that he was a very hard worker. Very dedicated to his job, very well groomed, and he had good morals and values. His parents are from Laredo. His dad originally, I found out later, was actually from Falcon, so they have roots here in Zapata."

After they had their first child, Javier, she returned to law school. "They would allow you to take your baby in a carriage and sit in the back of the room and listen to the lecture." She worked at Texas Rural Legal Aid while she was finishing. She also had her second child, Angela, at that time. Sometimes, the classes at Reynaldo Garza were held at the Echo Motel because the law school didn't have a permanent home. The college wasn't accredited at the time, so she and classmates had to lobby the state legislature to give the college the permission to let its students take the Texas state bar exam, which licenses attorneys. That was her first experience lobbying.

"It was just incredible to see all those green lights going on and at that point, I could not believe the power that they had. They actually had our lives in their hands. We had invested a lot of money, a lot of time, our families sacrificed a lot for us to just finish school, and it was just a wonderful feeling that I will never forget when we had the majority of the votes that would allow us to take the bar."

She had considered applying for a job as an attorney with Texas Rural Legal Aid, where she worked, but they only hired Anglos. "I think that the director at that time, made me feel that it may have been because of my being Mexican American."

So she took a job with the Zapata County District Judge, Manuel Flores. She was his docket coordinator and was assigned to monitor the Commissioner's Court. It was just after her father had been defeated in his reelection bid for the court. She knew it was just a matter of time before she got involved in politics. She thought of running for justice of the peace, just to get her feet wet, while learning more about politics. But she and her father and others noticed how bad things were getting on the Commissioner's Court.

"Things were bad. Somebody needed to speak up. Somebody needed to stand out and say, 'We are not going to take this anymore.'"

But nobody was willing to run against the incumbent, Jose Luis "Pepe" Guevara.

"I have never believed in impossibilities and things needed to change. They needed to change and nobody was willing to take him on. And I said, 'Well, if they are not, I will. I have nothing, absolutely nothing to lose and it will be a good experience for me.'"

At first, her dad had tried to shelter her and the rest of the family from politics because it was very dirty. But later on, he supported her decision to get involved. Norma remembers him telling her that, "if I believed that I could make a difference and that if I accepted the fact that it was going to be the hardest challenge that I could have, that he would support me totally and full. And I think, another thing that made me run or get involved in politics was the fact that I had a particular individual that said, 'Who do you think you are? You are a woman and what do you think you are going to do to this county judge? Don't even try it!' And I said, 'Oh, really? Well, you know what, nothing is going to change my mind.' I guess what offended me the most, in general, was for someone to tell me that I couldn't do it."

Her husband had discouraged her from getting involved in politics, but she did it anyway. "He did not want me to get involved in politics. I can see now why he was concerned about my safety and well-being if I got involved in politics, but my mind was made up." She talked to some people in the community to see how they would feel about a woman running for that position. She was encouraged to run.

"I didn't know how the people were going to respond to me and actually, when I started my campaign, I went door-to-door. The first house I ever went to was in San Ignacio. I was about to knock on the door and I went back, my sister was driving me, and I said, 'Lety, you know what? I can't do this. What if they tell me no?' And she said, 'Oh, you know, if they tell you no, you knock on the next one. Go on. Try it.' And all it took was going to that one house. And, of course, my dad helped me tremendously. With his propane gas business, by the time I would get to see some of the constituents, he had already been there."

She adopted her father's strategy of meeting people face-to-face. She went all over the county. She lost forty pounds during the time. "At the time, I was exhausted. I had visited everybody. My uncle Felipe got bitten by a dog at one of the houses. We had lots of coffee, *pan dulce* (sweet bread). The welcome was just so good. The response from the community was excellent. I recall maybe only three homes where they flatly said, 'We will not help you.' And, you know, it is appreciated when they speak to you with the truth. If they were to say, 'Well, look, I don't think that you are experienced enough,' or 'I am committed to helping the other person,' that is fine."

In the March primary election, she lost by only 45 votes against the incumbent, even after he had been indicted in an FBI investigation into fraud and other allegations.

"You see, it had been a practice for them to open up the locks on the ballot boxes, either put additional voted ballots, change them, or do whatever needed to be done, to ensure a victory for the candidate of their choice.

"And I really do believe that when my father lost that last time, they cheated him out of his election. I was a poll watcher and there was such little power that I had that I couldn't stand it. I was seeing what was going on. and it was real difficult for me to cope with it, but nevertheless we lived through that and it was a learning experience and an eye opener for me. So, the first thing that I did, I got a copy of the Election Code, because I didn't know what the law provided and I wanted to make sure that things were going to be done accordingly and that if I was going to lose, I was going to lose because that was really the people's voice and vote. That I was not going to let anybody cheat me out of an election." Other things that Guevara was accused of doing had to do with misusing funds.

"You had a political candidate who would come in (to the county purchasing department) and they would get a P.O. to pay for the *panchanga* (political social event).

"We knew that they were mishandling the moneys from the indigent program and they came under grand jury investigation. But because of politics, it didn't travel further out, other than just staying there and not doing anything about it. It was just a number of things that were just so out in the open that it was just *una verguenza* (an embrassment) for those of us that have lived here for years. And so two weeks before the primary elections, they come down with the indictments."

After her defeat, the incumbent was quoted in the *Monitor* newspaper as saying, "The people elected me because they know that I am innocent and they didn't want her because of her father."

This made Norma very mad, and she said at that time, "Oh, really! Well, I will tell you something. I have news. I am not going to let it go because I know who voted, and who was qualified and who was not qualified to vote. So, why don't we just go through the experience of filing an election contest?"

Others discouraged her from pursuing her suspicions that people had voted illegally. "Basically they were like, leave it alone. Leave it alone. You know, the people have spoken and I said, no, they haven't. I wasn't convinced that they had spoken. We are locals. We have lived here for a long time. We know the people and one of the, well, one of the most interesting aspects of that March primary was that I knew that illegal votes were coming in. I called everybody that I could, the secretary of state, attorneys, everybody, and basically, the response was, there is nothing you can do at this time except document and when the election is over, you can file an election contest."

While she was at the county clerk's office speaking on the telephone to someone in the secretary of state's office, the FBI busted in and started searching and confiscating documents pertaining to the fraud investigation.

"I will never forget that. They had the big guns. They had a box. And in his wallet, if I am not mistaken—it was a white card, like a credit card—and it had black letters that said, FBI. And they started searching. And it was funny that people started saying that the FBI came in because I was calling them on the phone."

Her opponent had been the target of an investigation for two years for misuse of funds, and for packing the ballot box in earlier elections. In this latest election, Norma accused him of bringing in ineligible voters, whom she recognized as recent convicts in the courtroom where she worked. Others who were registered to vote gave as their address the same address as the incumbent's garage. She filed an election contest while he awaited trial on the other charges.

"This is South Texas politics for you. We had the county judge giving out money to people. He gave a truck to one person that I know. He was actually buying votes." They also had barbeques all over town to win the election by feeding everybody in town. There were many irregularities, and the court ruled in Ramírez's favor. The appeals court upheld the ruling, and ordered a new election.

The new election was held in July, and Norma spent very little money, but returned to visiting people all over the community, except in her opponent's strongholds. She used leftover cards, just changed the date on them by hand. This time, she won. She still had the November election to go before she was officially elected, even though there was no Republican candidate. Her opponents tried one last dirty trick to derail her election. When the incumbent was arrested, the county commission appointed one of their own, a standing county commissioner, in his place as interim county judge. In turn, that commissioner appointed a nineteen-year-old to replace him on the court temporarily, with the understanding that the boy would relinquish the seat once the commissioner wished to return. The commissioner, while he was judge, then decided to appoint a woman in his place, simply so that Ramírez would not be the first female county judge in Zapata County. But Ramírez's supporters got an injunction to stop that from happening, and she was finally sworn in in January of 1995.

When she took office, it was a disaster. The office had been turned inside out by the FBI. The records were a mess, and the county was $500,000 overbudget. She could not get anybody's cooperation and has been battling every corner since her election. As a result, she has become very disillusioned by politics.

"I had a different idea of what it was about, but never in my wildest dreams did I ever contemplate or in addition that really. I mean, bottom line is if you have money or people in high places, that is how you are going to get things done. I, I am just real disappointed. County government is not what I thought it was. . . . For instance, there is things that I would like to get accomplished, but without the support of the commissioners, I can't do it. . . . Like you can argue a point in Commissioner's Court, you can have justification written. It is black and white and it is not going to sell unless you have something to bargain with and I hate that bargain for exchange.

"There is a lot of things that I don't agree with, but I don't have the majority to stop it. You know, like for instance, the purchasing is what gets, gets me the most. Commissioner's Court approved, I think it, they went right under the fifteen thousand mark so that they don't have to go through the biddings, although my personal feelings is that for anything that you purchase, get estimates, get bids, even if they are not required, just for purposes of accountability and documentation and so forth. *Fueron con un mafioso a comprar trocas . . .*

"The exchange there was that the seller gave the water plant manager a freebie, a car for the daughter that is in college. You see, but now we have to dig it up and prove it, you know, and, but I don't agree with that, you know. I mean, if you are going to purchase a vehicle, I would rather that you purchase a brand new, one brand new vehicle than two that don't work. *Alla entre ellos se arreglaron* (between themselves they worked the deal). Their minds are made up. I am not going to make a dent in their decision making, and sometimes it is not even feasible to go on the record, you know, because I will need them for other things. You know, you know what I mean? It is real hard. Bottom line is that I am not a politician nor do I aspire to be one because you just cannot be honest and you know, you can't take care of the whole business on your, on your own.

"I came in with the belief or the thought that I was going to change everything around; that everything was going to be in order; that everybody was going to start following policy; that we would be more careful of the spending of our moneys; and it is not like that. *No puedo hacer nada*" (I can't do anything).

Still, she would encourage others to try. "I think that it can be a self-rewarding job if you have done the best that you can. and in your heart, you know that.

Now, her only suggestion for real change is to impose term limits to keep self-serving politicians from becoming entrenched in office. Politics has also cost her a lot of heartache in her home life. Her husband, Javier, who never wanted her to run for office, has had to deal with harassing phone calls and other threats.

~

# CHAPTER TWENTY-FIVE

# Guadalupe "Lupe" Valdez

A small woman in size, a giant in political stature and growing on the national scene is Lupe Valdez, elected Sheriff of Dallas County, Texas, in 2004. Dallas County had been a bastion of Republicanism and home to many of its famous supporters and even a presidential candidate, Ross Perot. Now it is at a demographic and electoral tipping point, and Democrat Lupe Valdez is largely responsible for tipping it over. In 2004, no one would bet that Lupe Valdez could win the Democratic primary nomination for sheriff, much less the general election. Lupe was a first-generation Mexican American woman born to a family of immigrants from Mexico, which came probably during the Revolution of 1910. She was a Democrat, a female, and an outed lesbian, three strikes against her in Republican Dallas County. But she beat all the odds with hard work and a tenacity never seen before.

As a small child growing up in an extremely poverty-stricken family of eight residing in San Antonio's West Side *barrio*, she was the youngest girl, born in 1947 to Plinio and Teresa Valdez. After birthing four boys and an older sister, Mama Teresa had few options to avoid another pregnancy. She prayed to the *Virgen de Guadalupe* (Mexican Catholics' Patron Virgin Mary) for a girl. When Lupe was born, she named her Guadalupe for the answered prayer. A drunk driver in a car accident hit the older married sister, Emma, and left her with severe brain damage and almost paraplegic. She had two children. After the accident, her husband left her, and the family took them in, raised the children, and cared for Emma around the clock. Lupe's task for Emma was to put out the bedpan and clean it.

Lupe and younger brother Ramiro were the last siblings born. In reality, for Lupe it was living within two families. One family was that of the parents, the older male brothers, and the incapacitated sister. The other family was her and Ramiro, the babies. They felt related in another family, having little connection with the older brothers or Emma.

The Valdez's were seasonal agricultural migrants that traveled in a dilapidated mobile trailer hooked to the family car from Texas to Michigan and states in between. The money the family earned on the migrant trail was good because of the labor production of the grown older brothers and that of her father. Every year with little money saved, dad and the boys would gather scraps of wood, bricks, cement, aluminum sheeting, tar paper, anything to build a home for the family. Although illiterate, her father learned by watching others' various trades where he worked as a manual laborer in carpentry, engineering, architecture, plumbing, electrical, landscaping, and insulation. Every year after the return from the Midwest, the house was improved in some way or another: another room, a sidewalk, a utility room, a new roof, more insulation, and even a garden. Lupe to this day recalls the light switches in her home being different from those in other people's homes. The father couldn't read but knew how to install lighting and electrical lines. He had installed the light switches throughout the house upside down.

She also recalls that her father never made her a separate bedroom. Her sleeping quarters consisted of a corner of the small living room with a sheet draped diagonally across the corner walls. She did have a window and slept on a twin bed. That was her "privacy" until she left the family home; no less than five people at any given time and up to nine in a two-bedroom home.

The migrant way of life lasted until Mama Teresa put her foot down and refused to travel another season in 1954. She wanted the babies, Ramiro and Lupe, to attend a full year of school in San Antonio, beginning with the first grade. As a result, Ramiro has an earned doctorate and Lupe a master's degree.

The schooling issue became the first major disruption in the relationship between Lupe and her dad. He was of the old school: Girls should get married and have babies; any education on them is a waste. Boys are important because they earn money and help the family. Dad Plinio was always opposed to Lupe getting any more education past the elementary grades at Storm Elementary. The schools in that *barrio* were known as the "Projects Schools" because they took in most of the children living in the subsidized federal housing project. While in Harris Junior High, Lupe was mentored by an interested teacher, the band director, who saw in her potential for higher education. He recommended she not attend the *barrio* high schools, suggesting instead she enroll at Jefferson or Edison or Robert E. Lee in the Anglo side of town in order to prepare her well for college.

During Lupe's school years, the schools in San Antonio were segregated by distinct school districts after 1954, by historical neighborhood segregation, and within school buildings. Lupe shared the teacher's advice with her girlfriends in the hopes of finding others to make the crosstown bus journey with her; she was dismissed as being crazy. When she told her mother, again she was told it was a crazy idea. When her father learned of the scheme, he flatly said, "No! It is going to cost more money. Take this bus, then that bus." Lupe enrolled at Jefferson anyway. And dad was right, not a day passed when Lupe had to find money for workbooks, towels for the physical education class, new shoes, ink pens, lunch money, and other school supplies. Her mother pinched pennies from the grocery allotment for her.

The shoes she wore became an issue. The streets in the *barrio* were not paved and did not have sidewalks. Lupe's shoes were always muddy on rainy days. Her classmates at Jefferson stared at her dirty, muddy shoes. Their streets were paved. They had sidewalks, and more importantly, they were driven to school by parents. Lupe learned to either walk barefoot out of the *barrio* and clean her feet before reaching the school building or wear her shoes but clean them before entering class.

The bus schedules and routes also became a problem that curbed any extracurricular activity for Lupe. The buses ran on time or nearly on time, but Lupe had to be waiting or the bus would leave without her. The school was some fifteen miles from the *barrio*. A missed bus meant a late arrival at home because the routes changed after school hours, and all buses drove into the inner city to pick up laborers. After a bus transfer, it was back out to the *barrios*. Dad was frequently furious at her for being late or having missed the bus.

His real fury exploded when she announced after high school graduation that she was enrolling in college, but it was in Bethany, Oklahoma. The Nazarene Church had befriended mom Teresa when the family suffered with Emma's disabilities and needs. The family changed affiliations from Catholic to Nazarene. Their pastor, Dr. Howard Gordon, and his wife had to come to the Valdez home to persuade her father to let her go. Dad finally relented but with admonitions to the pastor to get her there, get her a job, and Lupe could pay her own way. Fortunately, her brother Ramiro also wanted to go, and Dad and Mom drove them to Bethany, Oklahoma. After Ramiro dropped out, father Plinio returned to his usual self and denied her any assistance. And Lupe just took that in stride. She managed to save some money and bought a Ford Falcon that got her there. Older brother Ricardo taught her how to drive the standard shift car. It took her six long years to graduate and many a sacrifice, but she managed it. She never returned home during this period of her life, but she did return to San Antonio. She tested for a summer job once and was denied, even though she was the highest scorer on the test. The Anglo interviewer told her so but added, "If I hire you, I'll be fired. I can't do this." This time Lupe never returned to San Antonio except to visit.

While at Nazarene College Lupe missed out on firsthand experience with the Chicano movement developing across the Southwest and Texas in particular. Moreover, while in Oklahoma she was often mistaken for a Native American, given her complexion and dark features. She did not resist the various identity labels imposed on her; just went with the flow, or as she puts it, "You were Latin. You were Mexican American. You were Hispanic. You were Chicano. You were Chicana. You were, you know, Spic. You were everything."

After college graduation she took various jobs. First, in Phoenix, Arizona, with a youth program affiliated with the Nazarene Church, then Kansas City also. These jobs came by way of her networking former college friends and church members. In Kansas she joined the Army National Guard to augment her measly income as a substitute teacher and help pay for her beginning work on a master's degree. Before she realized it, the military called her for basic training, and off she went to Fort Jackson, South Carolina, and then Fort Gordon for her advanced occupational training. During these months she learned of opportunities to enroll in officer candidate training school for the Women's Army Corps. Lupe was among the last officers commissioned in that corps before it was integrated into the regular army. She rose up in rank while in the military over the years.

When her parents got up in age and began to be ill, especially her mother, she began planning on returning to Texas. She resigned her military position at the rank of captain while still attached to the Kansas City unit and began looking for a job. Her career with law enforcement was to begin as a jail guard. When she decided to make the return to Texas in 1979, she landed a job with the federal corrections facility in Seagoville near Dallas, Texas. Her career got off to a bumpy start because she was among the first women hired as commissioned officers authorized to carry weapons. The all-male staff and supervisors harassed her and other women constantly, trying to force them out of the career. Lupe fought back and survived and also looked for a way out and up, if possible, within the federal system.

She found an opportunity with the General Services Administration, Criminal Division. Her job was to ferret out fraud and corruption in the buying of goods and supplies by the various agencies of the federal government in the state of Georgia. Investigations led her to a transfer to the U.S. Department of Agriculture to investigate fraud in the Food Stamp programs in Arkansas. Lupe became an ace undercover agent, making buys and busts of grocers and others involved in scheming with food stamps. Her skills at this type of undercover work got her assignments in small cities across the country, never the major ones. She protested these assignments; she wanted the big time. After thirteen years of this type of law enforcement, she made her move to the U.S. Customs Service at age forty. She bought a home in Dallas and joined the Metropolitan Community Church, a place of worship for gay and lesbian believers. She found herself and came out of the closet, "I allowed myself to come out because I understood I was okay with God."

As a seasoned and mature federal officer, she had a trial to attend in San Antonio. During those days she visited the family and arranged to meet her father at the senior citizen center for lunch. Her father was so proud of her being a federal law enforcement officer that he literally pulled her from one person to another introducing her as such and pulling out her badge from her pocket to prove it. This began the period of reconciliation between her and Plinio, but not the older brothers, who still resented her lesbianism. They grew to accept her and her partner. "We don't like it but she is our sister and we love her." Regrettably her parents passed away before the events that led to her greatest accomplishment came to fruition. Her father died from a fall on the sidewalk and steps he had built. He hit his head on them and died at age 93, some fifteen years ago. Her mother had died in 1973, and both parents are buried in San Antonio.

Having earned a regular paycheck with substantial benefits, Lupe began to plan on retirement from the federal service. She was tired of the international travel to Bolivia, Uruguay, Venezuela, Chile, Mexico, and Colombia working on drug interdiction. She visited the local Democratic Party Chair in Dallas County, Susan Hays, and inquired as to how best serve the community via public service. She asked, "Do you think it would be okay if I ran for like constable or justice of the peace?" An aide to Ms. Hayes, however, said to her, "Don't say no right away, but I want you to hear me out." They pitched her the idea of running for sheriff instead. Lupe was in shock at the suggestion and began to grapple with the enormity of the task were she to accept the challenge. She had previously abandoned her Republican mind-set early in her law enforcement career. When she saw firsthand the discrimination leveled at minorities in the criminal justice system and toward her, she told herself, "This is not me." She became a Democrat.

While still with Customs and planning on retirement, she put her toe into local politics by helping a school board candidate in Dallas win office, Jose Plata. She learned the ropes of campaigning, fund raising, get-out-the-vote, and networking with community groups. She turned to Plata for advice on whether to make the race for sheriff or not. She turned inward and reflected on the decision to run and risk losing her savings and jeopardize her plans for retirement. Initially her plan was to get to be debt free, then retire, and then run. Now she had to decide. She consulted her brothers in San Antonio, which was a mistake. They tore her down. They said, "No, you're stupid. It's a Republican area. You're gonna get killed. You're a lesbian. They're gonna drag it all over. . . . They are going to tear you apart." She left the encounter in tears.

When she mentioned her interest in making the race to her nieces, they were ecstatic. These young women, unlike the older brothers, offered not only encouragement but also volunteer labor to help her win. Lupe was in the race. She took $60,000 out of her retirement as a first loan and hit the campaign trail. She never looked back. She recruited a handful of volunteers and filed for the position. Running against her in the Democratic primary were three men: Jim Foster, Sam Allen, and Charles "Chuck" Munoz. On the Republican side were four Anglo males. She did not win outright and had to face a runoff election against Jim Foster to win the Democratic Party nomination. And she did with 70 percent of the vote. In the November election she faced Danny Chandler, the favorite of the incumbent sheriff.

Her successful strategy against Chandler was to target her potential voters in key precincts. She joined other Democratic women candidates and did mail-outs to 60,000 registered women regardless of party affiliation and voting record. Three of these candidates posed for a postcard with the caption: "The Right Women. The Right Time." And Lupe kept her campaign from going negative in its message and tone. She kept the high road and focused on the issues. The sheriff's department had been the target of many investigations, scandals, and upheavals in the past few years under the incumbent Republican sheriff. The voter's choice was simple—real change or the same good ole boys. The voters, including some 10,000 Republicans, crossed over and went with all three Democratic women and a few others, all Democrats. Lupe's victory and race was the national story that election night in 2004. She has become the poster figure for all types of groups: Latinos, Gays and Lesbians, Women, Law Enforcement, and Democrats. She is called on for public speaking and appearances nationally and internationally.

In 2006, Dallas County Sheriff Lupe Valdez heads the seventh-largest police department in the nation, has nearly 2,000 employees, and a multimillion-dollar budget. She is busy reforming the department and dealing with the multiple issues she inherited. She is also planning her reelection in 2008.

∼

# List of Interviews by
# Name, Location, and Date

| NAME | LOCATION | DATE |
|------|----------|------|
| Berriozabal, María | San Antonio, TX | July 16, 1996 |
| Canales, Alma | Arlington, TX | October 23, 1997 |
| Castro, Rosie | San Antonio, TX | July 1, 1996 |
| Chacón, Alicia | El Paso, TX | June 22, 1996 |
| Chávez, Norma | El Paso, TX | June 21, 1996 |
| De León, Gloria | Maxwell, TX | February 2, 1998 |
| Escobar, María | Albuquerque, NM | July 17, 2000 |
| Flores, Diana | Dallas, TX | November 3, 2001 |
| Gámez, Trini | Amarillo, TX | February 26, 1998 |
| Gutiérrez, Elfida | El Paso, TX | August 5, 1996 |
| Herrera, Rose | Arlington, TX | January 28, 2003 |
| Jiménez, María | Houston, TX | January 22, 1998 |
| Severita Lara | Crystal City, TX | July 22, 1996 |
| Levario, Lena | Dallas, TX | February 27, 2003 |
| Martínez, Anita | Dallas, TX | October 26, 1998 |
| Medina, Socorro | Amarillo, TX | February 26, 1998 |
| Mireles, Irma | San Antonio, TX | June 6, 1998 |
| Muzquiz, Virginia | Crystal City, TX | September 24, 1996 |
| Peña, Olga | San Antonio, TX | April 14, 1997 |
| Ramírez, Norma | Zapata, TX | July 5, 1996 |
| Reyna, Elvira | Mesquite, TX | February 12, 1998 |
| Tagle, Hilda | Corpus Christi, TX | June 14, 1998 |

| NAME | LOCATION | DATE |
|---|---|---|
| Tijerina, Rosa | Albuquerque, NM | July 3, 2000 |
| Van de Putte, Leticia | Albuquerque, NM | August 13, 2003 |
| Yáñez, Linda Reyna | Edinburg, TX | January 14, 1997 |

# APPENDIX B

~

# Library References

The following womens' original videotaped and transcribed interviews are housed at University of Texas–Arlington Special Collections Library under the Center for Mexican American Studies. The number indicates the reference number for the special collection. The Tijerinas' interviews are housed at the University of New Mexico Zimmerman Library.

002  Chacón, Alicia
007  Ramírez, Norma
013  Lara, Severita
026  Chávez, Norma
033  Berriozabal, María
047  Rangel, Irma
051  Gámez, Trini
060  Medina, Socorro
076  Mireles, Irma
096  Jiménez, María
100  Reyna, Elvira
105  Yáñez, Linda
108  Peña, Olga
110  De León, Gloria
111  Gutiérrez, Elfida
116  Tagle, Hilda
123  Castro, Rosie

# References

Adler, N. J. (1999). "Global Leadership: Women Leaders." In *Advances in Global Leadership*, vol. 1, ed. W. H. Mobley et al., 49–73. Stamford, CT: JAI Press Inc.

Adler, N. J. (1996). "Global Women Political Leaders: An Invisible History, an Increasingly Important Future." *Leadership Quarterly* 7:133–61.

Allsup, Vernon Carl. (1976). *The American G.I. Forum: A History of a Mexican-American Organization*. Austin: University of Texas.

Arrizon, Alicia. (1998). "Soldaderas and the Staging of the Mexican Revolution." *The Drama Review* 42(1): 90–113.

Baca Zinn, Maxine. (1980). "Gender and Ethnic Identity among Chicanos." *Frontiers* 5:18–23.

Blake, R. R., and J. S. Mouton. (1964). *The Managerial Grid*. Houston, TX: Gulf Press.

Blea, Irene I. (1992). *La Chicana and the Intersection of Race, Class, and Gender*. New York: Praeger Press.

Brady, Henry E., Sidney Verba, and Kay Lehman Schlozman. (1995). "Beyond Ses: A Resource Model of Political Participation." *The American Political Science Review* 89(2): 271–94.

Burns, Nancy, Kay Lehman Scholzman, and Sidney Verba. (2001). *The Private Roots of Public Action*. Cambridge, MA: Harvard University Press.

Cordova, Teresa et al. (1986). *Chicana Voices: Intersections of Class, Race and Gender*. Austin: University of Texas Press.

Cotera, Marta. (1977). *The Chicana Feminist*. Austin, TX: Information Systems Development.

Cotera, Martha P. (1976). *Diosa y Hembra: The History and Heritage of Chicanas in the U.S.* Austin, TX: Information Systems Development.

De la Garza, Rodolfo O., Martha Menchaca, and Louis DeSipio. (1994). *Barrio Ballots: Latino Politics in the 1990 Elections*. Boulder, CO: Westview Press.

Díaz del Castillo, Bernal. (1997). *Historia de Conquista de la Nueva España*. Madrid: Espasa.

Drath, W. H., and C. J. Palus. (1994). *Making Common Sense: Leadership as Meaning-making in a Community of Practice*. Greensboro, NC: Center for Creative Leadership.

Ferguson, Kathy E. (1987). "Male-Ordered Politics: Feminism and Political Science." In *Idioms of Inquiry: Critique and Renewal in Political Science*, ed. Terence Ball. Albany: State University of New York Press.

Flores, William V. (1997). "Mujeres en Huelga: Cultural Citizenship and Gender Empowerment in a Cannery Strike." In *Latino Cultural Citizenship: Claiming Identity, Space, and Rights*, ed. William V. Flores and Rina Benmayor, 210–54. Boston: Beacon.

Flores Niemann, Yolanda, Susan H. Armitage, Patricia Hart, and Karen Weathermon. (2002). *Chicana Leadership*. Lincoln: University of Nebraska Press.

Garcia, Alma. (1997). *Chicana Feminist Thought: The Basic Historical Writings*. New York: Routledge.

Garcia, F. Chris, ed. (1988). *Latinos and the Political System*. Notre Dame, IN: University of Notre Dame Press.

Garcia, Ignacio. (2000). *Viva Kennedy: Mexican Americans in Search of Camelot*. College Station: Texas A&M University Press.

Garcia, Ignacio. (2002). *Hector Garcia: In Relentless Pursuit of Justice*. Houston, TX: Arte Publico Press.

Garcia, Sonia. (1998). "Running as a Latina: Building a Campaign." Presented at the annual meeting of the Western Political Science Association, Los Angeles.

Garcia, Sonia. (1997). "Motivational Factors for Latinas in Electoral Politics." Presented at the annual meeting of the Western Political Science Association, Tucson.

Gonzalez, Gilbert G. (1999). *Mexican Consuls and Labor Organizing: Imperial Politics in the American Southwest*. Austin: University of Texas Press.

Gutiérrez, José Angel. (1998). *The Making of a Chicano Militant: Lessons from Cristal*, Wisconsin Studies in American Autobiography. Madison: University of Wisconsin Press.

Hardy-Fanta, Carol. (1993). *Latina Politics, Latino Politics: Gender, Culture and Political Participation in Boston*. Philadelphia: Temple University Press.

Hemphill, J. K. and A. E. Coons. (1957). "Development of the Leader Behavior Description Questionnaire." In *Leader Behavior: Its Description and Measurement*, ed. R. M. Stogdill and A. E. Coons. Columbus: Ohio State University, Bureau of Business Research.

Hero, Rodney E. (1992). *Latinos and the U.S. Political System: Two-Tiered Pluralism*. Philadelphia: Temple University Press.

Hernández, Daisy, and Bushra Rehman, eds. (2002). *Colonize This! Young Women of Color on Today's Feminism*. Emeryville, CA: Seal Press.

Hillman, R. (1999). "Iowa Straw Poll to Test of Bush, Rivals GOP Hopeful Using Funds, Food, and Celebrities in Quest for Momentum Event Can Provide." *Dallas News*, August 13.

Hosking, D. M. (1988). "Organizing, Leadership and Skillful Process." *Journal of Management Studies* 25(2): 147–66.

Ix Chel Goddess of Creativity: http://www.lvcm.com/tao.

Jenkins, W. O. (1947). "A Review of Leadership Studies with Particular Reference to Military Problems." *Psychological Bulletin* 44:54–79.

Jensen, Robert. (1998). "Fighting the Power at UT." *Texas Observer*, November 20, 12–14.

Justiceformypeople.org. (2002). *Justice for My People: The Dr. Hector P. Garcia Story.* www.justiceformypeople.org.

Kinder, D. R., and D. O. Sears. (1981). "Prejudice and Politics: Symbolic Racism versus Racial Threats to the Good Life." *Journal of Personal and Social Psychology* 40:414–31.

Kirt, P. (1998). *Sor Juana Inés de la Cruz: Religion, Art, and Feminism.* New York: Continuum Publishing Co.

Klenke, K. (1996). *Women and Leadership: A Contextual Perspective.* New York: Springer Publishing Co.

Macias, Anna. (1980). "Women and the Mexican Revolution 1910–1920." *Americas (Acad. of Am. Franciscan Hist.)* 37(1): 53–82.

Mann, R. D. (1959). "A Review of the Relationship between Personality and Performance in Small Groups. *Psychological Bulletin* 56:241–70.

Marin, Marguerite V. (1991). *Social Protest in an Urban Barrio: A Study of the Chicano Movement, 1966–1974,* vol. 1. Lanham, MD: University Press of America.

Martínez, Elizabeth. (1998). *De Colores Means All of Us: Latina View for a Multi-Colored Century.* Boston: South End Press.

Marquez, Marisela. (1997). "Redefining Politics: Survey on Chicano and Latina Political Actors." Presented at the annual meeting of the Western Political Science Association, Tucson.

McConahay, J. B. (1986). "Modern Racism, Ambivalence, and the Modern Racism Scale." In *Prejudice, Discrimination, and Racism,* ed. J. F. Dovidio and S. L. Gaertner, 91–126. New York: Academic Press.

McIntosh, Peggy. (1988). *White Privilege and Male Privilege: A Personal Account of Coming to See Correspondences through Work in Women's Studies.* Working Paper No. 189. Wellesley, MA: Wellesley College, Center for Research on Women.

Mendoza, Louis. (2001). *Historia: The Literary Making of Chicana and Chicano History.* College Station: Texas A&M University Press.

Meza Gutierrez, Arturo. (1999). *Mosaico de Turquesas.* Mexico City, Mexico.

Mirande, Alfredo, and Evangelina Enriquez. (1979). *La Chicana: The Mexican American Woman.* Chicago: University of Chicago Press.

Monaghan, Patricia. (1981). *The Book of Goddesses and Heroines.* St. Paul. MN: Llewellyn Publications.

Montoya, Lisa. (1996). "Latino Gender Differences in Public Opinion: Results from the Latino National Political Survey." *Hispanic Journal of Behavioral Sciences* 18(2): 255–76.

Montoya, Lisa, Carol Hardy-Fanta, and Sonia Garcia. (2000). "Latina Politics: Gender, Participation, and Leadership." *P.S. Political Science and Politics* 33(3): 555–61.

NALEO Online (1999). http://www.naleo.org/CenterFNWSpeech.html; Center for the New West Speech delivered on September 29 in Colorado Springs, Colorado, by Arturo Vargas, Executive Director, NALEO Educational Fund.

Nanfito, Jacqueline. (2000). *El Sueno: Cartographies of Knowledge and the Self.* New York: Peter Lang Publishing.

Navarro, Armando. (1998). *The Cristal Experiment: A Chicano Struggle for Community Control.* Madison: University of Wisconsin Press.

Navarro, Armando. (2000). *Mexican American Youth Organization: Avant-Garde of the Chicano Movement in Texas.* Austin: University of Texas Press.

Noyola, Sonia Adriana. (Spring 2000). "Votando en el Valle (Voting in the Valley)." Presented during a communications seminar held at the University of Texas–Pan American.

Pachon, Harry, and Lourdes Arguelles. (1994). "Grass-Roots Politics in an East Los Angeles Barrio: A Political Ethnography of the 1990 General Election." In *Barrio Ballots: Latino Politics in the 1990 Elections,* ed. Rodolfo O. de la Garza, Martha Menchaca, and Louis DeSipio. Boulder CO: Westview Press.

Pardo, Mary. (1998). *Mexican American Women Activists: Identity and Resistance in Two Los Angeles Communities.* Philadelphia: Temple University Press.

Pardo, Mary. (1990). "Mexican American Grassroots Community Activists: 'Mothers of East Los Angeles.'" *Frontiers* 11(1): 1–7.

Paz, O. (1997). *Sor Juana Inés de la Cruz: Las trampas de la fe.* México, D.F.: Fondo de Cultura Económica.

Ramos, Henry. (1999). *The American G.I. Forum: In Pursuit of the Dream, 1948–1983.* Houston, TX: Arte Publico Press.

Ruiz, Vicki L. (1998). *From Out of the Shadows: Mexican Women in Twentieth Century America.* New York: Oxford University Press.

Schlozman, Kay Lehman, Nancy Burns, and Sidney Verba. (1994). "Gender and the Pathways to Participation: The Role of Resources." *Journal of Politics* 56:963–90.

Schmidt, Ron Sr., Edwina Barvosa-Carter, and Rodolfo Torres. (2000). "Latino/a Identities: Social Diversity and U.S. Politics." *P.S. Political Science and Politics* 33(3): 563–67.

Sears, D. O. (1988). "Symbolic Racism." In *Eliminating Racism: Profiles in Controversy.* (Perspectives in Social Psychology) ed. P. Katz and D. Taylor, 53–84. New York: Plenum Press.

Sears, D. O., C. van Laar, M. Carrillo, and R. Kosterman. (1997). "Is It Really Racism? The Origins of Whites' Opposition to Race-targeted Policies." *Public Opinion Quarterly* 61:16–53.

Sierra, Christine. (1997). "From Activist to Mayor: The Controversial Politics of Debbie Jaramillo in Santa Fe, New Mexico." Presented at the annual meeting of the Western Political Science Association, Tucson.

Soto, Shirlene. (1990). *Emergence of Modern Mexican Woman: Her Participation in Revolution and Struggle for Equality, 1910–1940.* Denver CO: Ardern Press, Inc.

Stogdill, R. M. (1948). "Personal Factors Associated with Leadership: A Survey of the Literature." *Journal of Psychology* 25:35–71.

*Survivors of the Shoah.* Visual History Foundation: http://www.vhf.org.

Taube, Karl. (1993). *The Legendary Past: Aztec and Maya Myths.* Austin: University of Texas Press.

Telesco, Patricia. (1998). *365 Goddesses: A Daily Guide to the Magic and Inspiration of the Goddess.* New York: HarperCollins Publishers.

Tlapoyawa, Kurly. (2002). *We Will Rise: The Rebuilding of the Mexika Nation.* Victoria, BC: Trafford Publishing.

Townsend, Richard F. (1992). *The Aztecs.* New York: Thames and Hudson Ltd.

United States Census Bureau, Current Population Survey. (1999). Ethnic and Hispanic Statistics Branch, Internet Release Date: March 8, 2000. http://www.census.gov/population/socdemo/hispanic/cps99/99sumtab01.txt.

Van Maurik, J. (2001). *Writers on Leadership.* London: Penguin.

Verba, Sidney, Kay Lehman Schlozman, Henry Brady, and Norman H. Nie. (1993). "Race, Ethnicity and Political Resources: Participation in the United States." *British Journal of Political Science* 23(4): 453–97.

Vidal, Mirta. (1971). *Chicanas Speak Out Women: New Voice of La Raza.* New York: Pathfinder Press.

Warren, Kay Barbara, and Susan C. Bourque. (1985). "Gender, Power, and Communication: Women's Responses to Political Muting in the Andes." In *Women Living Change,* ed. Susan C. Bourque and Donna Robinson Divine. Philadelphia: Temple University Press.

Weber, Max. (1947). *Max Weber: The Theory of Social and Economic Organization.* Translated by A. M. Henderson and Talcott Parsons. New York: The Free Press.

Zamora, Emilio, Cynthia Orozco, and Rodolfo Rocha, eds. (2000). *Mexican Americans in Texas History.* Austin: Texas State Historical Association.

~

# About the Authors

**José Angel Gutiérrez** is a professor of political science at the University of Texas at Arlington. He received his PhD in government from the University of Texas at Austin, a jurisprudence doctorate from the University of Houston Bates College of Law, an MA in government from St. Mary's University in San Antonio, Texas, and his BA in government from Texas A&M University at Kingsville, Texas. He is the author of *The Making of a Chicano Militant: Lessons from Cristal* (1998); *A Gringo Manual on How to Handle Mexicanos*, 2nd ed. (2001); *A Chicano Manual on How to Handle Gringos* (2003); *We Won't Back Down!* (2005); and the editor and translator of the autobiography of Reies López Tijerina, *They Called Me "King Tiger": My Struggle for the Land and Our Rights* (2000). He has also published numerous articles in both Spanish and English. Dr. Gutiérrez is the founder of the Raza Unida Party and former national chair of that political party, former county judge for Zavala County, Texas, and member and president of the board of trustees of the Crystal City Independent School District.

**Michelle Meléndez** is a Chicana from Albuquerque, New Mexico. She is the mother of two girls, a traditional Aztec dancer, and cofounder of mexika.org. She is a community organizer in Albuquerque and was appointed by the Bernalillo County Commission to the board of trustees of the University of New Mexico Health Sciences Center after many years of grassroots community advocacy to improve affordable access to health care, to reduce racial health disparities, and to increase community participation in hospital policy

271

making. She earned a BA from the University of New Mexico and Loyola Marymount University in Los Angeles and was a newspaper reporter and journalist for twelve years in New Mexico, Texas, and Mexico. After several years working in public health, she became director of community programs for St. Joseph Community Health. She is currently finishing graduate work in public administration at UNM Anderson School of Management.

**Sonia Adriana Noyola** is currently pursuing her PhD in curriculum and instruction from the University of Texas–Austin while also serving as a social studies teacher at Moody High School in Corpus Christi, Texas. She has extensive experience in the educational field, with jobs ranging from educational advisor (LULAC National Educational Service Center) to coordinator for student development (University of Texas–Pan American). Sonia has taught courses at community colleges as well as public and charter high schools. Her educational background includes an MA in political science from Rice University, an MPA in public administration and an MS in educational technology from Texas A&M University–Corpus Christi, and a BA in government and a BS in radio/TV/film from the University of Texas–Austin.